Kick Me

ADVENTURES IN ADOLESCENCE

PAUL FEIG

THREE RIVERS PRESS

NEW YORK

Grateful acknowledgment is made to **Folkways Music Publishers, Inc.** for permission to reprint an excerpt from the song lyric "Black Betty" new words and new music adaptation by Huddie Ledbetter. TRO-Copyright © 1963 (Renewed) and 1977 by Folkways Music Publishers, Inc., New York, NY. Reprinted by permission of Folkways Music Publishers, Inc.

Published by Three Rivers Press, New York, New York.
Member of the Crown Publishing Group, a division of Random House, Inc.

www.randomhouse.com

THREE RIVERS PRESS and the Tugboat design are registered trademarks of Random House, Inc.

Printed in the United States of America

Design by Leonard Henderson

Library of Congress Cataloging-in-Publication Data
Feig, Paul.
Kick me : adventures in adolescence / Paul Feig.
ISBN 0-609-80943-1
1. Teenage boys. 2. Feig, Paul. I. Title.
HQ797 .F38 2002
305.235—dc21   2002018121

ISBN 0-609-80943-1

10 9 8 7 6 5 4 3 2 1

First Edition

To no one . . .

I mean, who in their right mind
would want this book dedicated to them?

Kick Me

WE STOOD IN LINE AT ELLIS ISLAND FOR *THIS*?

There is no God.

I mean, there can't be. Think about it.

If there were, then things in life would have to be fair. There would be no suffering, there would be no war, there would be no poverty . . .

. . . and none of us would be born with last names that could make us the brunt of adolescent jokes for the entirety of our school careers.

In a truly just universe, no child's last name would be Cox, Butz, or Seaman. No teenager would come from a family named the Hardins or the Balls. A young Richard Shaft wouldn't have to come home from school crying each day. An underendowed Lisa Titwell wouldn't beg her parents to let her finish her education at an all-girls' school. And an adolescent Paul Feig wouldn't have had to endure hearing the letters *e* and *i* constantly taken out of his last name and replaced with the letter *a*.

But, alas, I did.

It didn't start out that way. Fortunately, or unfortunately, when I was in grade school, there was a TV commercial for Fig Newton cookies that featured a man dressed up in a giant fig costume who performed a jingle called "The Big Fig Newton." He would dance and sing the words "Chewy, chewy, rich, and gooey inside . . . Golden, flaky, tender, cakey outside." At the same time, he performed a goofy, vaguely Egyptian-type dance, and then, after a few more product-endorsing verses, would wrap up his corporate caperings by saying "Here comes the tricky part," whereupon he would stand on one leg and grandly sing, "The Big . . . Fig . . . New-tonnnnnnn!"

The commercial was very popular and something every kid in my school district strove to memorize in the hopes that he or she could then perform it in front of his or her peers and obtain big laughs. Because of this, and thanks to the free association of youth, I, Paul Feig, became known as "Fig Newton."

At first, I hated it. I mean, who among us really is happy when we're assigned a nickname? It's never a situation where we get some cool handle like "The Big Hurt" or "The Yankee Clipper" or "Stud." It's always some lame, obvious play on our names, turning the once proud crest of our ancestors into something that either has to do with a body part, a reproductive organ, a mental shortcoming, or an insensitive term for a person who practices nontraditional sexual unions. The kids I grew up with could bend the most innocent name into something you wouldn't want to be called, even if it was preceded by the phrase "and the Oscar goes to . . ." Names as harmless as Smith and Jones could easily be twisted into Smegma and Boner, and so the journey from Feig to Fig Newton was little more than a quick trip to the local humiliation mart.

The name spread fast and soon none of my peers could resist it. The greeting "Hey, Fig Newton" became so prevalent in my life that by the age of ten I didn't even respond to my actual name. Paul Feig was someone from my past, a free spirit who had once played happily in his room, unaware that the world was filled with people who, unlike his mother and grandmother, didn't think he was "The Boy Who Could Do No Wrong." I was now Fig Newton, the kid who was known to burst into tears at the drop of a hat, who talked too loud and had trouble paying attention in class, and who had strange nervous tics like blinking his eyes, shaking the hair out of his face, and constantly tugging at the crotch of his pants because of a minor case of undiagnosed Tourette syndrome. No, Paul Feig was a private citizen, but Fig Newton was a walking target. And I wasn't very pleased about it.

The irony was, as with many things in life, I had no idea how good I really had it until it was too late.

It happened on the first day of junior high. I entered the building, fresh from seven relatively safe years in kindergarten and elementary school, and was feeling both nervous and excited about this upgrade in rank. To be a seventh grader didn't just mean you were one year older than a sixth grader. It meant that you had gotten through the first and longest leg of your precollege journey. You'd done seven years of the basics and were deemed worthy to step up to the next level. Life was going to be less about reading drills and times tables and using your finger to put spaces between the words you wrote with oversize pencils and more about scholarly pursuits. Feeling wise and mature, I marched proudly into my new homeroom and sat down near some friends from grade school. The teacher came in, and my excitement at my new academic surroundings grew. He was a handsome, too-cool-to-be-teaching-junior-high-school guy in his early thirties named Mr. Parks. He was the only teacher I'd ever seen at that point in my life who had a beard, and his cool quotient grew immediately once word got out that he had a guitar in his office. Mr. Parks started to call off our names from an attendance sheet. All of my classmates answered in the standard twelve-year-old's socially backward mumble of "Here" or "Present." I wanted to be different. I wanted to celebrate my new life in junior high with a hale and hearty "Right here, Mr. Parks," just to let him and the world know that I was going to be a force to be reckoned with. I could hardly contain my excitement as he worked his way through the Ds.

"Drabelski?"

". . . here."

"Drummond?"

". . . yeah."

When he got to Fazio, I knew that I would be next. I read-justed in my chair and took a breath, filling my diaphragm with a mouthful of air that was about to be transformed into my debut moment. Mr. Parks stared at the list, as if he were trying to figure something out. And then, uncertainly, he said my name.

Now, for the record, my family has always pronounced our last name "Feeg," which has stirred a lot of debate among my parents' peers. In some countries, citizens pronounce the second vowel in a pair, which would make our name come out as "F-eye-g." In other lands, people make the first vowel the dominant sound, as my ancestors had chosen to do. Well, for some reason, the melee of pronunciation rules in Mr. Parks's head made him take the squishy middle road through the world of articulation, and he tortured out a version of my name that sounded exactly like this:

"Paul . . . Fffff–aaa–ay–g?"

The laughter was deafening. In grade school, I had always attempted to make people laugh and had been semisuccessful at it, but suddenly I was getting the biggest reaction of my life and I hadn't done anything. And, more importantly, I didn't want it. Because I knew that it wasn't the good kind of laughing. I wasn't entertaining my classmates with a pithy set of observations about the fact that the cafeteria menu for that day featured something called "Ben Franklin Beans," nor was I pressing the heels of my hands against my mouth and blowing hard, creating the always laugh-inducing monster fart sound. And the phrase "we're not laughing *at* you, we're laughing *with* you" wasn't anywhere to be found. I looked around at my school chums, quite perplexed at the response, thinking that these laughs were far too big for a simple mistake in pronunciation. It was at that moment that some kid I didn't know who was sitting a couple of rows away looked right at me and said, "Paul *Fag?*"

More laughs exploded, and I knew that I had just witnessed the birth of something horrible. It was bound to happen and, in all honesty, I don't know why it didn't happen sooner. The word "fag" had started to float around on the outer fringes of my peer group right around the fifth grade. But I guess that in grade school, a fig-filled cookie was funnier than a cruel term for something we didn't understand. However, as I was about to find out, junior high was where the term flourished, and I had just been dubbed the Keeper of the Flame. As Mr. Parks tried in vain to quiet the class and regain order, I sat in the stunned realization that I had just seen the next several years of my life laid out for me.

Fig Newton was dead. Long live Paul Fag.

Even though it was of little consolation, I would come to find out that every guy was called a "fag" at one point or another during the day in junior high, and usually multiple times. There was no escaping it. Anything you did could cause you to be labeled a "fag." If you carried a lunchbox, you were a fag. If you wore a wool cap on a cold day, you were a fag. If you carried your books in a knapsack, you were a fag. It all added up to fag. The only time you weren't a fag was when you were calling somebody else a fag. And so, I guess that's why everyone was always calling everybody else "fag" all the time. If an army's shooting at you, raise a white flag, walk across the battlefield, and join them.

The irony was that few of us had any idea what the word even meant. There was a vague knowledge that it was a derogatory term for a guy who likes another guy. But we all had friends who were guys and we all "liked" them in the most widely accepted usage of the word. And so, by that simple definition, I guess we all *were* fags. But as we moved to the next level of semantic understanding and were told by others in our group that the term referred to guys who liked to *kiss* each other, then we started to catch on. No matter how liberal or conservative our families were, no matter if our parents had brought us up to be tolerant and understanding of others or not, there was one thing we all knew we

didn't want to be accused of in junior high, and that was being a
guy who liked to kiss other guys. And so began our six-year quest
to not be called fag.

But there was no escape. The word "fag" was part of the lexi-
con when I grew up. Guys couldn't form sentences without it.
They couldn't articulate greetings. It was as if "fag" had been programmed into all of their DNA and set by Mother Nature to ac-
tivate the minute they walked through the junior-high doors.

That and the word "dick". In some ways, "dick" was more
popular than "fag".

"Hey, ya *dick!*"

"What are you looking at, *dick?*"

I think its vogue was probably due to the fact that we all knew
exactly what a "dick" was. Which somehow made it even more
painful.

Guys whose actual names were Dick had it worse than I did
with the name Feig. Because if you were named Dick, then you
really *were* a Dick, and so you couldn't even get mad or report
your tormentor to the teacher because he could get himself out
of it with an innocent look and an "I was just calling him by his
name." The more industrious Dicks in my town would always
show up for their first day of school as Richards, but no self-
respecting twelve-year-old looking to oppress would ever fall for
that. To them, a Dick by any other name . . .

There was only one way for a Richard to avoid being a Dick
and it all had to do with the genetic lottery. Dorky Richards were
automatically Dicks. But if a guy was good-looking and tough and
cool and could actually kick the crap out of you if he heard you
call him Dick, then that Richard would be called "Rick."

I always hated guys named Rick. Because *anytime* you heard a
group of girls talking about who they were in love with and who
they'd give a million dollars just to have as their boyfriend, it was
always a Rick.

"Oh, my God. *Rick* is sooooooooo cute. I can't believe it."

"*Rick* is a total FOX."

"I'd do anything to go out with *Rick*."

Rick, Rick, Rick. It felt like every girl I ever had a crush on in school was in love with one Rick or another. And I never met a Rick who wasn't a handsome guy. It always made me wonder if hospitals had some kind of naming service to properly identify different types of babies.

"Well, Mr. Ramsey. It looks like your son is going to be quite a handsome lad, and one who will probably persecute and humiliate all the other male babies in this room someday. Might I suggest the name 'Rick'?"

So, the basic rule we learned early on was never call a Rick a dick. Or a fag. But the rest of us were fair game. There we were, trapped in our cinder-block prison, making our way through the endless days of homework assignments and pop quizzes, being called "fags" and "dicks" and "queers" and "homos" and any additional combination of those terms coupled with one or more parts of our anatomy. "Dick-head" or "fag-face" or "queer-ass" were all wonderful ways for your oppressors to break up the monotony of their daily name-calling grind.

But around *me,* they were purists. There was no need to invent any new terms when fate had provided them the perfect target—to the guys in my school, I was, and always would be, Paul Fag.

Except on the days when I accidentally wore white socks. Then, for some reason, I was called a "Polack."

Man, did I hate school.

ARMY-ISSUE ELF

I was selected to play the lead elf in my school's Christmas pageant when I was in the first grade.

I'd like to think that I was picked because someone thought I was bursting with unharnessed talent, that by merely looking at me they could see I was something special, a miniature Laurence Olivier just waiting to spring my talents upon the performing world.

Unfortunately for my ego, that's not the case. The only reason I got the part was because my voice was louder and better suited to be heard in a cavernous gymnasium than any other kid in my class.

I don't really remember the specifics of my recruitment into the world of theater. I just remember that one day I came home and told my mother I needed an elf costume.

"An elf costume? Hmmm . . ." My mother had an annoying habit of pondering things that I felt a person should immediately grasp. She and I had seen plenty of TV shows and commercials with elves in them. We'd watched the perennially creepy Rankin-Bass production of *Rudolph the Red-Nosed Reindeer* on TV together at Christmastime enough for her to know what one of Santa's miniature helpers wore. Personally, I was always terrified by the stop-motion antics of Herbie, the elf who wanted to be a dentist, and his tribe of oddly articulated cohorts, whose mouth movements were almost as upsetting as the way the Abominable Snowman's fur moved around unmotivated whenever he walked. But Herbie and company were the fashion standard for any elf wanna-bes and a good guide for any parent looking to outfit his or her son. The problem was, it seemed that my mother had never really focused on the show in all the times she'd watched it with me, and now it was going to be my job to help her figure out how the hell an elf dressed.

When my father came home that night, my mother informed him of my wardrobe needs. "We're supposed to make an *elf* costume for Paul," she said in a tone that bordered on incredulous.

"An *elf?*" said my father, immediately annoyed. "How are we supposed to do *that?*"

"I don't know. You'd think the school would make the costumes *for* them."

This then sent my mother and father into a half-hour-long discussion about where their tax dollars were going and what disrepair the school district was in.

It's not that my parents couldn't afford to outfit me. On the contrary, my father owned an army surplus store called Ark Surplus and had done quite well for himself. My dad called the store Ark Surplus for two reasons. One, he was a religious man and felt that the word *ark* represented protection and security, a name and image that would give his customers the reassurance to know his store would be there for a good long time, taking care of all their army-surplus needs like a nurturing mother hen. The second, and far more important, reason that he called it Ark Surplus was that by having his store start with an *A,* he was guaranteed to be the first business listed in the Yellow Pages under the heading "Army-Navy Surplus." Apparently, if you're a person who's looking for stuff the army doesn't want anymore, the first name in the book is good enough for you.

If a kid's father could own any kind of business, an army-surplus store is about as good as it gets, falling short only of a toy company or a roller-coaster factory. Ark Surplus was packed to the rafters with every kind of tent and hat and canteen and army uniform ever made, not to mention all kinds of low-rent sporting goods, products that were a name brand only if you lived in Taiwan or China. Spelling and syntax mistakes on the packages were more numerous than in a first grader's "How I Spent My Summer Vacation" essay. Items such as rubber rain ponchos sold in packages emblazoned with phrases like "Puncho to keeping rain off arm and logs" and "Super hi-fi re-inforce zipper tooths," which featured artists' renderings of a man in a poncho whose ethnic grab-bag of a face indicated that his parents must have been an American GI and a Vietnamese prostitute, were but the tip of the iceberg of merchandise for sale in my father's store. He was fond of saying that he had made most of his money off the "hippies and yippies" who, in the mid- to late 1960s, descended on his store to buy all his army jackets, shirts, and fatigue pants as part of their protest garb. The Vietnam War was a dark period in our history, but to my dad, it was all green.

His store was also where almost everything we used in our house came from. For years my father had brought home small bottles filled with a yellow liquid that the army had produced as insect repellent for soldiers in the jungle. It had a toxic smell and turned your skin into an arid wasteland within minutes of application. However, it definitely kept the bugs away. Whenever I'd see my friends' mothers spraying them with Off!, I'd feel a sense of superiority, knowing that I was warding off mosquitoes courtesy of the United States armed forces. It wasn't until I was sixteen years old that my father informed me the government had made him stop selling his bug repellent several years earlier because no one knew what was in it, and indications were good that whatever its active ingredient was, it wasn't something that should be put on human skin.

"Why'd you let us keep *using* it?" I asked incredulously.

"I don't know—it just worked really well" was his disturbing answer. And that was my dad in a nutshell.

I also never encountered a real piece of toilet paper until I went away to college, because my father would stock our bathrooms with the industrial toilet tissue that he bought at a discount from his government wholesalers. It had all the softness and absorbency of typing paper and acted more like a frosting spreader than a piece of toilet tissue. Once, while on a sleep-over at a friend's house, I went in his bathroom and for the first time in my life used a piece of quilted toilet paper and had a religious experience. It was around this time that I started to curse the day my dad ever owned an army-surplus store.

However, as a first grader who was simply trying to get an elf costume for the Christmas pageant, I knew exactly where that costume was going to be pieced together.

"All right," said my father with a sigh. "I'll take him down to the store this weekend and we'll figure something out."

A few days later, we went into Ark Surplus and started scouring the aisles for anything that was vaguely elflike.

"This looks like a hat that an elf would wear," said my mother, picking up an olive drab green watch cap, similar to the one worn by Mike Nesmith of the Monkees.

"What kind of pants do elves wear?" my father asked as he poked through a shelf filled with hunting clothes.

"I think they wear shorts," offered my mother.

"Yeah," I chimed in. "They wear shorts with suspenders."

"Well, I don't have any shorts here. At least, none that'll fit *him,*" my father said, frustration rising in his voice. It was Sunday, the only day my father closed his store and the vision of himself passed out in his chair with the Sunday paper lying uselessly on his stomach was obviously dancing in his head as he tried to unlock the fashion mysteries of the North Pole workforce.

I don't know why my parents didn't try to find a book that had a picture of an elf in it that they could have used for reference. Maybe it was pride, or maybe it was the fact that my parents had no real use for the accoutrements of Christmas. My father always bought our tree at the local YMCA but that was about as far as Christmas decorating went in our house. The same red spray-painted foam balls with macaroni glued to them that I had made in preschool adorned our trees until I left for college. My mother had no patience for decorating, so one rather moth-eaten-looking Santa doll she had won in a Kiwani-Queens bingo game became the sole representative of holiday cheer in our house. My father spent most of my childhood telling everybody at Christmastime, "Christmas is a holiday for kids. Anyone over eighteen who expects to get Christmas presents should have his head examined." This Scrooge-like theory stopped at his store's cash register, however, since he still made lots of money off Christmas surplus shoppers, scary people who liked to buy old army helmets, bayonets, and dummy hand grenades as presents for their loved ones. But whatever their true feelings about Christmas were, my parents felt they could pull an elf costume out of all this former soldier gear. And I had no choice but to trust them.

We came home that afternoon with a bag full of army issued goods. The search for elf shorts resulted in my father's grabbing a pair of olive drab (or "O.D.," as surplus hipsters called it) green U.S. government boxer shorts and two black nylon straps. These straps were usually used to lash down an ammunition box but were now going to serve as my merry suspenders. The question of footwear had stumped all three of us, and so a long pair of O.D. green socks and a lengthy piece of foam rubber had been harvested in the hopes of approximating an elf shoe.

"Okay," said my father with determination, "let's get to work."

He and my mother went about constructing my elf outfit. I put on a white button-up shirt from my closet and stepped into the army boxers, which my mother then hoisted up, practically lifting

me off the ground and giving me an army-issue wedgie. My father took the black nylon straps and taped the ends inside the front
and back of the boxers, creating a suspender-like effect.

"What the hell do elves' feet look like anyway?" my father
asked, staring at the long army socks.

"They have shoes that curl up," I offered.

"I think it's their *feet* that curl up," my mother said, as if the idea
that only their shoes curled up was an absurd notion.

My father thought for a second, then grabbed a knife and went
to work on the piece of foam rubber from his store. He cut two
large banana-shaped curls that were almost a foot long and then
stuffed one inside the toe of each sock.

"Here, put these on," he said, handing them to me with a look
that said he was convinced he was almost finished with his cos-
tuming task.

I pulled the socks on and stood up. My feet now looked like
two dark green pontoons. Instead of curling upward, they gently
rose at about a fifteen-degree angle. In addition, my feet were
now each about twenty-four inches long. My father looked at my
"shoes" for a couple of seconds, then nodded his approval.

"Those look like elf feet to me," he said, satisfied with his crea-
tive skills.

My mother pulled the watch cap down onto my head and then
she and my father stepped back to inspect me. Their stares made
it quite clear they had no idea whether I looked like an elf or not.

"It feels like there's something missing," my mother said, hand
on chin, thinking.

"He looks like an elf to me," said my dad with a sigh that alerted
the world he now had about five more seconds of elf duty left in
him.

"I know what's missing," said my mom excitedly and sprinted
off to the bathroom.

As I stood there with my dad staring at me with a perplexed
look on his face, I didn't know how I felt. I liked being in a cos-

tume, and since I wasn't able to see myself, I imagined that I looked every inch an elf.

"Why are you playing an elf anyway?" my father asked in a tone that sounded like he was insulted by the very thought of his son portraying a mere peon in Santa's organization.

"I don't know," I said, surprised at my father's question. "I guess they think I look like one."

"You don't look like an elf to me. Well, except for the costume."

Before my father's disapproval could scar me for life, my mother ran back in with some cotton balls and a bottle of Elmer's glue.

"This is what was missing," she said and proceeded to put glue on three cotton balls. She took two of them and put one on the toe of each sock. Then she took the third cotton ball and stuck it on top of my hat.

She stepped back and looked at me proudly. "*Now* he looks like an elf."

My parents stared at me. Several seconds passed.

All of a sudden, my mother burst into laughter. After a few seconds, my father caught the fever, too, and soon my parents were sitting on the floor, helpless with hysterics.

I knew tomorrow would not be a good day.

I headed off to school the next morning with my costume in a paper grocery bag. The pageant was scheduled for the end of the day and was to be attended by the entire school. Older kids were going to play the bigger roles in the show like Santa and his reindeer, while it had been left to my class to be the army of elves, mainly because we were all the correct height. Since I had been blessed with a loud voice and good speaking skills, I was to portray the skeptical elf, for whom the pageant was being held. In an act of Charlie Brown plagiarism, my character apparently had problems deciphering what the true spirit of Christmas was and it was up to everyone else in the show to convince me that Christmas wasn't just about presents and food. Which was ironic because to every single one of us in that elementary school, presents and food were *exactly* what Christmas was all about. But, like the celebrity who endorses a product he'd never use in a million years, we in the pageant were going to try to sell this altruistic bill of goods to our fellow students.

I had a queasy feeling in my stomach all morning. While I was looking forward to being the star of the Christmas pageant, I was having great angst over my elf costume. The sight of my parents helpless with laughter had shattered whatever confidence I had at six years old and so I was quite worried about the reaction I was going to get from my peers.

"What's your elf costume look like?" I asked my friend Brian.

"I don't know," Brian said with a shrug. "It's pretty stupid."

I started polling the other kids in the class. They all seemed to think that their costumes were not really very elflike.

"My mom made mine, but I don't know if she really knew what she was doing," offered up Amanda, the girl who sat across from me.

"Yeah, my dad made me wear the same crappy elf costume that my brother wore a couple of years ago," said Mike, a kid who always had some form of bright green visible around the vicinity of his nostrils.

I started to take heart. Maybe my costume wasn't so bad. True, I looked a little more combat-ready than any elf I'd ever seen but that was just about color. The cotton ball on my hat looked fairly pixieish, and I liked that my foam-filled socks gave the impression that my actual foot was big and not just merely a normal foot encased in an oversize curly shoe. And in my faux lederhosen, I almost looked like one of the kids from *The Sound of Music*. Well, except that I had freakishly large feet.

No, I thought, maybe I was going to be okay.

After lunch, our teacher, Miss Connor, informed us it was time to change into our costumes and get ready for the pageant. She shepherded the girls off to another room to change, and we boys went about the business of transforming ourselves into Santa's army.

What I saw next worried me.

Out of every bag, my peers produced gaily colored costumes. Bright reds and greens and crisp clean whites made the room glow. The infusion of hues seemed to have an almost magical effect on our otherwise colorless classroom. My friends all started donning their vibrant costumes, shorts with white fake fur around the waist and matching suspenders that actually crossed in the back. Some of the kids even had green or red tights. And everyone had shoes that looked like they came from a Hollywood studio costume department. These were the most realistic-looking elf costumes I had ever seen, better than the ones worn by the teenagers who worked at the mall and dragged you over to Santa to have your picture taken. And it was in this atmosphere that I pulled out my United States military elf attire.

"What color is *that?*" asked Brian in the same tone of voice he would have used if I had pulled a turd out of the bag.

"It's O.D. green," I said defensively.

"What's *odie* green?"

"*O.D.* stands for *olive drab,*" I said disdainfully, hoping to make Brian realize how uneducated he was in the vernacular of our country's military.

"Elves aren't that color," piped in Mike. "You're gonna look like a booger."

This got a round of laughter, as any reference to bodily functions or emissions always did back then, and it was quite clear I had a long afternoon ahead of me.

I put on my outfit and became the focal point of the room.

"What's wrong with your feet?" another kid said incredulously.

"They're elf feet. They're *sup-posed* to be big."

"Elves' feet aren't big," said Brian. "Their *shoes* are big."

"No they're not," I countered. "It's their *feet*. They're big and curly. My mom said so."

"Well, your mom is wrong."

Miss Connor came back into the room and looked us all over.

"Very nice. You all look wonderful," she said with a smile that showed she was overcome with the cuteness of the scene. Then she saw me. "Oh . . . my" was all she could muster as she stared at me with a furrowed brow that seemed to say, "Maybe I should call Child Services."

"He doesn't look like an elf, does he, Miss *Con-nor?*" Mike said, throwing a mocking glance my way. He always had an annoying habit of using Miss Connor's name like a weapon to prove my stupidity.

"I don't know," said Miss Connor. "I think he looks exactly like the kind of elf who would have doubts about Christmas."

Touché. I had spent the last several months unsure whether I should have a crush on Miss Connor or not, and now I found the scales tipping in her favor. It had been a toss-up between Miss Connor and Amy Lepnick, the blond-haired girl who sat at the front of my row. But since Miss Connor had just given me a great defense for my costume and Amy had just that morning informed me, "Your ears are too big," Miss Connor was now the love of my life.

"That's right, Miss Connor. That's why my parents made me dress like this," I said, giving Miss Connor my most sincere teacher's pet smile. Mike rolled his eyes.

Miss Connor brought us out into the hallway, where the girls were waiting. They, like my fellow male elves, all looked like they had been professionally outfitted by the costumer of the Ice Capades. Each girl was wearing a red or green short dress with white fur on the hem and on the ends of her sleeves. They had on matching stockings and shoes that all seemed to have just the right amount of curl. Their shoes also made their feet look actual size.

I guess even in Christmas Town, obscenely big feet are a no-go for the upwardly mobile female elf.

When the girls spotted me, they stared in disbelief. I saw a few of them stifle laughter. Amanda, despite her Coke bottle glasses, blinked at me and said, "You look weird."

"I'm an elf who doesn't know the meaning of Christmas. I'm *sup-posed* to look this way," I said in a haughty tone.

"You look like a booger that doesn't know the meaning of Christmas," piped in Michelle. It got a huge laugh from both the girls and the guys, even though Mike had already gotten a laugh with the same lowbrow reference earlier. One thing's for certain in grade school—a booger joke will *always* land well with your audience.

We all headed down the hall to the gym, where the pageant would be taking place. I straggled at the back of the group, trying to avoid my classmates' stares and comments. "You look like an elf who lives in a garbage dump" and "They should call you Stinky the Retarded Elf" were just a few of the zingers my fellow North Pole inhabitants got off at my expense. In addition to the slings and arrows my peers were hurling my way, I was having a lot of trouble walking, since my socks had no soles to provide traction and had thus reduced every step I took to that of walking across an ice skating rink in new leather-soled shoes. The effect was more of an elf with a drinking problem than a kid whose parents had sent him off to school with improper footwear. After a few minutes, however, I discovered that slippery socks could be fun and started skidding back and forth down the hall like a big-footed hockey player, well in my own world.

Just then, Miss Connor stopped. "Oh, shoot. I was supposed to tell Mr. Kavich's class to come down to the gym in five minutes." With this comment, she looked back at us and noticed that I was at the rear of the group. "Oh, Paul, run down to their room and tell them, would you?"

My heart sank. It was the last thing I wanted to do. Mr. Kavich's class was sixth grade. Even though I knew they were soon to see me in the pageant festooned in my government-surplus elf gear, there was something about their seeing me out of context that I knew spelled trouble.

"But . . ."

"Hurry up. If we forget, we won't have any upperclassmen in the audience. Now go on," Miss Connor said, giving me a smile that to her said "Be a good boy and make me proud" but that to me said "I'm in love with you, Paul Feig. Do this for me and I'll dedicate the rest of my life to you."

Having crushes on teachers is the surest way of relinquishing any and all power over your dignity when you're a kid.

I smiled at her and ran off to deliver my message. I glanced back and watched the rest of my class head off to the other end of the hallway and disappear around the corner. As they marched away from me, I was struck by how authentic they all looked in their elf costumes. It made our hallway look like one of those cheesy movies about Hollywood studios, where the street outside the movie sound stage is always filled with extras dressed like centurions and astronauts and Vegas showgirls. Seeing my classmates looking so elfinly accurate and not being in front of a mirror to see myself made my own costume start to morph into something magical inside my head. The noncommittal olive drab that dominated my army/navy outfit started to turn a Santa-approved kelly green as I ran and skidded down the hallway. My boxer shorts suddenly sprouted fur trim and my night watchman's cap with the cotton ball on top became much more like a hat that Robin Hood would be proud to wear, complete with a razor-sharp pheasant's feather as a plume. On top of that, there was no greater pleasure than to be out of class and in an empty hallway when you knew that behind all those closed doors you were passing were students wishing they were in your shoes. Or foam-filled socks, as the case may be. No, I was one light 'n' lively elf, roaming the countryside delivering good cheer to the poor unfortunates, ready to transform their holiday season from simple commercialism into Yuletide magic.

I slid up in front of Mr. Kavich's classroom door. I could hear him lecturing behind it. The weirdest thing about being in a hallway when classes were in session was hearing all those teachers lecturing to all those students and knowing that each lecture was about things you didn't know yet. From behind Mr. Kavich's door I could hear him talking about the roots of grammar and to me at the time it sounded as erudite as if I had been standing outside a quantum physics lecture in a hallway at MIT. Feeling very cool to be seconds away from entering a sixth-grade classroom as a lowly first grader, I confidently knocked on the door.

"Come in," said Mr. Kavich.

I opened the door and stepped inside. "Mr. Kavich, Miss—"

That was as far as I got.

I've always heard that Sammy Davis Jr. kissing Archie Bunker on the cheek was the longest laugh from an audience in television history. If that's true, then I must officially nominate the response I got from this class of sixth graders as the longest laugh a first grader ever got from a room full of upperclassmen in the history of the Macomb County school system. As I stood there, watching both the students and Mr. Kavich become helpless with laughter, I pondered whether this was the kind of joy and goodwill I, as an elf, was supposed to be bringing to the world. I had certainly put them in a holly-jolly mood. Anybody could cheer another person up by giving him or her a present, but to be able to fill people with happiness just by entering a room . . . well, I figured, that took talent. Granted, this wasn't so much happiness as it was ridicule, but in the world of the elf, the theory had to be "Whatever it takes." And I was definitely taking one for Santa's team.

But, after all, 'twas the season.

The pageant was a blur to me. There are unsettling home movies from the event my father dutifully took that show me reciting my skeptical-elf routine so loudly that you can almost hear my voice coming through the soundless eight-millimeter film. Behind me in a sloppy line are my fellow elves, fidgeting and shifting their weight and picking their noses and engaging in general unprofessional stagecraft. I, on the other hand, despite my nontraditional garb, was the very picture of professionalism. I had overcome the handicap of my costume, the mockery of my peers and schoolmates, the stifled laughter of every teacher and parent in the audience, and I discovered the true meaning of Christmas. They had all laughed at the skeptical elf and made fun of his clothes, but the skeptical elf had learned that it was about more than just clothes and presents and decorations. He had learned what this holiday was all about, and he hadn't done it for them, not for himself, and, no, not even for Santa.

No, the skeptical surplus elf had done it all for one thing and one thing only . . .

The United States Army.

GROWING UP THROWING UP

When I was in grade school, it seemed like everyone was always throwing up. Every time I turned around, I'd hear a splat and see some queasy-looking kid standing over a puddle of puke. And then, seconds later, I'd get a whiff of that unmistakable throw-up smell. This always announced the imminent arrival of a janitor, who would enter carrying a large broom and a dustpan full of red sawdust to dump on top of the offending pool of barf, which was then swept back into the dustpan and spirited away by our unlucky custodian.

What a gig.

I've never been able to forget that red sawdust. I always knew when it was around because of its own distinct odor, something akin to an extremely cheap bottle of Grandma perfume, a sort of subdued peppermint smell with just a hint of mothballs thrown in. Throw-up smells terrible and, because of that, the red sawdust always smelled pretty good when it arrived. It wasn't something you'd want to smell every day, but when the air is ripe with the aroma of what was formerly inside of a kid, red sawdust was about as welcome a smell as fresh home-baked cookies on a rainy day. That is, until it was dumped on top of the vomit, where the two opposing fragrances would battle for superiority and produce a tangy, sour bouquet, like a pungent French cheese gone horribly wrong in the back of a hot car.

As a kid, I never knew why janitors always used that red sawdust or where it came from. Years later, when I was working in the warehouse at my father's store, I learned that it was actually a manufactured product called sweeping compound, and was made to both soak up spills and keep dust from going into the air as you swept a dirty floor. Not knowing this back then, I figured that the red sawdust was just something the janitor had found lying around in the wood shop and decided was as good a substance as any to camouflage a puddle of throw-up. Because he had to do something so that we kids didn't have to look at it. All school professionals know that if one kid sees another kid's throw-up, that kid will then also throw up. And then another and another. Throwing up is contagious. One kid with a nervous stomach can set off a chain reaction in a crowded classroom that could seriously deplete the world's supply of sweeping compound.

I never understood how my peers could throw up so easily. To me, throwing up is about the worst thing that can happen to a person. The stomach-twisting retches. The complete lack of control of one's body. The hellish sounds of air being forced through the upwardly traveling bile. To this day, I think I'd rather die of food poisoning than have to throw the tainted food back up. I think I've only thrown up about three times in my life. But never in school. Things were bad enough without adding regurgitation to my list of problems.

My most vivid experience with throw-up happened in the second grade. It was show-and-tell day, and I had brought in a brand-new Hot Wheels fire truck that I was dying to show off and tell about. That truck, which I had wanted for months, was everything I had dreamed it would be and more. Bright red and so new that all four wheels were still straight. They hadn't had a chance to bend inward yet like Hot Wheels cars always did after a few play sessions, so that when the car was rolled, it would simply go into a spin and tip over. No, this Hot Wheels fire truck was pristine. It even had a little ladder that you could move up and extend out. I'd been trying to get my mother to buy it for me for what seemed like a million years and had finally guilted her into it. The day before, she had accidentally thrown my favorite troll doll in with the laundry and had turned his bright red hair pink, and I played her like a royal flush. My tears could only be stopped by a trip to the toy store and, lo and behold, the fire truck was mine. And now I couldn't wait to impress my peers with it.

The teacher, Miss Drulk, had gone out of the room for a minute, and I was busy making the truck race to the scene of a fire on my desktop, complete with screeching tires sound. I was good at sound effects and was convinced that no one could do the sound of a car getting into an accident and blowing up better than I could. True, I couldn't do a machine gun as well as my friend Gary, and when it came to helicopters, Stephen Crowley was the king. But when it came to automobiles, the rest of the class could simply step aside. I was the master.

As I sat there, lost in my own noisy world, making the truck go into a catastrophic slide that saw it heading for a fall off the side of my desk—where it would then burst into flames in super-slow motion—Chris Davis, a perpetually dirty kid who sat behind me, tapped me on the shoulder.

"Hey, Paul, that's a neat truck. Can I use it for show-and-tell?"

What? I thought. No way. This was mine. I'd been waiting all day to show this baby off. "No. My mother just bought it for me."

"Aw, c'mon. I don't have anything to show. My family can't buy me anything. We're poor."

For a kid who was poor, he sure said it a lot. I'd always heard that poor people were proud, but the only thing Chris was proud of was telling you how poor he was. He was always talking about how his family lived in a shack, how they didn't have any clothes, and how they had to eat birds in order to keep from starving. I never knew if I believed him or not. I couldn't imagine anyone's family sitting around naked eating robins and sparrows. But my mother had always drilled into my head that I had to be nice to people who were less fortunate than we were because we, too, might be poor someday. Did she know something I didn't? I would wonder. Were we on the verge of bankruptcy? Because I was terrified of the thought of having to walk around in front of my parents naked.

I stared at Chris for a few seconds, deliberating. He stared back at me with a pathetic look on his face. I stared at his hands. They were filthy. His clothes had food stains down the front. His hair was dirty and looked like it hadn't been combed in days. I wasn't sure if this meant that he was poor or if it was simply proof that the guy was a slob. However, my Sunday school teacher's voice rang out in my head: "Do unto others as . . ." Yeah, yeah, yeah. All right. I get it. Stupid Bible.

"Well . . . okay. Here. But be *careful* with it."

Fortunately, I had brought along one of my less cool Hot Wheels cars and I figured I could show it instead. I don't know why I didn't give Chris the less cool car, but I didn't. I guess I wasn't good at thinking on my feet when I was seven.

Miss Drulk came back into the room. I had a huge crush on Miss Drulk. She was beautiful. She always wore short dresses and her hair was done up in that 1960s straight-down-to-the-shoulders-then-flipped-up-at-the-ends style that I thought was just the most feminine thing imaginable back then. Simply put, she had blond *That Girl* hair. And she was always extra nice to me, too. Miss Drulk knew that the other kids picked on me and she always seemed to be coming to my defense. Once, when some third graders made a dog pile on top of me at recess, Miss Drulk came running over and made everyone get off. I was crying, as usual, and so she took me into the teacher's lounge and gave me carrot sticks out of her lunch. I really fell in love with her that day. Even now, when I eat carrot sticks, I occasionally think about Miss Drulk. Her or Carl Slanowski, who used to secretly shove carrot sticks up his nose, then give them out to teachers.

Anyway, Miss Drulk came into the room and announced that it was time for show-and-tell. When she said it I felt a twinge of excitement. But then I quickly remembered that it was going to be the poverty-stricken Chris Davis, and not myself who would be showing off the brand-new Hot Wheels fire truck. I immediately felt mad at the guy for guilting me out of my first moment ever of potential coolness.

And then suddenly, out of nowhere, I heard it.

SPLAT.

Oh, no, I thought. It couldn't be.

I turned around to see Chris Davis sitting behind his desk, which was now covered with throw-up. COVERED. For a poor kid, he sure had a lot in his stomach. And what was buried under the lake of vomit?

My fire truck.

Chris had barf running down his chin and was about to start crying. Kids always cried after they threw up. Probably because throwing up was so disgusting, there was nothing else to do *but* cry. And if you cried, the odds were you didn't have to clean it up yourself. But when I saw Chris about to start bawling, I just wanted to slug him. I mean, if anyone had the right to cry, it was me. Couldn't he have pushed my fire truck out of the way when he felt the vomit coming? I mean, throw-up gives you a couple seconds of warning before it arrives. It doesn't just appear. You've got at least a few solid moments of nausea and tingling in the back of your throat that lets you know you have time to push a brand-new three-inch-long Hot Wheels fire truck that doesn't belong to you out of the goddamn way. And didn't the kid even know he was sick? He must have at least felt queasy when he was talking to

me. A person just can't feel great one minute and the lose the entire contents of his stomach the next. I guess he'd had a bad bird
for breakfast.

Chris started crying. Miss Drulk came over and pulled him
away from his desk. The massive amount of vomit was starting to
migrate down his desktop and spill over the edge onto his seat. It
was truly disgusting, but the worst part of it was seeing that faint
outline of a fire truck–shaped lump underneath it all. Miss Drulk
hustled Chris off to the bathroom. I heard him crying all the way
down the hall and even heard his sobs echoing out of the boys'
room. Mr. Carowski, our mysterious janitor, a mountain of a man
from some unknown country who spoke to us in an unintelligible
mixture of garbled English and rumbling bass tones, came in with
the famous red sawdust and dumped it on top of Chris Davis's
desk. All my classmates were over at the window trying to get
some fresh air, since the room was now filled with the unmistakable odor of stomach stew. Mr. Carowski then took a hand broom,
swept the whole vomity mess into a bucket, and sprayed the desk
with disinfectant. The disinfectant smelled even sweeter than the
red sawdust, but that didn't make me feel any better. Mr. Carowski
took his bucket, mumbled a few indecipherable words that I think
were supposed to convey the warning "Don't touch his desk until
it dries," and departed. I looked down at where my fire truck had
once sat. Nothing was left but the memory.

I never asked Mr. Carowski about my fire truck, and I never
saw it again.

And I never got over my anger at Chris Davis. Especially when
I found out that he lived in a house twice as big and way nicer
than mine.

I AM BETRAYED BY A GIRL

Childhood is built on bad decision making. In fact, if it weren't for all the bad decisions we were constantly carrying out as kids, there's a good chance that none of us would have figured out all the things we weren't going to do when we became adults.

A few of the more obvious lessons I learned as a kid were:

- Don't ride a bike with no brakes down a very steep street that dead-ends into a feculent, stagnant river.
- Don't hold a lit firecracker in your hand to see if it'll hurt when it explodes.
- Don't save your urine in a flowerpot for more than a week in a hot garage if you don't want your parents to find it.

All obvious conclusions. All painfully learned.

The good thing about those epiphanies was that they stuck with me. Once I'd done them and realized how stupid I'd been to do them in the first place, I never did them again.

Unfortunately, this was not the case with all of my bad decision making. Because there was one area where I just kept making the same mistakes over and over again:

Girls.

I know that most people have ill-fated stories concerning their interactions with the opposite sex. But they usually don't begin to appear until their junior-high or high-school years. For me, my stupidity with girls started as soon as I walked out of my preschool.

As a kid, I was somewhere around the mean average when it came to emotional maturity and intellect. I wasn't the dopiest kid in the class but I wasn't the most advanced, either. The kids who you could tell were going to "go places" were already starting to show the beginnings of leadership qualities even at an early age. While it didn't manifest itself in anything as overt as some future class president's jumping up on his third-grade desk and leading us in a revolt against our teacher's unfair demand that we hang up our coats or organizing a sit-in next to the teeter-totters in order to protest the shortness of our recess periods, you could just see that some kids were the types that other kids followed.

That wasn't me.

Fortunately, I wasn't a member of the paste-eaters either, the underachievers I would routinely observe digging their fingers deep into the inner reaches of their noses to extract something green that would immediately be snuck into their mouths as a sort of chewing tobacco for the younger set. These were the kids who routinely fell off the monkey bars and peed their pants and threw off the rhythm of the teacher's lessons by raising their hands and uttering such pithy phrases as "What?" and "Huh?"

No, I was not one of them either. I was a youngster who clearly fell in the middle of the social bell curve. Except for the fact that I liked girls.

I'd always liked girls, ever since I was five. Maybe it was because I grew up next door to a house with eight kids, five of whom were girls. Of them, my best friend Mary and I started playing together when we were babies. And so I was quickly broken of the "euw, cooties" instinct before it ever had a chance to take effect. This set me apart from my male classmates, many of whom were still begging one another well into the sixth grade to "spray" them after they had been brushed against by a girl. (For those of you who didn't grow up in my neighborhood, "spraying," was the act of holding an imaginary aerosol can about six inches away from your friend's cooties-infected area and making a *psssssht* sound while moving the imaginary can back and forth over the offending patch of skin, thus decontaminating the victim from whatever disease was believed to result from contact with a female.) No, I was a much more worldly five-year-old who had watched too many sappy romances with my mother on the *Afternoon Million-Dollar Movie* and had thus been transformed into a pint-size Lord Byron who decided that girls were to be sought out and wooed, not sprayed against and run from.

And it was because of this that, when I was six years old, I had a girlfriend.

True, it was in the most patronizing sense of the word, usually uttered by my parents at bridge games to their friends in the form of "You know, Paul has a little *girlfriend* now." Their fellow bridge players, upon hearing these words, would look over at me as I sat there watching TV and give me one of those annoying "isn't he cute in his ignorant six-year-old way?" smiles that I now find myself giving to little kids no matter how hard I try not to. But whether they or anybody else chose to believe it, Patty Collins *was* my girlfriend.

At least for half a day.

It was a warm, sunny morning in the summer between kindergarten and first grade, and I had walked the four blocks over to Patty's house to play. When I arrived, the day started out like all the others we had spent together. We played a few games of Candyland and the ironically titled CootieBug and were having a nice time. It was then that our play date took an unexpected turn.

"Do you want to set up a tent?" she asked me.

"A tent?" I asked, uncertain. "Why?"

"I don't know," she said with a shrug. "We could play inside it."

It seemed like an innocent enough idea to me. After all, when you're a kid you always seem to be desperate to hide inside things. Whether it's a plastic cube at the top of the playground slide or an appliance box or a makeshift fort made by taking your mom's wooden fold-out drying rack and covering it with a blanket, we as kids always seemed to enjoy sequestering ourselves away from the rest of the world. I think when you're that age that it's the only time you seem to have any control over your life. Hiding places were safe havens where we couldn't be forced to eat brussels sprouts and could cough without covering our mouths and could make goofy faces without fear of being told our faces were going to "freeze that way." Inside our boxes and forts and treehouses, we were kings and queens. We were our parents, and we had ultimate authority. Or at least we did until somebody yelled at us to get out of there.

Patty and I took three old blankets and went out to her driveway. We tied one blanket to the fence, so that it could hang down and block her neighbors from seeing us through the chain link. We put another blanket on the ground, then tied the third to the top of the fence. Then we pulled this blanket out at an angle and used a couple of bricks to hold it in place. And now we had a tent.

We looked at our creation proudly. "Let's get inside," Patty said, giving me a strange smile.

Patty and I crawled inside the tent and sat there. It was a hot day, and the blankets gave off the scent of the fabric softener Patty's mom had washed them in. Pools of sunlight danced on the blanket hanging in front of us, the shadows of the leaves from the oak tree in her yard silhouetted on our tent's fuzzy surface. The movement of the branches in the slight breeze that day made the shadows of the leaves float back and forth, and we stared at this peaceful light show for a while. I would occasionally look over at Patty. She looked pretty, sitting there staring at the sunlight. She had bigger eyes than most girls I knew, and when they focused on something, they had a hypnotic quality. The breeze would occasionally drift through the tent and lightly move the ends of her hair and everything started to feel like a dream.

Patty looked over and saw me staring at her. She smiled, then got a look in her eyes that I had never seen before.

"You wanna kiss?" she asked me with a small smile.

I can't quite describe the feeling I had at that moment. I guess it's hard to explain what it feels like when your human sexuality pops like an egg in a microwave. It felt like someone had set off a small firecracker in the back of my head. The world seemed to flash white for a split second, after which my body started to go numb. I blinked at her. A barely audible "What?" was all I could muster in response.

"Let me kiss you," she said with a bigger smile and a look that I had only before seen on the faces of kids who were trying to talk you into doing something that was going to get you in trouble. We were both sitting cross-legged on the ground, and she turned her body to face me. She stared at me, her big eyes filled with anticipation.

My scalp tingled. Hot flashes shot up and down the back of my neck. I had wanted to kiss a girl ever since I'd seen Jimmy Stewart and Donna Reed kiss in *It's a Wonderful Life,* but I never dreamed it would actually happen, at least not before my voice changed. The inside of my chest felt like it was filled with helium, and I knew right then that there was nothing I wanted more in the world than to kiss Patty Collins.

So . . .

What happened next will have to go down in my Book of Bad Decisions, planted firmly in the chapter entitled "I Have No Idea What I Was Thinking."

For some strange reason, I said, "No."

But it wasn't a simple "no." It wasn't a single word said in a tone that implied "We can't do this, it's wrong." It wasn't said in a way that confessed "I can't kiss you because I'm afraid." Nor was it said in a manner that indicated "Euw, you're a girl, and I don't want your germs."

No, for some bizarre reason, my brain told me that I should become coy.

And so the word *no* came out of my mouth in two distinct parts. The first part was an extended "nnnnnnnnnn" sound, which had a slowly rising pitch that indicated I was considering the idea and was working my way toward the rendering of a decision. Accompanying this "nnnnnnnnnn" was the action of rolling my eyes to the side, also meant to show I was deliberating the request and was more than likely to agree to it. Following the "nnnnnnnnnn" was the second part: a quick and debate-ending *"oh,"* which was accompanied by my eyes snapping back to meet hers with a look of "I know you want me, but you can't have me."

In short, I had answered Patty's sweet request in exactly the same way a stuck-up girl would in an *ABC Afterschool Special*.

I don't know why I did this. I'm sure a part of me was simply scared of kissing her. However, I know that a bigger part of me, my Jimmy Stewart side, wanted to kiss the Donna Reed sitting next to me. Maybe I said no because I'd heard my cousins Leslie and Laurel talking about playing "hard to get" with guys. Maybe it was because I'd heard my father tell my mother that the more he told salesmen he didn't want to buy anything from them, the harder they'd try to sell him something. Or maybe it was just something I'd seen Gilligan do. I'm not sure, but all I know is that I was certain this was the way to handle the situation.

Well, surprisingly enough, my two-part "nnnnnnnnnn-*oh*" had the effect I was looking for. Patty smiled again and scooted up closer to me.

"C'mon, Paul. Let me kiss you."

In my six-year-old head, I knew I had her. And I suddenly felt like the coolest guy in the world. There was no reason to change my tactic.

"No," I said again, this time with more of a raised-eyebrow

"Didn't I already tell you once?" playfulness that I remember thinking was the perfect way to keep the game going and myself as appealing as ever.

Patty laughed, moved closer, and asked again. I refused again, and so began several hours of some disturbing gender-reversed game of The Cowboy Tries to Kiss the Little Lady. During our time in the tent, Patty would (a) put her arms around me and try to pull me close, (b) try to force her face into mine to deliver a peck on my lips, (c) tickle me to try and get me to give in, (d) stare at me with a pouty look meant to guilt me into kissing her, and (e) several combinations of all the above. And during her repeated advances, I would alternately (a) giggle like a girl, (b) pretend to be very serious and upset with her, (c) cover my face with my hands, (d) do a singsong "no no no" chant, and (e) make a complete ass out of myself.

As the morning passed, I remember that I was having the time of my life. There I was with a pretty girl I really liked who was desperately trying to kiss me and devoting every ounce of her energy and attention to accomplishing her task. Life didn't get better than this. I had suddenly found myself cast in the role of a miniature Hugh Hefner and was now certain that life would no longer be the same for me. And the one thing I knew for sure was that Patty could never possibly get tired of this. Ever.

But, alas, she did.

In retrospect, how couldn't she? If I were her, I would have given up after the first minute. I would have figured that I was repulsed at the thought of kissing myself and slunk away, my confidence in tatters. But Patty was too secure in her femininity to have that happen. Simply put, she knew that she was pretty, she knew that she was kissable, and she just got bored with the dork in the tent.

It happened slowly. Her romantic assaults began to lose their vigor. I, of course, found myself cluelessly misinterpreting her deceleration to mean that I had to resist even harder. I figured that

Patty's letting up was a clever ruse to con me into succumbing, that her new plan was to dangle in front of me the threat of not wanting to kiss anymore, thus getting me to let my guard down, whereupon she would throw her arms around me and we would consummate our lovers' game.

I said "no" again and waited for the next onslaught.

Patty leaned back, looked at me with bored contempt, and said, "Let's go watch *The Banana Splits.*"

At that moment, I knew I had overplayed my hand. Before I could figure out what to do, she got up and left the tent. I was stunned. How could she just walk away? Wasn't she enjoying this little passion play as much as I was? Wasn't she getting a thrill out of showering me with attention and affection? Didn't she realize how much fun I was having? I quickly scrambled out of the tent in the hopes of luring her back, but she was already inside the house. I pulled open the screen door and went in, thinking that maybe Patty was tricking me into continuing the game in her room. However, I quickly saw that she had indeed come in to watch *The Banana Splits.* She was sitting on her couch, slouched back with her knees sticking up, wearing the impassive look all kids get when they watch television. I stared at her and thought I saw a look of disappointment on her face. Unfortunately, upon closer inspection, I could see that it was something far less flatter-ing than disappointment. Disappointment would imply that I had denied her something she truly wanted. What I saw on her face was the realization that she had wasted an entire morning on an idiot. I came over to her on the couch and tried to start the game again, pathetically leaning in to her and saying, "I bet you still want to kiss me," but she was now far too engrossed in the low production-value antics of Fleegle and Snorky. I stared at her, waiting for her to laugh at the success of her newest ploy, then grab me and deliver the much anticipated soul kiss. But she didn't. When I leaned in to her again, my nose mere inches from her cheek, she pushed me away and said, "Cut it out." The game was truly over.

And suddenly, all I wanted to do in the entire world was to kiss her. My brain spun as I tried to think of ways to get her re-interested. I acted goofy, trying to make her laugh. I stared at her with what I thought was a kiss-inducing face. I even tried to get her back outside and into the tent with me. But when her dad came in and asked us if we wanted him to take our tent down and she said flatly, "Yeah, we're not using it anymore," I knew I had blown my chance. Patty Collins would not be kissing me anytime soon.

That night, I had the most vividly erotic dream I've ever had in my life. I was dressed as a bee and was standing around in some crappy-looking beehive set from a grade-school play. Patty, also dressed as a bee, was lowered down from the sky. She smiled at me, then backed her stinger into my stomach and dragged me away as I had what I now believe was my very first orgasm. What the symbolism of this image was or why it resulted in such a strong physical reaction, I have no idea. All I know is that I woke up feeling light-headed and giddy. I was now completely in love with Patty Collins and desperate to get back inside that tent with her.

But I never did. She and I only saw each other at school after that, and our interaction consisted solely of saying hello. What-ever romantic feelings Patty might have had for me had died in that tent made of blankets on her driveway one tragic summer morning when I decided it would be cute to be coy.

Over the next few years, as my male classmates were spending their days trying to become proficient at tetherball and playing the drum solo from "Wipe Out" on the edges of their desks, I was busy developing crushes on girls.

It's hard to say why we have crushes on anybody at that age. It's not like we're that in touch with who's beautiful and who's not, or who would make a good girlfriend or boyfriend. Many times our crushes are simply based on people's hair or their nose or the way they dress or if they're nice to you. In the third grade I had a big crush on Teresa Andrews, and in her case, I liked her because she was smart. She always seemed to get answers right and was usually the first one in the class to raise her hand. Maybe it was her confidence that attracted me, or maybe it was simply that she was the only girl I knew who wore glasses. I would spend hours of class time drawing pictures of her in the back of my notebook. Once our teacher, Miss Patton, caught me not paying attention during class as I was adding yet another artist's rendering of Teresa to my already stalkerlike notebook gallery. Fortunately, Miss Patton found my lovelorn doodlings to be heartwarming, and so she simply gave me a sympathetic smile, closed my notebook, and told me to pay attention. Even Miss Patton could see what a good couple Teresa and I would make, I figured. And by the middle of the school year, I decided that it was time to make my move.

I didn't know Teresa very well, even though she rode the same school bus that I did. I never had the nerve to talk to her because I was always too shy to talk to girls I had crushes on. Instead, I would try to figure out ways to get them to notice me. With Teresa, I knew I could impress her by showing her how smart I was. There was just one problem—I wasn't that smart. My grades always hovered around the letter C, and I knew it would be hard to win her over by reciting the alphabet or stammering my way through times tables I hadn't yet committed to memory. And so I knew I would have to default to the only means available to me to grab her attention . . .

I would try to make her laugh.

It had worked before with several other girls over the past couple of years. It wasn't that they would hear one of my supposedly funny comments and fall in love with me, but it at least opened up the lines of communication and gave me hope that one day I might get them to the point where they would drag me into a tent and try to kiss me. And so it was decided—this was the strategy I would use on Teresa.

The next day, I got my chance. We were studying science and Miss Patton broke us off into pairs to work on our reports. As luck would have it, she paired me with Teresa. I wasn't sure if Miss Patton had done it because of my crush or if the Fates had simply been on my side that day, but I was grateful and vowed not to squander this opportunity.

"What do you want to do our report about?" she asked me. I stared into her glasses and found myself unable to think.

"I don't know," I said, a bit too politely. "Whatever you want to do, Teresa."

She gave me a strange look that seemed to say "Thanks for all the help, jackass" and leaned back in her chair to think. I watched her furrow her brow as she pondered our report, and I tried to imagine what our children would look like. I envisioned her and me holding hands as we strolled along on the college campus where she would be a professor and where I would not be a professor. I saw us out camping, as she kissed me in a tent and I let her. Our life together was unrolling before my eyes, and the mere thought of it made me all the more desperate to crack my first joke and break the ice between us. However, the academic mood was proving to be an obstacle.

"Let's look through a science book and see if we get any ideas," she said as she stood up, talking more to herself than to me.

"Great idea, Teresa" was my enthusiastic reply, even though she was halfway across the room by the time I said it.

Teresa returned with a large book titled *Science and You*. She sat down and opened it. I moved my chair next to hers so that we could read the book together. She didn't look at me as I leaned my head in beside hers to read along, and I found myself waxing poetic over her concentration skills, as if her ability to read without being distracted was yet another good reason to dedicate my life to her. Teresa had the book open to a chart that showed man's ascension from ape to human. There were about eight apes in various stages of development, going from the hunched-over primitive ape-man up to the fully erect *Homo sapiens.* The fourth ape was a semihunched half ape–half woman whom the illustrator had decided to endow with hairy sagging breasts. Being a third grader, I immediately found this funny but instead of just laughing and pointing at the breasts like one of my less erudite peers might have, I decided that Teresa could only be won over by a more sophisticated quip. My opportunity had arrived. Science and comedy had merged. I thought hard and after a couple of seconds, I realized I had a real zinger, sure to melt Teresa's brainy heart.

I looked around to make sure the coast was clear, leaned in to Teresa, pointed to the picture of the ape-woman, and whispered in an amused tone, "Teresa, look, it's Miss Patton."

Whereupon Teresa immediately raised her hand and blurted out loudly, "Miss Patton, Paul said you look like the ape in this book."

My jaw dropped. As quickly as that, I was thrust into the spotlight. Miss Patton came over and looked at the picture, as did several other kids. You'd think that out of a roomful of third graders, somebody would see the picture of a hairy, saggy-breasted ape and deem my comment funny. But whether they were afraid to because Miss Patton was standing there or because they had suddenly all become sophisticated connoisseurs of highbrow comedy, nobody laughed. Instead, they all looked at me with a mix of contempt and disbelief. And Miss Patton, my onetime ally in the world of romance, was highly insulted. She told me that my remark was insensitive and immature and then made me go sit in the corner for an hour.

Teresa Andrews never gave me the time of day after that, although she had never given me the time of day before that, either. But I couldn't get over what a tattletale she was. And I was now completely confused as to what my relationship with women was going to be in the future. Was I destined to be the dope in the tent who felt compelled to push away the things that he wanted in life? Or would I be the clueless buffoon, pointing at pictures of ape-women with no idea when he was going too far in his search for love and acceptance?

Or would I just be the guy who overanalyzes everything and makes a big deal out of a stupid mistake? Sitting in the corner that day, listening to my peers living their lives behind me while I counted holes in the cinder block, I knew that only time would tell.

But I had a feeling the answer wasn't going to be good.

OUT OF THE CLOSET

Seek and ye shall find" is a quote that I believe comes from the Bible. I'm not quite sure, though, since thankfully I haven't had to go to church or Sunday school in about twenty-five years. For all I know it could have been a line of Spock's from the "Trouble with Tribbles" episode of *Star Trek*. But seeking and finding were two things that I did quite well as a kid.

One of the things I used to constantly seek was my yearly stash of Christmas presents. Or at least I did once I found out there was no Santa Claus.

On Christmas Eve, when I was seven, as my mom and I made a last-minute trip to the mall to buy a copy of *The Naked Ape* for my radical cousin Leslie, my mother had finally cracked under the pressure of having to lie to her only child about the jolly fat man for all these years. Doing so violated every ethic she had ever learned in church, and she resented having to do it simply because as a parent she had been ordered by society to march in lockstep with the wishes of the corporate world. Whenever a gift-getting holiday would roll around in which unearned gains were supposedly delivered by a mystical third party, I always forced her to tell me more and more about these Santa Claus and Easter Bunny and Tooth Fairy people. I think that deep in my heart I never really believed that these enigmatic, science-defying figures existed, but since all my friends seemed to be so into them, I wanted desperately to believe, too. As we drove around the mall parking lot looking for a space while Christmas music played on the car radio, I guess I finally pushed my mother too hard for a concrete answer.

"There really *is* a Santa Claus, isn't there?" I asked her point-blank.

She was silent for several moments, and then she deflated. Looking almost as if she was going to cry, she simply averted her eyes, shook her head, and uttered an embarrassed "no." It was the answer I'd been expecting, having recently deduced the impossibility of the physics of Santa's single night of worldwide gift distribution after watching a movie about clocks and time in my second-grade class. But still, I made a grand show of my mortification, dropping my jaw and making the standard "I can't believe you would do this to me" face that kids become so adept at pulling out in any circumstance in which they are denied some impulsive whim. I even forced myself to start crying, asking tearfully, "Then who eats the cookies and milk I put out on Christmas Eve?" My mother confirmed what I had always suspected and yet didn't want to believe—it was my father. In a colossal act of grief management, I decided to seek revenge. I ended up mixing a devil's brew of spices, cooking oils, vinegars, and spit in order to teach my lie-mongering father a lesson about deceiving his only son. However, as I mixed the vile-smelling cocktail in the kitchen sink while my mother watched, amused and somehow relishing my plan, as if she had wanted to get back at my father for all the years of lying he had forced her into, something happened. I was suddenly overcome with a strange mixture of disgust, grief, nostalgia, and love for my father. The image of my dad bringing out presents that he and my mother had taken the time to research, buy, and wrap was too much for me to take. He was only trying to be a good dad, I thought. I just couldn't reward his earnestness with a poisoned glass of swill. And so I ended up dumping the nauseating liquid down the drain, pouring my father a fresh glass of milk and putting it out next to a plate of just opened store-bought cookies. And when I unwrapped my presents the next morning, I pretended to be excited that Santa had arrived during the night, even though my mother threw looks at my father that showed they both knew I no longer believed but was somehow trying to squeeze one more year out of the Santa lie.

But I couldn't. Santa was dead. Rest in peace, you goddamn, fat-assed liar.

After that, whenever my parents would leave me alone in the house in the month of December, I would turn into a junior McCloud and scour my parents' bedroom for the gifts that I knew I was going to get anyway, albeit sometime in the not-near-enough future. One year, when I found a particularly good batch of toys my parents had successfully figured out I wanted, I spent the next several weeks pulling out the not-yet-wrapped presents from the back of my mother's closet whenever she left the house. I would carefully extract the toys from their packages and then play with them nervously, one ear focused on the door in our family room, listening for my parents' return. It wasn't particularly fun playing with these illegal toys but the thrill of doing something I wasn't supposed to be doing made it feel dirty and exciting.

However, my skulduggery skills proved to be far superior to my judgment skills. On Christmas Eve, when my father asked me what presents I thought I was going to get that year, I put on a big act of divining and ended up naming every single present in my mother's closet in excruciating detail, including an exact description of an obscure knock-off version of a G.I. Joe scuba outfit made for a low-rent action figure transparently named "Army Jack." My mother and father exchanged disappointed looks with each other as I made matters worse by pretending to have no idea what they were upset about.

"What? What's the matter? Why are you guys looking at each other like that?" I said, performing one of the most unconvincing portrayals of an innocent person ever perpetrated on stage or screen. My guilt was complete when, the next morning, I got up only to find my presents lying under the Christmas tree un-wrapped, and my mother sitting on the couch drinking a cup of tea, saying disappointedly, "What's the point of wrapping them? You already know what they are anyway."

After that, I vowed never to seek out my Christmas presents again. However, within weeks, the lure of the backs of my par-ents' closets proved too strong to resist and I returned to my pry-ing ways, justifying my snooping by reassuring myself that I wasn't looking for presents—I was just being nosy. I couldn't help it. It was just too tempting. Our house always seemed to offer up a never-ending wealth of poorly hidden treasures. My mother was a bit of a pack rat, a trait that I have inherited from her in spades. I am loath to throw out even the most disposable of items, for fear that some day in the near future, I will (a) find myself in need of an old *Time* magazine even though its contents are much more conveniently archived on the Internet, (b) figure out a way to re-fill and repair that old disposable "Makin' Bacon" lighter I found several years ago, or (c) mourn the nostalgic boost I'd miss if I threw away that stack of completely out-of-focus photos of my backyard taken for insurance purposes. No, mother and son Feig would save everything, and I was always stumbling upon bizarre items from my past in our closets.

My mom had saved the first book I ever wrote, an obtuse little tome titled "BananaLand" that I penned in the first grade and then tried to bind into a book using construction paper and a sta-pler. Unfortunately, I laid it out completely backward, so that it had to be read from back to front like the Torah. I found my old handprint plaques from preschool, uncomfortable little craft items made out of plaster and spray-painted gold. I found my mother's old mortarboard from her high school graduation, and, when no one was home, I would parade around the house wearing it and carrying a rolled-up comic book that served as my diploma from the College for Gifted Goofballs. It always made me happy that my mom saved everything I ever did, because there's nothing more terrifying to me than people throwing out your past while you're still alive. After you're dead, I guess they can just toss everything on the scrap heap, but I know I don't want to be an old man who sits around saying, "You should have seen me when I was a kid. Man, was I good-lookin'." With photographic evidence available, I could quickly be brought back to my senses despite the onslaught of my aged delusion.

Even though my dad was the "if you don't use it for twenty-four hours it goes in the trash" sort of guy, it was actually his few saved items that offered the greatest treasure-hunting finds. When I was seven, I would frequently sneak nervously into his den, a room that sounds much more ostentatious than it actually was. It was the smallest room in our already small house, a place where he could balance his store's accounting books in peace. He had a tiny desk in there, a small countertop, and shelves along one wall that Mr. Lufthauser from down the street had built for him. Into the middle of it all my dad had crammed in a large reclining chair, where he'd spend his days off trying to catch up on politics and end up open-mouthed and drooling after falling asleep two minutes into an attempted reading of the Sunday *Detroit News*. But it was the closet next to his chair that was the gateway to adventure every time I was brave enough to venture inside it. It had sliding aluminum doors that had been painted orange to match the rest of the burnt umber and dark-paneled room. I always remember the forbidden thrill of putting my hands on that cold door and slowly sliding it to the side as it rumbled with a metallic shudder. Even though I knew nobody was home, I'd get completely paranoid and have to run out into the living room several times to convince myself that the rumbling door noise hadn't masked the sound of my dad's station wagon pulling into our driveway. Then, on hands and knees, I'd slowly work my way into the piles of old brown paper grocery bags in which my dad had stored all the selected items from his past.

On most occasions I'd only get far enough in to find old home-movie equipment and bags of forgotten sweaters and shoes. Once I came across an old tool kit sitting under some of the bags. The beat-up metal case contained ancient power and hand tools that even Ethan Allen would have rejected as being too clunky and an-tiquated. I took out an old drill and something that looked like a pointy egg beater and started to pretend they were deadly weap-ons that only I had the power to control. After a few minutes, I became convinced that my dad had memorized the exact way the tools had been laid into the box and spent the next half hour in a panic, trying to rearrange them back inside the case so that their disruption could pass the scrutiny of my father's probing eyes. Looking back, I'm sure my father hadn't thought about those tools in years and wouldn't have known I had disturbed them if I had put a note inside the box that read "I swear I didn't touch your tools." But, like any good intrigue worth its salt, paranoia was an essential part of espionage.

And, unfortunately, the one time I erased paranoia from the equation was the time I almost got my family into big trouble.

One day when I was eight, while scavenging in my father's closet, I made a strange and exciting discovery after making it all the way to the very back and bottom bag. I had dreamed of going in this far for a year now but had never had the nerve. However, having earlier that day won the first and only game of tetherball I would ever win in my life (because I had challenged a right-handed kid whose right arm was in a cast—a kid I *still* almost ended up losing to), I found the courage to boldly go where I hadn't gone before. What I ended up finding as I dug into the de-caying bag was my father's stash of memorabilia he had collected during his time as a GI in Europe during World War II. My dad would occasionally tell me stories about how his division had landed at Normandy, albeit on the day *after* D Day, but I found this to be quite impressive and always told my friends that my father was a war hero. And now I found myself quite excited that I was finally getting some tangible proof. I opened the musty-smelling grocery bag and looked inside. On top were some old army clothes, including a shirt that had my dad's name written over the breast pocket. Sticking up along the side of the bag was a green handle. I pulled it out carefully and found that it was a folding army shovel. I was impressed that these were things that actually belonged to my father during World War II. But since he sold both old army clothes and folding shovels in his store, I realized that I'd have to dig deeper in the bag if I wanted to find something really good. I pulled out an old boot and another pair of green army pants. And then I uncovered two items that blew my eight-year-old mind.

I reached in and pulled out a long, sleek-looking dagger in a sheath. I stared at the knife in disbelief. It didn't look like something an American soldier would carry. Knowing nothing about military history, I deduced from the old war movies I had seen my dad watching on TV that this was a knife that had belonged to somebody important and scary in the war. I slid the dagger out of its sheath. The blade was about a foot long and thin and looked practically new. I lightly touched the edge and realized it was sharp enough to cut me if I so much as put my fingers on it with any sort of additional pressure. The handle was covered with a thin layer of leather and between the blade and the handle was a medallion with a strange-looking eagle on it. I was immediately in awe and terrified of the dagger. I slowly swung it around, trying to act in a way that I thought someone with a knife like this might act during a war. But I was soon struck with an image of me accidentally dropping the knife and cutting my leg off. And so I quickly put the knife back in its sheath, carefully set it aside, and looked back into the bag.

I saw something brightly colored and pulled it out. It looked like a red bedsheet that had been folded up. Confused, I started to unfold it slowly, remembering exactly how I was doing it so that when I refolded it, it would tell no tales. After a few unfolds, I saw a large patch of white sewn onto it. Another unfold revealed part of a black symbol stitched onto the white area. One more unfold and I realized that it was a flag. What I didn't know at the time was that it was a Nazi flag. Another unfold revealed a large black swastika in the center of the white circle. My eight-year-old brain was enthralled. I remembered seeing flags just like this in those war movies my dad had watched, the movies that I didn't pay much attention to except when bombs were exploding and guys were flying through the air. All I could think was, Wow, this is something my dad brought back from World War II. Beyond that, I had no idea what the flag or the strange symbol that looked like four sevens in a circle stood for. The only thing I knew for sure was that, compared with the old shoes and Christmas presents I was used to finding in our closets, I had just found something very, very cool.

I took the flag and unfolded it completely. It was big, about six feet by four feet. I carried it around the house for a while, pre-tending to be a general leading my army into battle. The flag was so crisp and new-looking that I was completely enamored with it. I remember thinking that my dad was so cool because he had saved this flag that was part of history and that if everyone else knew my dad had done this, they would think he was cool, too. Maybe they'd even say he was a war hero and he'd get to be in the paper. Our local paper was always running pictures of wrinkled old veterans in their McDonald's trainee–like army caps every Memorial Day and Veterans Day, and each year I thought that my dad should have his picture in the paper, too, since he probably did more than any of those old grandpa-looking guys ever did. I mean, my dad had landed at *Normandy*. One day after *D Day*, for cryin' out loud.

Overcome with love for and pride in my father, I figured that

I should let the whole neighborhood know just how great a guy my dad really was and decided right then and there to hang the Nazi flag in our front window.

I got some string and tape from the kitchen drawer and rigged up the top corners of the flag so that I could tie them to the curtain rod over our living room window. Once it was secure, I let the flag hang down and adjusted it so that it was centered. Satisfied that I had presented it in the most aesthetically pleasing manner, I went outside to take a look. From our driveway, the Nazi flag looked quite handsome. It filled the entire front window of our house. I walked all the way out to the street and checked it out from there. Yep, it was fully visible to any passing car. I felt good. I felt proud. People were going to love my dad when they saw that flag hanging in the front window of our house, right in their very own neighborhood.

As I stood there admiring my handiwork, my mother drove around the corner and onto our street unexpectedly. At first I was nervous, scared I'd get in trouble for going through my father's closet. But the more I thought about it, I was sure my mother would be quite pleased that I was performing such a selfless act to show the neighborhood what a cool guy my dad was.

I waved at my mom as her car approached. She waved back with a smile. She turned into our driveway and suddenly her car screeched to a stop. Wow, I thought, she must be really surprised. I bet she's going to be so proud of me she'll take me to Dairy Queen. As I stood there debating whether I would order a Mr. Misty Float or a Dilly Bar, my mother immediately jumped out of the car, wild-eyed.

"Where did *that* come from?!" she sputtered.

"It's Dad's. I found it in his closet," I said proudly. "I thought I'd hang it up for everybody to—"

"Oh, my *God*," said my mother. And with that, she sprinted away from her still-idling car and ran into the house. I'd never seen my mother run before, especially in a pair of low-heeled pumps.

And the next thing I knew she ripped the flag down from the window and closed the curtains.

I didn't get to go to Dairy Queen.

That night, my father gave me a lecture on the horrors of the Nazis and told me that he had saved the flag and the dagger because most of the guys in his division had done the same thing, wanting to keep a few souvenirs of the enemy from their time in the war. Apparently he had picked up the flag and the dagger after his battalion had gone through France when the Germans had been defeated. He told me about friends of his who were killed during the war, and a wave of embarrassment at what I had done overtook me as I tried not to cry. Seeing this, my dad gave me a pat on the shoulder and said, "Hey, it's okay. At least now you know."

Since he knew I'd thought I was doing something nice for him by showing off his flag, he thanked me for trying to make him a war hero and told me that he was going to donate the flag and the dagger to a war history museum where they could be properly displayed in the right context. And then he grilled me over and over again to make sure that no one in the neighborhood had driven by and seen the flag in the window.

Fortunately for all of us, nobody had.

Well, that would have been one way to get my dad's face in the paper.

MY FIRST AND BESTEST GIRLFRIEND

I met my first real and true girlfriend when I was in the second grade. It turned out to be the beginning of a very long and faithful relationship.

We met in gym class. It was about a month into the new school year when our teacher, Mrs. Handler, informed us that we were going to learn how to climb ropes. We looked over and saw a two-inch-thick cotton cord hanging down from the very high ceiling. I had seen those ropes stored up in the rafters before but always assumed they were there to keep the roof from blowing away if a tornado tore it off. Beneath the rope was an extra-thick mat, signaling to us all that severe injury was possible. Mrs. Handler, making it sound simple, informed us that we were to grab the rope and use our hands to propel ourselves upward. She said that as we climbed we should use our thighs to pinch the cord and hold ourselves in place to prevent us from sliding back down and negating whatever progress we might be making before we reached the top. I was immediately terrified because it looked to me like the ceiling was about one mile up, and if I were to get up there and then lose my grip and fall, the mat would only prevent my body from breaking apart upon impact as I was killed. But like all things in any gym class, we had no say in the matter, and so we lined up to wait for our turns. I watched as each of my friends, both boys and girls, scurried up the rope as if it were the easiest thing in the world. Maybe this wouldn't be so bad, I thought. It sure didn't look like anyone else was having any problems. However, nobody else in the class cried when they got a mosquito bite, either. So I had no idea what to expect.

When my turn arrived, I approached the rope and awkwardly took it in my hands. It was hard and a bit slick-feeling, not at all what I was expecting. I assumed the rope would be soft and easy to grip, a magical Nerf rope of sorts that would render me weightless and carry me up to the gym ceiling like Mary Martin in that creepy TV version of *Peter Pan* my parents made me watch. But the minute I touched that rope, I knew my success was going to depend strictly on how much strength I did or didn't have in my arms and legs. I reached up as high as I could on the rope and tried to pull myself off the ground. It was almost impossible. I've never had much upper-body strength, and at age seven I couldn't defeat a newborn baby in an arm-wrestling tournament.

"Just pull yourself up," Mrs. Handler said in an encouraging tone, assuming I was a newcomer to the ways of gravity on this planet.

"And spit on your hands," said Norman, a future bully who was on this day still about five years away from making my life a living hell.

I looked up the rope and decided that if I could jump up and grab it, at least I'd be off the mat. I sprang up a few feet and gripped the rope. I immediately wrapped my legs around it and hung on. It felt like I had gotten myself pretty high up, but when I looked down, I saw that I was about one foot off the mat. I looked over at my classmates, who were staring at me impassively. My aunt Sue was an Avon lady and she had given my dad a Soap-on-a-Rope for his birthday once. I suddenly knew what the soap felt like.

"Keep going," Mrs. Handler said politely, although there was already a hint of "Jesus Christ, just climb the goddamn rope already" in her voice.

I peered up and tried to figure out the best way to accomplish this. A couple of kids had done it using nothing but their arms, kicking their legs wildly as they climbed. I knew this wasn't an option for me and so I fixated on the kids who had taken the teacher's advice and held the rope tightly between their legs as they pulled themselves up hand over hand. I readjusted myself so that the rope was firmly pinched between my thighs and started to pull my body up. And to my amazement, I was actually getting up the rope. Mrs. Handler is quite a teacher, I thought. I pulled and locked my legs, pulled and locked my legs, pulled and locked my legs.

And then something happened.

All of a sudden, I felt this strange wave coming over me, a powerful sensation that seemed to be building inside my body but I didn't know from where. It almost seemed to start in my chest and expand outward. I felt it in my butt, in my legs, in my arms . . . but especially in my pants. (These were the days when you wore your school clothes in gym class. I guess this was either because we didn't sweat at that age or because we *always* smelled bad, so what was the point of making us change into clothes whose job it was to get stunk up anyway?) I stopped climbing and held on to the rope. The feeling was building stronger and stronger. And the weird thing about it was that it felt good. Better than anything I'd ever felt in my life. Suddenly, my body started to pulse and, the next thing I knew, the entire sensation rushed into my groin area and specifically into my—as the girls who lived next door to me used to call it—"thing." It was a strange, wonderful pounding sensation, a velvety version of the pile driver that almost crushed Bugs Bunny during a Warner Bros. cartoon I had seen about a construction site. Boom boom boom. All my muscles tightened and I was frozen in a blend of ecstasy and utter confusion. Was I having a heart attack? Was this what a stroke was? I had no idea what they were and figured that maybe this was what they felt like. But the biggest thing I remember was that (a) I didn't care if it was a stroke and (b) I didn't want it to end. Ever.

"Paul? What are you doing up there? Are you stuck?" Mrs. Handler called up.

". . . no . . ." was all I could muster. I was now guarding this moment and I wasn't going to let anything interrupt it. I was afraid that if I moved, it would stop. And I couldn't move, even if I wanted it to stop.

"Can you go up any higher?"

"I don't know." The sensation continued to pound in my privates. My head seemed to fill with fog.

"Well, either keep going or come back down. People are waiting."

"Uh, okay." The feeling was starting to subside and so I cautiously began to let myself down. As I slid slowly down the rope, it happened again. This time it hit harder and actually made me gasp. I froze again. Another wave of euphoric muscle contractions swept through my midsection. Boom boom boom.

"Paul, I don't know what you're doing but please hurry up."

This time the feeling faded quickly. But it was now indelibly etched in my brain. And I knew it was something that I was going to make happen again, even if I had to dedicate my life to it.

I got to the bottom of the rope and put my feet on the mat. As I tried to walk away, I almost fell onto the gym floor. My legs felt like Jell-o and I was having ghost pangs of the feeling. It was like my body was now vibrating slowly like a car that's about to stall because of a dirty carburetor. I walked among my fellow students but everything was a blur. I had experienced something that felt almost religious in its scope and I was quite sure that no one else in the gym that day could even begin to understand what I'd just been through.

A few hours later at recess, I decided to find out if I was the only one who'd experienced "the rope feeling." I asked my friend Brian if he'd felt anything during his climb.

"My hands really hurt after it" was all he offered up.

"Didn't you feel anything else? Anything that was really good?" I didn't want to get more detailed than that for fear that I would be informed of some life-ending disease that had as its main symptom "an intense, pleasurable sensation when climbing ropes in gym class." Kids were always interpreting any abnormality or injury I had as the tip-off of a fatal disease. Once I had a scratch on my arm and a kid in my class saw it. He told me that if you have blood poisoning, it looks like a red scratch on your arm that runs along one of your veins and when the red scratch reaches your heart, you drop dead immediately. Of course I spent the rest of that day staring at my scratch, convinced it was growing longer, and well on its journey to kill me. But as far as "the rope feeling," Brian just shrugged at my question.

"I didn't feel anything. What did it feel like?"

"I don't know," I said, trying to figure out how to verbalize it. "It was like I was floating or something. It felt really good."

"Huh. I don't know. Maybe you have cancer."

The next day in gym, the rope had been put back up into the rafters and I stared at it longingly. "Can we climb the ropes again today?" I asked.

"Paul, you were the only one who couldn't make it up the rope yesterday. Why do you want to do it again?" Mrs. Handler said as she bounced a kickball, clearly more excited at the prospect of teaching us a new competitive sport.

"I don't. I was just wondering if we were going to do it again."

"Not today. We'll try them again next Wednesday." She then launched into a lecture on the fundamentals of kickball and I stood there trying to calculate how many hours separated me from next Wednesday.

That night, I was watching TV in my usual position, lying on my stomach with my chin on my hands and my legs bent at the knees behind me, my calves and feet slowly moving back and forth. Then something strange happened. The rope feeling started to come back again. It wasn't as strong this time but it was definitely creeping up on me. As I had on the ropes, I immediately froze. I stopped moving my legs. The feeling pulsed a bit, then started to fade. I was very surprised and stunned. What happened? I began moving my feet back and forth again and the feeling started to return. I stopped breathing, hoping that it wouldn't fade again. I kept moving my legs and the feeling continued to grow. I started to move my feet faster, as if I were swimming in the air. When I started to go too fast, the feeling began to fade again. And so I held a steady pace with my legs. My brain was now beginning to overload with the joy I was experiencing at the return of my new best friend, "the rope feeling." As the sensation built, my father walked in the room.

"What are you watching?" he asked.

At that moment, I had no idea what I was watching. I was numb with intense feeling as the pounding returned. Boom boom boom.

". . . nothing . . ." was all I could get out.

"Well, you shouldn't lie so close to the TV. You're gonna hurt your eyes. Move back."

It was as if the world were conspiring against me. I started to think that maybe what I was feeling was somehow forbidden and so God had sent my father in to put an end to it. But once again, I couldn't move.

"Okay, I'll move in a minute."

"Move *now*," my dad said impatiently.

I slid myself back and the feeling immediately peaked. I gave a little gasp.

"What's the matter? Did you get a carpet burn?"

I couldn't summon the breath to speak and so just shook my head no, pretending to be too engrossed in whatever it was I couldn't see on the TV through my orgasm-hazed eyes.

"Well, just be careful that you don't get so close to the TV. You'll end up having to wear glasses."

Whereas bath time used to be an opportunity to make my G.I. Joe perform all sorts of underwater adventures in his Army Jack scuba gear, my time in the tub was now transformed into a quest for knowledge. It had become apparent where the feelings were emanating from. I just didn't know exactly how to re-create them. My mind fixated on the idea that if I could somehow figure out how to replicate the circumstances under which "the rope feeling" occurred that didn't involve sliding a twenty-five-foot-long piece of braided cotton between my legs, then I would discover the key to overwhelming joy. The incident in front of the television had given me hope. Re-creation of "the rope feeling" apparently had something to do with pressure or contact between my private area and another surface and movement or friction between them. The bathtub became a virtual testing ground as I tried everything within reach to create the necessary ingredients. Shampoo bottles, sponges, washcloths, soap bars, the side of the tub—yes, I'm afraid even G.I. Joe was called into duty—but nothing seemed to work. "The rope feeling" was to remain elusive for another day, it seemed.

However, as with all great inventors, a breakthrough occurs when one least expects it.

Somehow, through a coincidental sequence of washing with soap, scrubbing certain areas harder than normal, and keeping my eye out for any possible disturbances in my lower reaches, I stumbled across what appeared to be a possible winning combination. There was a stirring deep within the part of my brain that had earlier frozen me to both the rope and the carpet that seemed to say, "You may be on to something here." Bath time lasted longer than usual that night and by the time I emerged, my skin wrinkled and puckered from too much exposure to water, I was a veritable Jonas Salk on the day he discovered his polio vaccine. I had cracked the code and found that my discovery worked every single time I performed the same sequence of events. And trust me, I had just test-driven it. Many, many times.

That night as I lay in bed, the universe seemed a strange and wondrous place. I felt as if I had discovered something that hadn't existed, at least not before I plucked it from the world of overlooked human abilities. I had found a mysterious way to manipulate my body that could produce a feeling of such intense pleasure and euphoria that now my only worry was how I would prevent myself from doing it constantly. Would I ever be able to leave my room? Would I be able to control this ultrahuman power I had stumbled upon? I was now a seven-year-old Clark Kent, possessing an awe-inspiring secret that I would have to hide from the world. Superman never used his powers to rob banks and so I vowed that I would somehow find the strength to keep my new ability in check.

But I knew it wouldn't be easy.

When next Wednesday arrived and I was reunited with my girlfriend, the rope, it was as if I were a formerly cornpone country boy who had returned to his sweet and innocent new bride after coming home from the war. Our first encounter the previous week had been a brief, fumbling union that found both of us inexperienced and awkward during our inaugural dip into the rivers of ecstasy, much like the virgin recruit who marries his best girl the night before he ships off.

But on this day I had returned a savvy, worldly-wise Lothario, bringing a week's worth of experience back from my travels and into the world of my braided cotton lover. As I ascended the rope that day, I knew what to expect and planned on taking full advantage of it. I had been struck with the notion that if, instead of freezing on the rope, I were to continue my climb as the feeling overtook me, I might find myself sailing into unthinkable new heights of pleasure. I was practically trembling with excitement and anticipation as I waited my turn to once again become one with my twenty-five-foot friend.

"Think you can make it all the way this time?" chuckled Mrs. Handler. Oh, I can make it, all right. Just make sure you all have something to distract yourselves with because I might be up there a while. If it's anything like it was last week, I might climb right up through the gym ceiling and take the rope with me.

I nodded and headed up the rope. At first, nothing was happening. I reached the point where the feeling overtook me last week but still there was nothing but the unpleasant realization that I was climbing a big, stupid rope in gym class. What had I done? Had I run through my life's limit of rope feelings in the past week? Had my momentous discovery revealed itself to be my Frankenstein's monster, turning on its master and taking all that is precious from him? I started to feel as if life had lost all purpose.

Fortunately, I found the fortitude to pull myself up one more time. There, at the ten-foot mark, I once again felt the stirrings that I had spent so much of the past week attempting to re-create. Another few pulls and the religious feeling returned. Boom boom boom.

I froze. Keep moving, I told myself. Stick to the plan.

But I can't, came another voice. If I move, it'll stop.

It'll get better, I swear.

It's already about as good as I can handle.

That's what you think.

Okay, okay, I thought. I'll do it. Muscles locked and tight, head spinning, throat clamped shut, I moved my hands up to pull. Unfortunately, my arms were Jell-o. My stomach suddenly seized into a cramp and my head and shoulders pitched backward. My legs flinched and contracted and the next thing I knew, I was plummeting downward. I heard a girl scream and Mrs. Handler yell "Stand back!" as I thudded heavily onto the mat.

"Maybe climbing the rope isn't your cup of tea, Paul," Mrs. Handler said sympathetically.

"No, I know I can do it," I said, my voice trembling from the continuing contractions taking place in my body. "I just think I need to keep trying. Is it okay if I come back after school today?"

That afternoon on the playground, my friend Brian came over to me with urgent news. "Paul, I felt it! On the ropes today!"

"You did?" I wasn't sure if I was pleased or not. I had been leading myself to believe that I was the Chosen, that "the rope feeling" was mine and mine alone, something that Mother Nature had given me to make up for the fact that I was so goofy and girls didn't seem to really like me.

"Yeah. It was weird. It felt really good."

I stared at him for a second, thinking. Should I let him in on the fruits of my bathtub research? All great scientists share their work in order to let others reproduce their results. And yet, was I hoping to have others benefit from my hard work or was I more interested in keeping this breakthrough for myself? Although I was convinced that I should probably just keep my mouth shut, the lure of bragging about my genius simply proved too strong to resist.

I leaned in close to him. "I figured out how to get that feeling without a rope," I said in the same way a guy in prison might tell a fellow inmate about a tunnel he'd been digging for years with a teaspoon. "You can do it in the bathtub."

Brian's eyes went wide and he immediately wanted to know everything. And so I filled him in. He sat, rapt, taking in every detail. I told him about all the different techniques I had tried, the ones that had failed and the one that worked. I mentioned that shampoo bottles provided an interesting feeling because of the smoothness of their sides when used in conjunction with the soapy bathwater. I impressed upon Brian that while the inside of my thigh seemed to be the surface of choice, he should experiment, too, and see if he could find a surface that was even better. By the time I finished, I could tell I had planted a seed in Brian that would grow into the same overwhelming crop that I myself had harvested all week—that he might feel that force of nature that makes you run, not walk, home from school and head straight for the bathtub.

The next day, I noticed Brian giving me dirty looks as we passed in the halls before school started. We weren't in the same class and so I didn't see him at length until recess. As I sat on a parking block, avoiding any and all competitive activity, Brian walked over and sat down next to me.

"Thanks a lot," he said angrily.

"Why? What happened?"

"I got my thing stuck in the shampoo bottle. My mom had to come in and take it off. She's really mad at me now."

I was flabbergasted. And then I was mad. Try to give a guy the keys to the city and all he does is open the door to the broom closet. "Why did you stick your thing *in* the bottle?"

"You told me to!"

"No, I didn't. I said to rub it on the side."

"Well, now my mom's making me read the Bible. She says she's even going to make me go to church camp." Brian looked at the ground and shook his head.

I immediately felt mature. I knew I was clearly way ahead of my classmates when it came to feeling pleasure and figuring out the mysteries of the human body. I studied Brian as he sat there, staring at the asphalt, knowing that his quest for sexual gratification had led him to ruin, and I kind of felt sorry for him. I could tell that his humiliating episode last night had probably soured him on ever trying to re-create "the rope feeling" on his own again. And while I celebrated the fact that I was now in possession of the greatest morale-boosting activity of which I could ever conceive, I felt bad that Brian wouldn't be able to attain the heights that I knew I would—many, many, many times—over the course of my life.

Oh, well. At least he didn't tell his mom that I was the one who'd told him how to do it.

Brian stood up and started to walk away. After a few steps, he turned back and looked at me, a bit sheepishly. "And my mom said I'm not allowed to hang out with you anymore. And she says she wants your phone number so she can call your parents."

Hello, church camp.

I WAS A POET AND, YES,
I *DID* KNOW IT

At some point in our lives we all want to be special. We all want to be that person who walks into a room and whom everyone immediately notices and says, "Hey, isn't that so-and-so? I'm a huge fan of his." And even though most of us know that the only real shot we have at achieving anything like this is through hard work and diligence, we all secretly dream that one day we'll sit down at a piano and miraculously bang out "The Minute Waltz" or pick up a paintbrush and quickly lay down the sequel to the *Mona Lisa*. But it never happens that way. And that's why most of our closets contain one abandoned saxophone or drawing kit or pair of tap dancing shoes. Because life's just not that generous.

At least, it's not supposed to be. And that's why I was so surprised when one morning, when I was in the third grade, the gods looked down from on high and for some unknown reason decided to make me a poet.

It's possibly the strangest thing that's ever happened to me. I awoke one day with a poem stuck in my head. But it wasn't a poem I'd ever heard before. No, by some bizarre twist of neurological fate, the neurons and synapses in my brain had combined and interconnected during REM sleep and formed a fully writ-

ten, ready-to-use poem that sat waiting for me in my frontal lobe.
I woke up and there it was:

> *I'm a knight in shining armor*
> *I'm the bravest man in town*
> *I fight off dragons from the queens*
> *I give kings back their crowns.*
> *The only thing that bothers me*
> *It gets me in the head*
> *By the time I get my armor on*
> *It's time to go to bed.*

Just like that. A humorous poem, delivered sight unseen to my
third-grade brain. I didn't know where it came from. I hadn't
watched any medieval shows or read any Arthurian books lately.
In fact, I didn't even *like* that kind of stuff. I searched my memory,
trying to figure out if maybe it was a poem I'd heard on TV or on
the radio or read in a book. But I hadn't. No, for some unknown
reason, a fully formed Round Table verse had just popped into my
head and now it was mine.

I went to school that day bursting with pride over my poem
from beyond. I wasn't sure how best to share it with the world, but
I knew that I wanted to impress Miss Patton with it. I'd always had
the feeling that she thought I wasn't very smart, especially since I
consistently pulled up short during our times-tables races in her
class. There was just something about the way she looked at me
every day, a hint of annoyance on her face that said, "I wish you
weren't really here." As a kid, you get used to people smiling at
you and acting like they're happy that you're around. They'd always seem to go into overdrive when they spotted you standing
with your parents, and their reactions could range from giving you
a quarter to the antiquated gesture of pinching your cheeks. The
latter didn't happen often, but if you were ever brought before an

old woman and heard the term "the Olde Country" used within a description of her, then the odds had it that you were in for a good ol' fashioned, capillary-bursting cheek pinch. But not from Miss Patton. Even before I compared her to the fourth level of human evolution, she'd never seemed that impressed with me. But now I had a chance to change all that.

And so, around midmorning, while the class was reading an assignment, I took out my binder, wrote the poem down on a piece of loose-leaf paper, and went up to her desk.

"Miss Patton, I wrote a poem."

"A poem?" she said. Miss Patton gave me a perplexed look, since she had neither requested a poem from me, nor had we ever even talked about poetry during class. She looked at the notebook paper and read my verse. Then, to my surprise, she laughed.

"Paul," she said, looking at me with what I can only describe as utter amazement, "this is *very* good. When did you write this?"

Not wanting to sound like I hadn't put any effort into it, I immediately embellished. "I wrote it last night." Not truly a lie but enough to make it seem as if I hadn't just dreamed the poem up with no thought process whatsoever. Which I had.

"Well, I am impressed." And with this she stood up and got the class's attention.

"Everybody, stop reading for a second and look up here. Paul Feig has written a poem and I would like him to read it to you."

She handed me my notebook paper and gestured for me to step front and center. My heart raced. Much like a guest host heading to the spot marked with a star on the floor where Johnny Carson stood to deliver his monologues on *The Tonight Show,* I was being invited to stand in the spot where Miss Patton, the woman in charge of our third-grade education, stood daily. On top of this, Miss Patton was now smiling at me in the same way that fans smile at their favorite celebrities. Through eight simple metrical lines, hewn out of a night of random brain activity, I had accomplished what throughout the year I'd assumed to be impossible—I had turned Miss Patton into my groupie. I walked up to the spot of honor and faced the class.

They were all staring at me, unsure. They knew me, since I'd been in the same class with most of them since kindergarten, and a few of them I could even call my friends, but at the same time, they'd never heard the words *has written a poem* spoken in the vicinity of my name. So it was clear no one had any idea what to expect. For all they knew, I was going to recite some flowery tribute to my cat or my grandma. I looked down at the piece of paper, took a breath, and started to read.

"I'm a knight in shining armor / I'm the bravest man in town / I fight off dragons from the queens / I give kings back their crowns. . . ."

When I read the final line of the poem, everybody laughed. It wasn't an uproarious laugh, the kind you could always get by pressing the heels of your hands against your mouth and blowing to create a fart sound, but it was a good, solid response. Miss Patton then stepped forward and had the class applaud for me. I couldn't believe it. It was mind-boggling. When I went to bed the previous night, I was just Paul Feig, the kid who was trying to figure out how to get girls to like him. But thanks to a random act of unconscious nocturnal wordsmithery, I was now getting a round of applause from my peers. Something in my brain snapped. Like getting your first shot of heroin, I was now immediately hooked on the forced adoration of my classmates. And I was overjoyed knowing that Miss Patton now viewed me as not just another third grader, but as an artist.

I returned to my desk and Miss Patton started to talk to the class about poetry. She said that she had wanted to teach us some fundamentals but didn't know if we were ready for it or not. But now that I, her eight-year-old poet laureate, had broken down the wall, she said that she was sure we could all handle it. And so she told the class that in the next two days, she wanted everyone else to write a poem, too.

When we were all leaving for home, Miss Patton called me over and told me how proud she was of me for doing something on my own. To her, the previous night I had decided to throw off the shackles of mindless television viewing, pull out a quill and parchment, and spend the evening indulging and exploring what was clearly a prodigious talent. "I wish that more students were like you," she said. "And I hope you'll keep pursuing this gift you seem to have."

Now I had a gift! It was getting better and better. Miss Patton was putty in my hands. I had broken through into a whole new world, a world in which I was my teacher's favorite student. I'd heard the term *teacher's pet* bandied about derisively in the past and always thought it sounded like something a person should strive to avoid being. However, I was now starting to see the other side of it. Becoming the teacher's pet could be a *good* thing. It could be the key to grade-school happiness. If I was her pet and she was going to start heaping praise upon me for the things I did, then my entire life would change for the better. I had to play this right. I had seen contests on the news where a kid would win the chance to push a shopping cart around a toy store for one minute and during that time anything the kid threw into the cart would be his or hers to keep. For free. I'd always been envious of the kids who got the chance to do that and was constantly outraged when they'd either dumbly fill their cart with a bunch of crappy cheap toys or else simply grab a Barbie's Dreamhouse or boxed G.I. Joe Army Jeep and shove it into the cart, thus insuring they couldn't fit anything else in there other than a few thin coloring books during their final fifty-five seconds of gratis shopping. I had always vowed that if I were to get that opportunity, I would figure out in advance the best toys to grab by making a preliminary trip to the store to calculate their weight, volume, and price. With a bit of planning, my shopping cart could be packed in such a way that the store would go out of business from lost profits. And this was how I knew I had to play my emotional shopping spree, courtesy of Miss Patton's newfound respect. Maximum effort to ensure maximum returns.

That night I stayed in my bedroom, working diligently, as my head slowly began to expand. Miss Patton had asked me to write out my poem on a large sheet of poster board to hang in our classroom, so that she could refer to it while she taught my fellow students how to analyze verse. I figured she wanted it up as a visual aid that she could use to show the other kids what I had done so right in my poem and what they were surely going to have done so wrong in theirs. As I drew light pencil lines on the poster board in order to keep my lettering straight, I imagined the poems that my classmates would bring in. Probably childish verses about trees or birds or their parents. Inferior works artistically equivalent to the "roses are red, violets are blue" school of greeting card poesy. All quite earnest and populist, true, but could anybody possibly hope to achieve the depth that my poem had? Could my fellow students transport their audience back through the ages, letting their words and images amaze and amuse the listener with tales of mythical knights in chivalrous times as I had? Would they be able to consider themselves junior Chaucers with their clumsy rhymes and *Romper Room* verse? Of course not, I mused as I carefully wrote out my masterpiece with a black Bic Banana marking pen. Poetry was for the Chosen. And you didn't choose poetry— poetry chose you. The best my peers could hope to achieve was to imitate my style and possibly scribble out some veiled homage to my masterpiece. I pitied them as I breathed in a nontoxic whiff of my Bic Banana.

The next day I arrived at school with my wall-sized poem. In addition to writing it out, I had also taken the time to draw pictures of a knight's helmet, a horse, and the head of a damsel who looked a lot like a princess I'd seen in an old Bullwinkle cartoon.

I'd had some trouble getting the poster board to school because it was an excessively breezy day and the large floppy piece of cardboard kept catching in the wind and flying away from me like a kite. I didn't want it to bend and so I ended up pirouetting around the school yard with it in order to keep from creasing it against my body. I didn't want any blemishes or imperfections on this placard to distract from my poem's grandeur. When I got into class, Miss Patton smiled happily and took the poster board from me, pinning it up on the corkboard in the front of the class. It was the centerpiece of the board that was normally covered with flash cards and posters of the presidents, and I couldn't have felt cooler.

During the course of the day, Miss Patton taught us all about the different forms of poetry, about meter and rhymes and even dipped into iambic pentameter. As she lectured, my attention was much more on the other kids in the class than on what she was teaching. First of all, I already knew what she was talking about. I mean, I didn't know the terms by name or by their official definitions but, as was quite clear, I was a prodigy. I knew that all this technical stuff she was talking about was for the benefit of those without the gift. If you had to be spoon-fed the basics of poetry, it was only because the gods had not chosen you to receive such an immense capacity for greatness. A prepackaged set of rules was your only hope for scaling the heights of creativity that just seemed to be preprogrammed in the small minority of we, the gatekeepers of art. I watched my peers' faces as Miss Patton lectured and saw looks of confusion at the concepts she was laying out before them. Occasionally, Miss Patton would throw me a look that said, "*You know what I'm talking about, don't you, my talented ward?*" Oh, yes, Miss Patton, I thought. *I* know what you're talking about, but heaven help these other poor saps who are being forced to perform in my wake. I'm sure that they, too, will one day discover they have some small talent in another area, modest though it may be. But what's the point of having prodigies if they are a dime a dozen? No, the burden of enormous talent is heavy, but it is borne for the sake of humanity. My suffering was worth the price.

That night in my house, alone with my muse, I sat down to compose my next poem.

There are times when our brains protect us from traumatic and embarrassing past memories, in order that we may continue to live our day-to-day lives unfettered by the pain of remembrance. In the years since third grade, time has erased from my memory and my records the words I composed that night. I remember sitting at our kitchen counter with a pile of notebook paper, waiting for the inspiration to hit me. Words started coming into my head and I wrote them as I heard them, secure in the growing genius of each. The words were forming some kind of verse about a parade going through a town. I didn't want to interrupt the flow and so simply gave in to my unconscious. Unlike my previous metered effort, my emphasis wasn't on trying to be funny or clever or even making sense this time. I simply knew that if I was channeling the same source that delivered the "Knight in Shining Armor" poem, then these words had to be good.

Instead of giving me another a-b-a-b sequence of couplets, my otherworldly inspiration was now giving me an a-a-b-b little ditty. The only lines I can remember from the poem are the following:

> *Oh, see what's in my hand*
> *It's a pin drop from the band*

What was a "pin drop"? I had no idea. And I didn't care. The words were coming and I was writing. I knew this was what inspiration was all about. Just sit back, I thought, and be the stenographer to the artist within. Take the minutes of the I'm-a-Genius-Poet club meeting and reap the rewards. "Paul Feig Has Done It Again!" is what the headlines would read after Miss Patton got a load of this new batch of poesy the ghost of Shakespeare was sending my way.

My pen scratched furiously as the last line of my latest masterpiece came through my hand and onto my lucky sheet of Smithsonian-bound paper.

Spent, I set down my pen, sighed wearily, and thanked the Fates for another job well done.

As I read over the poem I had written in forty-five seconds, I remember wondering if it was any good at all. But I quickly put such destructive thoughts out of my head. Of course it's good. How could it not be? *I* wrote it. And once Miss Patton read it and saw that I had segued out of humorous verse and into abstraction, her admiration for me would grow exponentially.

I walked into class the next day and saw my fellow students busily looking over their poems, making changes and handing them in to Miss Patton. I remember walking into the classroom think-ing that my peers would fall silent, feeling the presence of the master among them and hoping that I would quickly read my lat-est creation aloud. But nobody seemed to notice me. I figured they were all too preoccupied with their quaint little verses and so took no offense. I walked right up to Miss Patton, who was busy sta-pling papers together, and said loudly, "Here's my new poem, Miss Patton."

It was the strangest thing. For whatever reason, Miss Patton took the poem from me like I was just another one of her stu-dents. There was no look of excitement, no calling the class to at-tention. There wasn't even a thank-you or a small conspiratorial smile. I was thrown at first but then quickly realized that she probably didn't want to appear to be showing favoritism by fawn-ing over my latest yet-unread work. She must treat my next master-piece the same way she was treating all the other stanzas that were being handed to her, I thought. My poem would have to stand on its own.

She had us all sit down and said she wanted each one of us to read our poems out loud.

Aha! I was right. This was how she was going to laud me. Let me present the poem myself without any prevoiced bias. Then let the accolades roll in. You're a clever one, Miss Patton. Clever like an art-appreciating fox.

She went desk by desk so that our selection would be impartial. Other students got up and read their poems. As I suspected, most were about their families or about their pets or about the beauty of a tree or a summer day or any other standard verse subject suitable for a Carlton greeting card. There was nothing approaching the quality of a Hallmark-worthy set of metered lines, but their attempts were sincere, if not inspired. One kid even got a laugh with a poem about his dog stealing food off the dinner table. I chuckled supportively, glad that he had succeeded, happy that my poem wouldn't have to be the only one worthy of praise. Of course, I knew my composition would be hands down the *most* successful work of the day, but that was like comparing apples to oranges. The depth of the lines I had written were beyond these childish verses. I looked up and started to resent my earlier success as I saw it pinned to the corkboard in front of me. To write about knights in shining armor is all well and good but to write an abstract poem about a parade was to break new ground. Once my new poem had succeeded, I figured that I would denounce my old work and take it down from the classroom wall, thus building my reputation as an artist who's "hard on himself" and "a perfectionist."

It was my turn. I stood up and cleared my throat. I launched into my poem, looking up at Miss Patton and the class alternately between each line. I read in a very grand, dramatic tone, so as to drive home the emotion and the irony of each line in this ode to a mythical celebration. When I got to the verse "Oh, see what's in my hand / It's a pin drop from the band," I looked up at Miss Patton, sure that she would be nodding with a small smile playing across her lips, amused and amazed at my use of Lewis Carroll–like abstraction. Miss Patton stared at me, slightly wide-eyed, with no real expression on her face. There was a hint of questioning in her eyes that I immediately interpreted as absolute awe. She was blown away by my poem and I wasn't even finished yet. I gave her a knowing smile and finished reading my magnum opus. When I concluded, I looked around at the class. They were staring at me with slightly confused looks on their faces. I nodded to Miss Patton knowingly and sat down. The lack of reaction from my classmates was what I had anticipated. They were new to the world of art and couldn't be expected to understand the difficult concepts I was tackling. But Miss Patton surely would.

She had the rest of the class finish reading their poems, after which she said she'd grade all our work that night. Then she announced that we had spent too much time on poetry and had better get back to our basic math and English skills. And with that, she started to talk about decimal points. I was confused and a bit disappointed, having expected at least some perfunctory lauding to reward me for the forty-five seconds of soul-wrenching work I had performed the night before. But, once again, I figured she was probably shying away from favoritism.

When she handed back our poems the next day, I saw that most students had gotten A's, with a couple of B's thrown in for two kids who wrote their poems about Spiderman and Fred Flintstone. Then she handed me my masterpiece back. A large red D was written on it.

I was shocked. Clearly there had to be some mistake. I looked up at Miss Patton but all I got from her was a slightly angry look that I interpreted to mean "Man, you're an idiot. What was I thinking?" It also seemed to carry the subtext "And *where* did you steal that knight poem from?" Then she turned and continued handing out the graded papers as I shrank down in my chair, too stunned to even turn my paper over to hide the terrible grade from the eyes of my peers.

There's a verse in a song by the group They Might Be Giants that says, "I've got just two songs in me, and I just wrote the third." Well, apparently I had just one poem in me and had faked my way

through the second one in a cloud of youthful arrogance and laziness. I never spoke to Miss Patton about the grade and she never
spoke to me about my failed parade poem. I was firmly back at
square one with her, no longer the boy genius of verse but once
again merely the kid who told Teresa Andrews that our teacher
looked like the saggy-breasted ape-woman on the evolutionary
chart. What one successful endeavor in the arts had erased, failure
and hubris had restored to its original luster like a bottle of mental Turtle Wax.

Success had come easily and had vanished twice as effortlessly.
I lay in bed that night feeling silly, mad at myself for squandering
my reputation, and embarrassed that I had entertained such cava-
lier thoughts about my abilities and such patronizing thoughts
about those of my classmates. Their poems had all been good.
They had been sincere and had obviously been written with a
fair amount of effort. I imagined how each kid had consulted his
or her parents, had sought out advice about what subject to write
their poems on, had toiled with finding rhymes, and had then read
their works aloud to their pleased families, fielding both sugges-
tions and praise. And while they were all bonding and challenging
themselves, I was quickly dashing down a set of nonsense lines I
knew deep in my heart were terrible so that I could spend the rest
of that evening watching TV and ignoring my parents, sure that I
was now far too advanced to need them around anymore.

Like the singing frog found by the construction worker in that
old Warner Bros. cartoon, my gift from beyond had ended up ru-
ining my third-grade life. Or at least my much coveted teacher's
pet status. I had shoved a Barbie's Dreamhouse into my shopping
cart and now discovered that I didn't even have room for a few
cheap coloring books of dignity. It was the most humiliated I'd
ever felt in my eight years on Earth, and I knew I had to do something to erase my arrogant act.

I got out of my bed and sat down at my desk with a piece of

notebook paper. Over the course of the next two hours, struggling with every word and rhyme, I wrote the following verse:

> *Miss Patton is so beautiful*
> *On this we all agree*
> *She tries to teach us every day*
> *Teach you and you and me*
> *And if there's something we don't get*
> *It's not her fault, it's ours*
> *That's why Miss Patton is the best*
> *Let's all give her some flowers.*

I never gave Miss Patton this groveling poem, but it didn't matter. I had written it and I was awake when I had written it and it was really hard to write and I knew that what I had written was pretty bad. In other words, it was exactly the way I would have done things had my brain not seen fit to curse me with the Knight in Shining Armor poem. I smiled at my ode to Miss Patton, buried it in the bottom drawer of my desk, and went back to bed, dreaming of a shopping cart filled with cheap but still very fun toys.

SCARED STRAIGHT

One Halloween, when I was ten, I decided to dress up like a girl.

For the past year, I had been playing around with a long blond wig my mother had in her bedroom. I'd discovered it a few years back while searching for my hidden Christmas presents. During my quest, I peered into the space between my parents' dresser and the bedroom wall and came across a thick, short blue tube with a picture of a woman's head on it. I took the top off the tube and found the flowing blond wig inside. It was the exact same style and color of hair that my second grade teacher, Miss Drulk, had when I was in love with her three years prior. Feeling as if I'd found some forbidden clue to the secret life of my perpetually big-haired mother, whom I had never seen wear a wig, I found myself overcome with the desire to put it on.

And so I did.

When I looked at myself in the mirror, I was amazed. Believe it or not, I actually looked like a girl in it. This was not major news to me because at that time I had rather long hair anyway and was constantly being mistaken for a girl by the old waitresses at the Canadian diner my mother and I used to eat in when we'd stay at my family's cottage. This was always a source of much angst for me. I'd be sitting at the table, dressed in a cool new jeans jacket that I was sure made me look like the kind of boy who would have girls throwing themselves at him, only to have some grand-motherly waitress come up to the table and say, "Oh my, aren't you a pretty little girl?" My mother would always correct the waitress, which felt even worse because it would bring on a cho-rus of "Oh, I'm sorry, you just look so much like a girl" and "With that long hair of yours, I could have sworn you were Elaine's daughter." Which would drive me into ten-year-old indignation. Didn't these women know what the style was these days? Weren't they up on the trends? Did they encounter no other men, right there in the early 1970s, who also had long hair? What a backward, one-horse hick town this place was, I would fume.

But suddenly, as I stood in my mother's bedroom wearing her wig and staring into her mirror, I was seeing what all those old waitresses were seeing.

I really *did* look like a girl.

I stared at myself a long time, then started mincing around, tossing the hair back and forth with a flick of my head, pretend-ing to be a shy woman at a ball, declining offers to dance, and ob-scuring my face coyly with my new, thick, long, luxurious blond hair. I did this for quite a while until the telephone rang and I im-mediately became self-conscious, certain that the caller could see through the phone and was now shocked at the state in which he or she had found me. I tore the wig off my head, stuffed it back in the tube, returned it to its home between the dresser and the wall, and ran away from the bedroom phone to answer the exten-sion in the kitchen, in order to prove to the caller that I hadn't been in my mother's bedroom experimenting at being a girl.

Over the next several months, when I had the house to myself, I would pull out the wig and put it on. More than anything, I sim-ply liked the way I looked in it. After a few times, I put on a string of multicolored beads my mom had in her dresser and decided that the addition of this accessory only enhanced my girlish quali-ties. This led to additional sessions that found me looking through my mom's closet, trying to spot a dress that I thought might complement my hair and beads. One afternoon, when I knew my parents would be away until dinnertime, I pulled out a short blue sleeveless dress and, feeling like I was going to have a heart attack, slipped out of my school clothes and tried it on. The transformation was even more startling to me. I could pass for a girl, I thought. From this came a search through my mother's shoes until I found a pair of high, white go-go boots that I had never seen my mother wear. I put them on and the transformation was complete.

I was a girl.

And, incidentally, I was a girl whom I found to be quite attractive.

Some geneticists say that we are drawn to potential mates who are physically similar to us, that it's part of our survival instinct to stay among and breed with like kinds. And as I stared at myself in the mirror, I was on my way to proving that theory true. I went cautiously out to the full-length mirror in our hallway and looked myself up and down. I had nice legs. The wig was extremely flattering and looked as if it were my own hair. And my rather full face suddenly seemed to make sense, framed as it was by the long blond *That Girl* locks that surrounded it.

There was no getting around it.

I was pretty.

I put my hands on my hips and sashayed back and forth in front of the full-length mirror, trying to move like the women on TV I had crushes on—Dean Martin's Ding-a-Ling Sisters, the go-go girls from *Laugh In,* the runway models on the fashion reports my mom used to watch. It was strange. The girl in the mirror was really turning me on. I almost felt as if I had found my perfect mate. I began wishing that somehow I could come out of the mirror and date myself. The message was clear. I had become completely enraptured with my feminine alter ego.

Over the course of the next few months, I would attempt to put on the full outfit again but seldom had any concrete guarantees that my mother would be out of the house long enough for me to spend any quality time with Mrs. Paul Feig, at least without fear of being walked in on. The few times that I could safely suit up and admire myself in the mirror, I found myself wishing I could let somebody else see me this way. I wanted to know if I truly looked as much like a girl as I thought I did, or if I was simply lost in some narcissistic haze that was keeping me from seeing the whole, like an unattractive girl who thinks she's pretty just because she buys some new clothes.

But when October rolled around, I saw my chance. It was time for this debutante to venture out into society.

Halloween seemed like the perfect excuse to let the girl in me go public. Guys dressed like women for Halloween all the time. I'd even seen a couple of my dad's Kiwanis buddies in dresses at a party and everyone thought they were really funny. Who would think anything of a ten-year-old boy putting on his mother's wig and go-go boots just to get some candy? It felt like the perfect plan. If I didn't look like a girl, people would laugh and I could pretend it was a joke. If they told me how good I looked, then I'd know my suspicions were correct. I wasn't really sure what I was going to do if I did indeed get the confirmation that I possessed a great deal of feminine pulchritude but that wasn't my concern at the moment. This was strictly my opportunity to burst upon the scene and beguile, like a young actress who gets an "And introducing . . ." credit in her big-screen debut. Excited and nervous, I went into the kitchen to enlist my unwitting mother in my cross-dressing plan. Not wanting to out myself on the spot, I did some quality acting as I pretended to dream up the idea in front of her.

"Hey, Mom, I think for Halloween this year, I'm going to dress up either as Groucho . . . uh, a spaceman, or . . . um . . . I don't know. Hey, you know what could be funny? I should dress up like a girl. Ha ha. That'd be pretty weird, wouldn't it?"

If they handed out Academy Awards for childhood deceit, I would have at least gotten a nomination.

"Dress up like a girl?" my mother said, pondering. Then she smiled and laughed. "That *would* be very funny. You know what? Wait here a minute."

She went into her room and I heard some rustling around. My heart almost stopped when she quickly reemerged with the familiar blue tube that held my blond wig in hand. Did she know what I'd been doing all these months and was now about to shame a confession out of me? I steeled myself and prepared several statements of denial in my head.

"I've had this wig lying around here for years," she said, excited. "I almost gave it away last month." My heart *really* almost stopped on that one. I made a mental note to self—*Hide that wig.* "I bet this would look good on you."

She slipped the wig on my head, then laughed, a look of amazement on her face. "Wow, I've gotta say, honey. You really look like a girl in that wig."

A wave of joy overtook me upon this confirmation of my feminine charms. I pretended to act surprised and went into another dramatic soliloquy.

"Really? You're kidding? I do? That's so funny. I can't believe that I look like a girl in this wig. I want to look in a mirror. I've gotta see if I really look like a girl or not. How funny if I did, huh?"

It's a testament to my mother's blind devotion to me that she didn't see through these terrible moments of overacting I was trying to pass off through the guilt and weirdness I was feeling. Even though it was going well, this whole encounter with my mother felt like the time she walked in on me as I was getting out of the bathtub and saw me fully frontal in my nudity. I had forgotten to lock the door that time but on this, my coming-out day, it felt as if I had left the door unlocked and asked her to come in so I could dance naked in front of her. I was enlisting my mother to validate this strange prepubescent game of dress-up that had become my obsession and something about it felt inherently wrong. But things were progressing at too quick and successful a pace to put the brakes on now.

We went to a mirror and I pretended to be shocked and amazed as I stared at myself wearing the wig I had already seen myself in oh-so-many times. Then my mother said we should pick an outfit for me to wear when I went out trick-or-treating.

"You can't just go out with a long hair wig and your regular clothes and expect anyone to know you're a girl," she said, getting swept up in the moment. "People will just think you're just a hippie. We need to pick you out a dress."

"You really think so, Mom?" More bad acting. "Well, okay, maybe you're right."

We went into her bedroom and she slid open the door to her closet. As my mother looked through her tightly packed clothes hanging on the closet's sagging, straining wardrobe bar, I pretended to be deliberating along with her as she stopped at different potential outfits. Then I went into my con.

"I think I should wear something, um, I don't know . . . maybe blue," I pondered aloud, making sure to perform the appropriate searching-face/vaguely-gesturing-hands action that went along with such a moment of fashion decision making.

"Oh, I think you're right. You'd look very good in blue. Especially if you're wearing a blond wig."

Feeling cocky, I almost overplayed my hand with a moment of superhuman eyesight. "What about that dress there?" I said, pointing vaguely at the mass of clothes.

"Which one?" my mom asked, scanning her outfits, unable to see anything other than thin strips of color in the overstuffed closet.

"That one right there," I said as I stepped forward, reached right into the dense crush of outfits, and pulled out the dress I had been wearing for the past several months.

"How did you see *that* in there?" My mom gave me a strange look that said either she was amazed at my bionic vision or she knew something was up. Fortunately for me, she would never have suspected that her only son, the boy whom she had taken to Sunday school every week since he was two, had been spending the better part of the past few months trying on her clothes.

"I just liked that color of blue, that's all." Careful, I thought. Don't blow this.

I went into the bathroom and put the blue dress on. When I came out, my mother laughed girlishly, much the way I had seen girls in movies laugh when they would put makeup on each other at slumber parties.

"Oh, Paul, that dress is *perfect*."

Her excitement growing, she started rummaging through her jewelry, looking for some appropriate accessories to enhance my natural beauty. While I had found the colored beads to be a good look for my Y-chromosomed alter ego, my mother had a more classic and elegant take on things. She pulled out a long string of fake white pearls and held it up to the dress. "Yes, I think these would go nicely," she said, becoming giddy as she put the pearls on me. It was at this moment that I started to wonder if secretly my mom had always wanted a daughter instead of a son. She was clearly as into this as I was and it was starting to dampen the experience for me. But with the end of the tunnel so close, I decided to press on.

"What kind of shoes should I wear?"

"Gosh, I'm not sure if any of my shoes will fit you. Maybe you should just wear your tennis shoes."

Perish the thought. I almost recoiled in disgust at my mother's lack of imagination. How would that possibly support the look we were so carefully creating? I suddenly realized that maybe it was a good thing she hadn't had a daughter whom she would encourage to walk around in dresses and tennis shoes like a rodeo clown. "No, I think I should wear women's shoes. Or maybe boots."

"I don't know. I don't think you'll be able to walk in them.

Plus, people might get the wrong idea if you get too girlish." My mother's sudden backtrack threw me. I became self-conscious.

"I just want to look funny," I said, my conviction wavering. "I think it's funny if I dress up all the way." As I stood there in my parents' bedroom, the room in which I was conceived, wearing my mother's clothes, jewelry, and hair, trying to force her into letting me also wear her shoes, I started to feel dirty. I began to envision God standing with his arms crossed looking at me and shaking his head slowly, muttering, "Oh, you're gonna pay for this, friend."

Fortunately, my mother saved the day.

"You know what? I've got these old white go-go boots that might work. I'll pull them out and you can see if they fit."

The plan was on.

When Halloween night rolled around, the girls who were my next-door neighbors came over in their costumes. We had all been going out together on Halloween for years, always with the master plan of making it to the rich neighborhood eight streets down from my house. Rumor had it they gave out giant candy bars and twenty-dollar bills. Our annual plan was to skip our streets and head directly for the rich neighborhood, get the costly booty we knew they were giving out, and then work our way back through the poorer, working-class houses that made up my immediate neighborhood. Every year, however, the lure of nearby candy would prove too tempting and we would convince ourselves that we could harvest all the treats from our blue-collar neighborhood as we worked our way toward the rich section, where we would then end the night on a high note of free cash and insanely big sweets. However, our energy would always flag after about four blocks in and so we'd hobble our way home, our pillowcases filled with normal lower-income candy, where we'd watch *It's the Great Pumpkin, Charlie Brown,* stuff our faces, and vow to bankrupt the rich neighborhood next Halloween. A cou-

ple of years later when we actually made it to the rich neighborhood, we were shocked to find out that half the houses were dark
and empty, and the rest were giving away the exact same Smarties
and "fun-sized" Snickers that my not-as-rich neighbors were
handing out. Our dreams of twenty-dollar bills and enormous
Hershey bars died along with our innocence that night, and it was
the last time we ever went out trick-or-treating. But on this night,
as I stood primping in my bedroom, fully outfitted as a girl, ea-
gerly awaiting my unveiling to my friends, the spirit of Halloween
optimism was strong in me.

My neighbors Sharon, Mary, and Stephanie, ages eleven, ten,
and eight, respectively, came into the house dressed in their standard costumes. Sharon was a bum, Mary was a cat, and Stephanie
was Little Bo Peep. My mother fussed over them accordingly as I
checked myself in the mirror to make sure I was looking my absolute best. An additional element had been added to my appearance now that my mother had gotten fully involved. Subscribing
to my "It's funny if I dress up all the way" theory, my mom decided that I should also add makeup to my look. As if I were a
young bride being prepared for her wedding night by the doting
married women in her family, my mother had spent the past half
hour sitting with me in front of her mirror, showing me the
proper makeup I would wear if I indeed *were* a girl. Lipstick,
rouge, mascara, powder—I was missing nothing. And with each
new application of color, my fascination with myself grew. I was
looking more and more girl-like with each stroke of the brush
and each pat of the puff. I was starting not to even recognize myself and so began to detach from my image in the mirror. It was
getting about as close as it could to a psychotic episode for me:
Act One of a Quinn Martin show, in which some crazy transves-
tite has a Narcissus experience, falls in love with his alter ego, and
ends up killing everyone who ever made fun of him until he's finally shot dead in a house of mirrors by Cannon or Mannix or

Barnaby Jones. I didn't know where this new phase of my obsession was going to ultimately lead me, but at that moment, I didn't care. Right then, as the song goes, I enjoyed being a girl.

When I finally came out and revealed the New Me to my next-door neighbors, my appearance had the intended effect.

"Wow, Fig Newton, you really look like a *girl*," marveled Stephanie.

"Hey, Fig Newton, nice legs," Sharon chortled. She was caught between amazement at my appearance and the overwhelming desire to make fun of me. Since her usual course of action was to get zingers off at my expense, I took her semi-stymieing as a compliment.

Mary, my best friend, whom I also happened to be head over heels in love with, stared at me, then shook her head and laughed. "Oh, my God . . ." was all she could muster. But the look on her face said she was thrown by the accuracy of my gender change. I was very pleased and started trying to envision myself in other, more provocative outfits.

My mom took pictures of us, and then we headed out into the night. As we went from house to house, the reaction that greeted me was exactly what I was hoping for. People thought I was a girl.

"What are you supposed to be, young lady?" asked Mrs. Galanski down the street. "A go-go dancer?"

"Mrs. Galanski," Stephanie said proudly, "that's *Paul*."

"Oh, my goodness. It is? Paul, you have such beautiful legs."

I had never been happier in my life. For all the times I had to suffer through the old waitresses' mistaking me for a girl, I was now getting that same recognition strictly because I was asking for it. This night it wasn't an insulting mistake. I was controlling my image and it felt good. And for the first time in my life, I was being considered attractive, albeit in the wrong gender. But what the hell? A compliment's a compliment.

The rest of the evening went off wonderfully. People assumed I was a girl, and soon I told Stephanie not to tell them I wasn't. If they knew me in real life, it was nice to fool them. If they didn't know me, the extra anonymity was freeing. It was like being in a different country where no one knows you and so you can act like you're considered cool and dangerous back in your hometown, walking with a scowl and not saying thank you if you don't feel like it and putting a pack of cigarettes on the bar in front of you even though you don't smoke. There I was, undercover in my own neighborhood. I walked among them, my Midwestern brothers and sisters, anonymous and pulling one over on them all. My ego was being stroked and there would be no real witnesses to my subterfuge other than my next-door neighbors. It was the perfect social crime.

That night as I lay in bed, I kept reliving the evening in my mind, trying to figure myself out. I still had the huge crush on Mary that I'd had since we were five, and, in fact, it had grown even more powerful after spending the evening with her in her form-fitting cat costume leotard, so I knew I hadn't gone so far over to the girl side that I was losing interest in the opposite sex. But there was no denying it—I loved myself as a girl. And I knew that I couldn't wait to get the outfit—the *full* outfit—back on again.

The next day, when I returned home from school, there was a note from my mother that she had gone out shopping and after that she was going to go directly to my father's store to do some work. She had recently started working in his office, adding up the hours on time cards and issuing paychecks to the employees. My mother had given up her career at the phone company when she married my dad, and, although she liked being a mom, she had always wanted to have a job again. And so my dad, sensing this, let her start doing these minor accounting jobs. She loved it, and I loved it because it meant more time after school that I could lie around and watch TV without being implored to go outside, practice my guitar, or do my homework. And on a day like today, I especially loved her working because it meant I could take my good old sweet time and once again get fully dressed up like a girl. Makeup and all.

I rushed into her room and pulled out the now familiar pieces of my outfit. I had become quite adept at getting dressed and could be fully outfitted in less than three minutes' time. However, having never applied the makeup on my own before, I settled in and vowed to do an even better job than my mother had done.

Once I was fully made up to my satisfaction, I started to parade around in front of my mother's bedroom mirror as usual. However, after having enjoyed the freedom of using the entire neighborhood as my fashion runway the night before, the five-foot-square carpeted area in my mom's bedroom now no longer seemed to be enough. And so I decided to venture out into the living room.

It was a sunny day outside and at first I was scared that somebody could see me through the front windows. But then I remembered that our house, which was surrounded by a row of scraggly-looking hedges, was fairly obscured from the street. And besides, when the sun hit our normally dirty windows, the glare was such that you really couldn't see in unless you got pretty close to the glass. Having a clear view of our driveway from the living room, I knew I had plenty of time to dash into the back of the house if any paperboys or neighbors looking to borrow a cup of sugar showed up. Feeling safe in this knowledge, I proceeded to begin mincing about the living room, looking at my reflection in the window of my mother's china cabinet. As I did this, I heard a distant screech of tires and a dull thud. Since our house was so close to a major truck road, a quarry, and some railroad tracks, strange industrial noises were just part of the pastiche that made up the air around my neighborhood. I continued to mince, pretending that I was entertaining guests in our living room, laughing at unheard jokes and inviting people to sit soft. My eyes were firmly glued to the china cabinet window, trying to get a glimpse of my alter ego's reflection as she performed her duties as the perfect hostess. I felt a pang of weirdness. While staring at myself in the mirror seemed to be about enjoying this other person I had created, and trick-or-treating had been about hiding my identity, what I was now doing in the living room started to feel like I was simply playing house with myself. Not only did it feel a little unnatural and creepy, I was starting to feel stupid. Wanting to get the buzz back, I decided that I had chosen the wrong activity to exploit my feminine side and so figured that maybe an activity that fully exploited my go-go boots would be the answer. I started to do a spastic version of the twist, trying to make my pearls swing around my neck like a Hula Hoop. Because the go-go boots had smooth plastic soles, I could really get a good swivel going on the thick green shag carpeting we had in our living room. I was busy trying to make my hair fly out to the sides and alternately hit the corners of my mouth as I danced when suddenly I heard a loud *TAP TAP TAP.*

I froze. Terrified, I turned and looked toward the window. There I saw three kids from my school with their faces pressed up against the glass, staring at me. My stomach shriveled to the size of a raisin. I felt like I was going to faint. I waited for them to start laughing. But they didn't. One of them gestured wildly for me to come to the door. Oh, no, I thought. How am I going to get out of this one? My mind spun, trying to come up with some reasonable excuses for why I was just go-go dancing by myself wearing women's clothing, a wig, and full makeup in my living room. There were none to be had. The surrealism of the moment was undeniable, and all I could do was simply walk to the door and prepare to take my lumps. I grabbed the knob and pulled the door open, which now felt as heavy as the door on an extra-large bank safe. The three kids, one girl and two boys, stood staring at me through the screen door, shocked looks on their faces.

I quickly went into overdrive. I made a goofy face and did a "girl" gesture, which consisted of waving my hand limp-wristed at them and doing a little bounce with my feet. Trying to be as light as possible, I said, "Oops, you caught me." I don't know what

I was hoping to accomplish with this. Was I thinking they'd assume I was just trying to be funny? That my appearance was a muffled cry for help? Did I feel some need to be discovered so that the therapy could begin? The kids looked at me but didn't react to my attempt to defuse the situation.

"Your mom was just in a car accident," the girl said, terrified to be the one delivering bad news.

I immediately went numb. Everything popped out of my head except the image of my mother lying dead and mangled in a totaled car. "Is she all right?" I squeaked out, my throat seizing up with rising emotion.

"I don't know. You'd better come quick," said one of the boys, ominously. "She's down at the corner. It's pretty bad."

And without another thought, I threw the screen door open and dashed out of the house, running full speed down to the intersection one block over. As I rounded the corner, I saw a large crowd standing around, looking concerned. Then I saw my mother's lime green Dodge Coronet in the middle of the street, the front end smashed and steaming. Broken glass and radiator fluid were all over the asphalt. On the other side of the intersection, I saw a van that had the words *A-1 Extermination* on the side. Its front corner was also smashed. Then, about ten feet in front of the van, lying motionless on its back, was a five-foot-long plastic cockroach that had been on top of the van before impact.

I ran up and saw that several people were helping my mother out of the car. She looked very shaken up but at least she was moving. The manager from my dad's store, John, was there with his arm around her, giving her support. What I later found out was that one of the neighbors had called my dad at the store but because he was out at his warehouse picking up merchandise, John had raced over to help. I ran up through the crowd of people and said tearfully, "Mom, are you all right?" She was quite unfocused and I couldn't tell if she was hurt or just stunned. She didn't really look at me and just kept moving away from the car, her arm around John's shoulder. John, however, had a very tense expression on his face and he threw a look over at me that said, "She's fine, just don't bother her right now." His eyes lingered on me another few seconds and I remember thinking he was mad at me, as if the accident were my fault. I couldn't figure it out, but it scared me. As he led my mother away, I stood there helplessly, trying not to cry but feeling the tears coming on. I looked into the car and saw a bag of groceries that had been thrown forward into the dashboard and scattered all over the floor. A couple of dinner plates that she had bought were broken in pieces among the boxes of Pop-Tarts and bathroom cleansers. The sight of the scattered groceries made me start to tear up, as I thought about my mom at the grocery store buying me all my favorite treats and now there they were all smashed and ruined. I was terrified and numb.

It was then, as I looked up at the crowd for sympathy, that I saw for the first time that everyone was now no longer staring at the wreckage of the accident but was indeed staring at me. Faces ran the gamut from slack jaws to furrowed brows to out-and-out smirks. What's wrong with you people? I thought. My mother was almost killed. I looked over at the girl standing next to me, hoping to find a sympathetic face. She was staring back at me, looking like she'd just smelled dog shit.

"Oh, my God . . . what are you *wearing?*"

I immediately snapped back to reality. The shock of the accident had somehow erased from my mind the fact that I was now standing in the middle of my neighborhood—in broad, non-Halloween daylight—in full drag. Some of the kids in the crowd started to laugh, which led to some of the adults starting to laugh and shake their heads in disbelief. The initial wave of humiliation I felt was quickly replaced by an anger that these people couldn't just overlook the way I was dressed out of respect for my mother. But clearly they couldn't. Who could? I certainly couldn't if I was standing at the scene of a non-fatal accident and a kid ran up dressed like an airline stewardess. I'd probably laugh even if it was a *fatal* accident.

Well, a chorus of hilarity went up and I headed off after my mother. When we got my mom back to our house, she was still shaken up and only wanted to sit down. She sank into the recliner in our living room with a cold compress on her head and cried about her wrecked Dodge Coronet that she liked so much. John went into the kitchen and called a doctor to come over to make sure she was all right. And I went into her bedroom and quietly changed back into my regular clothes. As I hung up my dress and put my boots back and returned my wig to its tube, I realized that I would never again dress up like a girl. I had been scared back into pants, concluding that somehow my desperate need to transform myself into the opposite sex had incurred the wrath of God, who then decided to fire a warning shot across my bow by almost killing my mother and embarrassing the hell out of me. It seemed like a rather drastic act for the Ruler of All Space and Time to do just because I liked the way I looked in a *That Girl* wig. I'd assumed He had bigger fish to fry. But, as my grandmother used to say, "The Lord works in mysterious ways."

Looking back, I think it was just my ego and a big dose of bad timing that got me in the end. I mean, I feel pretty certain that there is no God, but just in case there is, then I can say one thing about Him . . .

The guy's a real party pooper.

'Cause I looked damn good in that dress.

I LEARN SOMETHING
DISTURBING ABOUT GIRLS

There's nothing like being told you're not allowed to know about something to really get your imagination racing. Especially when you're a kid.

The irony was that people were always telling us things they wanted us to know when we were in school. They were constantly trying to force us to listen to them and remember their words and concepts, warning us that everything they were teaching was for our own good and that it was information we'd definitely need to know later in life. Clearly, no one in the educational system had ever read *Tom Sawyer*. Their misguided attempts to "make learning fun" were never effective because learning *wasn't* fun back then. They simply should have figured out what the most important subjects were that we would need later in life and then told us that they were forbidden to teach those things to us. We would have paid every penny of our allowances just to hear tales about the taboo isosceles triangle or the verboten declarative case, and the con job would have been complete. But, no, they would simply try to convince us how important these subjects were and so the only attitude we rebellious children could possibly adopt was one of total indifference. It's because of this that I've always felt the school system is designed completely backward. Because when you're in school, the last place you want to be is in school. And once you graduate and get out in the world and start learning just how much stuff you should have paid attention to when they were teaching it, school's the only place you truly want to be. And yet by that time, you're stuck smack-dab in the middle of the adult world, and going back to school at that point just makes you seem like kind of a . . . well . . . loser (Grandmas and divorcées not included). It's like that grouchy guy on the porch in *It's a Wonderful Life* said when Jimmy Stewart wouldn't kiss Donna Reed:

"Aw, youth is wasted on the young."

Amen, my chunky black-and-white friend. Amen.

Across the board, the things we want to know throughout our lives are the things people tell us we're not allowed to know, and those things are more enticing to us than the world's most sugary dessert.

Case in point . . .

When I was in the fourth grade, something happened that my friends and I were excluded from that really got our minds racing. It was something I like to call:

"The Day The Girls Got To Get Out Of Class."

One morning, we were all sitting in Mr. Dukowski's math class. My head was in its usual state of perpetual swimming as I tried once again to grasp the idea that numbers could actually be combined in a predetermined manner using set rules that would then result in a definitive answer. Everyone else around me always seemed to be able to grasp this concept and apply it in order to produce the right answers to the problems in our math books. However, for me, all the numbers and division signs and fractions were some type of ancient hieroglyphics, symbols of a lost civilization that were fun to look at because I knew they probably held the answers to some pretty interesting questions. The problem was that Mr. Dukowski and the school board wanted *me* to learn how to translate this strange language. I tried and tried throughout the years with only limited success but, alas, the art of numerical computation ultimately eluded me. I wasn't proud of this and tried in earnest to conquer math, but the prosecution had already built a pretty strong case that any attempt I made to nurture a science or accounting career would prove to be a war as unwinnable and ill-advised as Vietnam.

As I sat there staring cluelessly at the number-covered chalkboard while Mr. Dukowski explained the concept of fractions to us, a female teacher came to the door of the classroom, cracked it open a few inches, and peeked inside.

"Pssssst!"

Mr. Dukowski looked over, along with the rest of us in the class, and saw her signaling for him to come into the hallway. Mr. Dukowski excused himself and disappeared. We all exchanged looks. Moments like this meant either that somebody was in trouble and was about to be dragged out of class or that there was some wonderful surprise heading our way. Unfortunately, "wonderful surprises" never occured in my school. But I had watched enough *Little Rascals* shorts on TV to believe that occasionally— and usually on the day that you played "hooky"—your teacher would throw you a cake-and-ice-cream party. I waited my entire school career for a cake-and-ice-cream party, and the closest I ever got was a tornado warning in which they let us all go home early so that we could be killed in our own houses instead of on school property.

Mr. Dukowski came back into the room and said, "All right, all the girls in the class should gather their things and go with Ms. Comforti."

The girls exchanged looks and did as they were told. As they scooped up their books and purses and bags and filed out, all of us boys in the class were at a loss.

"What are they going to do?" asked Rob Leffert, a friend of mine whom I admired because he could draw cartoons of Wile E. Coyote that actually looked like Wile E. Coyote.

"Something that you're *not* going to do," Mr. Dukowski said with a sarcastic smile. These are the retorts that I now know seem really funny when you're an adult but just bug the hell out of you when you're a kid.

"Well, why do they get to leave when we have to stay here?" complained Mark Bennett, being far more aggressive than any of my circle of friends would ever dare to be. At age nine, Mark was definitely a cool guy in the making. I remember in my freshman year I saw him hitchhiking when I was driving with my mom. I asked her to stop and pick him up, thinking he'd be really happy to get a ride from someone he knew, and yet he just looked upset when we pulled over and told him to get in the car. After we drove less than a quarter of a mile he said we could let him out. I was confused until my mother informed me that she was sure that Mark was hitchhiking in order to meet girls. This blew my backward thirteen-year-old mind and it was then that I realized I was the most sexually ignorant kid in my school.

Mr. Dukowski gave Mark a look and then told us, "You guys are unfortunately stuck with me," but that we would have our own fun learning how to add fractions. He chuckled again at his quip, and the feeling in the room was palpable. There was a great injustice taking place that the girls were benefiting from and it was quite clear that none of us were going to take it in stride.

As my friends and I walked through the hallway to our next class, we noticed that the girls were still nowhere to be found. It was as if we were in some science fiction movie where all the females had been taken away to another planet and we males were left to unravel the mystery. Discontent was everywhere.

"This is *so* unfair," said my friend Mike.

"What do you think they're doing?" I asked.

"I bet they're getting to have a tea party or something," chimed in the perpetually greasy-haired Art.

"No, I bet they're letting them watch TV," said Mike.

"Why would they do that?"

"Because they're girls and they get to do all kinds of fun stuff like that," groused Mike, who had been complaining about the unequal treatment he and his sister had been getting for a couple of years now. "My mom's always taking my sister to buy stuff at the mall and eat out and go to ice-skating lessons. My mom won't do any of that stuff with me."

"Do you *want* to go to ice-skating lessons?" Art asked, obviously ready to accuse Mike of being a girl.

"No, but I'm just saying that girls always get to do cool stuff."

As we young males suffered through our next class, our collective minds were spinning as we tried to figure out what the girls had done as a group to entitle them to all this time away from their desks. I had visions of them sitting in a room pajama party–style, passing around chips and cups of pop and exchanging stories about how stupid all us boys were. I saw flashes of the girls walking around at the zoo, being presented with the keys to the city, getting manicures and pedicures, being given bags of money and jewels, all for the simple reason that they were girls and had a different set of chromosomes than we did. Girls always seemed to get special treatment like that. We were told to be nicer to girls and that we weren't allowed to fight with them. Girls could stay in the bathroom longer and seemed to be able to get out of all the activities I hated to do in gym. Girls didn't have to play dodgeball or flag football and even had their own tetherball court and a much easier way to do push-ups—they got to keep their knees on the floor. I could have done hundreds of push-ups that way and won multiple Presidential Fitness Awards if only they'd have let me, but I was always forced to do push-ups the proper boy way with my knees straight and could therefore barely do ten. No, girls had all the advantages and there wasn't a thing we boys could do about it.

But getting out of class because of being a girl? Well, that was just too much.

When the teachers told us it was time for recess, we all headed out. The unbounded enthusiasm we usually had for the playground had been cut by our collective angst over the missing girls.

Recess now seemed to us like a cheap consolation prize for having been born a male. The girls had now been gone for over an
hour and it wasn't sitting well with any of us.

"They took them roller-skating, I'm telling you. I *know* they
took them roller-skating." Mike now seemed on the verge of
tears, his frustration high at the gender injustice to which we were
being subjected. "My mom always lets my stupid sister go roller-
skating and she won't even let *me* hang out at the *creek*."

"Maybe they transferred them to another school," said Art.
"Maybe they're gonna turn this into an all-boys' school. My cousin
goes to one and they make him wear a *tie*."

Before we could really take time to be horrified by this
thought, we walked out onto the playground only to find that, lo
and behold, the girls were already out there.

They had returned.

What happened next I can only describe as a grade-school
reenactment of the Rape of the Sabine Women. Before any of my
friends could even process the reappearance of the girls, gangs of
other boys from our grade saw them, stopped, and yelled, "There
they are! Get 'em!" The boys burst past us and sprinted across the
parking lot toward the girls. The girls' instincts seemed to immediately tell them that there was trouble afoot because they all
screamed and started running, too. The gangs of boys swarmed
around them like border collies, breaking them into smaller groups
and herding them into different parts of the playground. Apparently the angst that had made me and my group of friends so curious about what had happened during the girls' sabbatical had
driven the other guys in my class to the brink of insanity. Suddenly, the playground was filled with the sounds of screaming girls
and the sight of boys strong-arming them into confessions. I saw
boys pushing girls back and forth between them, backing them
up against walls and the trunks of cars. I remember feeling very
strange—that I was witnessing something inherently wrong. Out-

side of showing a girl a worm or pointing a spider out to her on a nearby wall, there weren't too many times in a boy's life when he actually got to hear girls scream in terror.

But today, screaming they were. Girls were crying, fleeing, trying futilely to escape to the top of the monkey bars, but there was no stopping the advance that was fueled by the adrenaline rush of a group of nine- and ten-year-old boys who felt they had been dealt a grave injustice. The message was clear: If you get out of class and I don't, then kiss your peaceful existence good-bye until you tell me what happened.

As my friends and I stood there stunned at the battle before us, Gary Winnik—a kid whom we knew but weren't particularly friends with because he was way cooler than we were—ran back in from the melee and came up to us.

"They saw a movie!" he reported proudly, like an enemy soldier who had just tortured sensitive information out of a prisoner.

"*See,* I *told* you so," Mike said to us, angry that he hadn't been taken seriously.

"What movie did they see?" I asked.

"It was a movie about being a girl."

"What kind of movie is *that?*"

"It's about going to the bathroom and underwear and girl stuff."

We were immediately thrown. This was not the answer that any of us were either expecting or hoping for. We wanted to be indignant but suddenly didn't know if we should feel cheated over not getting to see a movie that none of us would really want to see in the first place.

"Yeah? Well . . . how come there's no movie about being a *boy?* That's not fair," complained Art. "Are we gonna get to get out of class tomorrow for *that?*"

As we all harrumphed in agreement, it was obvious that our indignation had given way to total confusion. A movie about being a girl? I remembered having seen a weird program on TV that showed girls sitting with their elbows in grapefruit halves, something that was supposed to make their skin softer. While this had perplexed me when I saw it because I couldn't figure out why anyone needed softer elbow skin, I now imagined that these were the kinds of tips the girls' mysterious movie had been filled with. My mind started to put odd pieces of a puzzle together. Since girls took longer in the bathroom, there must have been something in the movie that explained exactly why this was or gave them advice about what they needed to do while they were in there to make sure they were doing things properly. I'd heard from my friend Mary that women sat down when they peed. Armed with this disturbing fact and the thought that an entire movie was required to teach girls the specifics of bathroom usage, my mind started imagining all sorts of strange activities that they might be doing in their marathon lavatory sessions. I envisioned girls performing contortionist-like exercises and having to take off all their clothes in order to properly complete their feminine toilet duties. If grapefruits on elbows led to softer skin, then who knew what kind of fruit on what part of the body was being used in the ladies' room, not to mention exactly what it might be softening. My head began to swim at all the details I realized I didn't know about the opposite sex. I suddenly felt relieved to be a male, a species so simply and externally designed that, like a blow-dryer or a transistor radio, we could operate ourselves without ever having to consult the owner's manual.

And yet it *still* didn't seem fair that the girls would be allowed out of class to learn something as mundane as how to relieve themselves.

As my friends and I waded out into the chaos, we saw the playground ladies desperately trying to restore order. These out-of-shape guardians of our recess activities were running from group to group saying such effective crowd-control phrases as "Stop that—now stop that right now" and "Boys, you leave those girls alone!" The sight of the rotund Mrs. Warner's enormous old-woman breasts bouncing out of control under her "World's Greatest Grandma" sweatshirt as she chased after a gang of marauding schoolboys would have been funny had I not been so consumed with my quest to decipher what this girl-movie was really all about. It was then that Tim Stepalonis, the dirtiest and skinniest kid in our school, ran up to us with more in-depth information. Tim was a kid who always scared me because, even though he was so thin that you thought he'd snap like a Pringle if you accidentally ran into him, he had an insane quality that made him seem like he would have no qualms about one day killing you when your back was turned. It was Tim who uttered the words "Man, if I did *that* my mom would kick my *ass*" when we were shown Gene Kelly's famous downpour dance number from *Singin' in the Rain*. But right now, Tim was the guy with the information I desperately needed and I couldn't have been happier to see him.

"You wanna know what that movie they watched was about?" Tim asked, out of breath from running to us, clearly relishing the information he held.

"Yeah, was it about going to the bathroom?" asked Art uncertainly, sounding almost fearful of hearing that it was anything more complicated.

Tim got a scary smile and said, "No, it was about them having their *periods.*" The way he said that sentence made it clear that this was information we were supposed to find very funny and forbidden. Unfortunately, his factoid landed on the wrong ears. My group of cartoon-watching misfits and I stared at him, unified in our shared misconception, all puzzling over the suggestion that the movie was about punctuation for females. Tim immediately knew we had no idea what he was talking about and shook his head.

"Don't you know what a girl's *period* is?" he asked, incredulous.

He said the word *period* as if he were saying the word *boobs* or *vagina,* two terms that all nine-year-old boys take great pleasure in overpronouncing.

"*Yes, of course* I do." Mike was loath to admit that he didn't know something, especially when it was something so clearly subversive as this mysterious girls' "period."

"Yeah? Then what is it?" Tim smiled smugly. He knew he had us all.

"Just tell us, Stepalonis," Mike said, too curious to be embarrassed about his failed attempt to make himself seem learned.

"It's when girls bleed out of their va-*gi*-nas."

I can't speak for my compatriots, but I know that the wave of horror that overtook me in that moment was as strong and mind-altering as the time I saw my next-door neighbor's mother accidentally step on a large praying mantis in our driveway. "Why do they bleed?" I squeaked out, my head spinning.

"Because all girls do. That's how they have *babies,* you retard."

It's hard to describe the dizzying assault of images that flashed through my brain at that moment; overscratched mosquito bites, scraped bleeding knees, and uncontrollable nosebleeds were among the highlights. But the most disturbing was the memory of something I had recently seen in a movie preview. The local Standard gas station by our house used to give away free passes to kids for a movie program that the Macomb Mall sponsored every Saturday morning. I used to go because the movie was generally along the lines of those harmless Disney *Charlie, the Lonesome Cougar*–type films, the ones in which a rambunctious forest creature would befriend a park ranger and reek madcap havoc upon an outpost's flour sack. But the previous week they had shown a trailer for the film *Dracula—Prince of Darkness.* And in it, Dracula had a woman hanging upside down over a white cement floor and before my mind could process what I was seeing, Dracula snatched a sword from its scabbard and swung it toward the woman's neck, whereupon the film cut to a shot of the white floor and then a tidal wave of blood pouring down on top of it. So disturbing was the image to me that, as I watched the zany misadventures of a pair of bear cubs in the low-rent Canadian nature film that was the feature presentation, all I could see were flashes of the crimson cascade that Dracula had caused. Even an adorable pair of gingham-stealing chipmunks didn't cheer me up, as I was now fixated on the thought that the chipmunks and the bears and even the befuddled forest ranger were also filled with copious amounts of blood. I felt faint envisioning that if Dracula were to show up and perform his dirty work, I'd be watching oceans of bear and chipmunk and ranger blood stain the meadows of golden wheat through which they were currently romping. The image haunted me all week and yet today that splattering blood wasn't part of a movie anymore. It was something I was now convinced I'd be witnessing on my wedding night.

Tim didn't really have much more of an explanation regarding a girl's period than simply giving it a name, and, from the looks on our faces, it was clear that none of us really wanted to know much more than that. I could tell that we were all dealing with this disturbing news in our own private way, bringing to it whatever personal plasma imagery we had available to us.

The conversation for the rest of recess was strained and awkward. When I got home that afternoon, I was tempted to ask my mom to explain the science of girls' periods to me but quickly decided that it was something I didn't really need or want to know for the next fifteen years. And even if I did, it was definitely *not* something I wanted to have my own mother explain to me as she stood in the kitchen mixing the ingredients to make a Texas sheet cake. And so I decided then and there to put the whole thing out of my mind by convincing myself that Tim Stepalonis was just crazy and wrong.

But a strange seed had been planted that day, a bipolar idea that a girl was both something I wanted to possess entirely and, at the same time, a thing of horrifying mystery, a blood-and-guts time bomb that seemed to be constantly ticking, always moments away from peeing unnaturally or unleashing a sea of blood or excreting a baby or any number of off-putting biological processes. The world of girlfriends and hand-holding and kissing and romance that I had so wanted to be a part of now looked like it might be a lot more *Dracula—Prince of Darkness* and a lot less *Charlie, the Lonesome Cougar.* I was starting to understand why other boys my age didn't like girls. It wasn't because of "cooties" or toughness or genetics but because of fear. We had never understood the way girls thought and now we had no idea how they even worked.

And yet, I couldn't deny that for all the strange things that must be going on *inside* girls, everything on the outside of them was far too powerful to walk away from. Like it or not, my fate was set. The fear would have to be overcome and the girls would have to be understood. Just not that day.

But I had a feeling it would all be worth it. After all, Dracula may have been scary, but let's face it. The guy was a perpetual bachelor.

LITTLE LEAGUE FAUNTLEROY

I've never been much for sports.

This doesn't mean I haven't tried. Throughout my life, I've attempted on several occasions to do two things—smoke cigarettes and watch sports. And both quests have always proven to be miserable failures. Because of a nicotine allergy, any awkwardly held cigarette I have disaffectedly tried to smoke has resulted in over two hours of chronic nausea and dizziness, erasing any cool quotient I was hoping the "butt" would lend me. James Dean I was not on the numerous occasions that I would smoke a cigarette and then have to sit on a curb with my head between my knees trying not to pass out as my friends looked on, unsure if I was on death's doorstep or just suffering from terminal loser disease. And because of a lack of competitive spirit and a short attention span, coupled with an overriding inability to figure out why teams of men scoring points should have any importance in my life, I've just never been able to get into sports, either.

I think part of the problem is that in order to enjoy watching sports, one must enjoy *playing* sports. And as my ill-fated encounters with kickball, softball, tetherball, basketball, dodgeball, and any other activity that ends in the letters *all* (or *olf,* for that matter) have shown, I enjoy playing sports about as much as I enjoy slamming my fingers in a car door.

It's not for lack of trying. Once, when I was ten, at the prod-
ding of my father, I joined Little League. I liked the idea of it,
having enjoyed attending Tiger baseball games in Detroit. However, in retrospect, I think it was the consumption of hot dogs, the
purchase of giant sponge "We're Number One" hands, and being
allowed to scream at the top of my lungs without getting in trouble and not the game itself that held the greatest allure for me.
When I put my Little League uniform on for the first time, I was
convinced that because I was dressed appropriately, I would be an
immediate baseball prodigy. There are pictures of me in our family album posing in my living room with my uniform on, mitt on
hand, hat on head, crouched in an enthusiastic attempt to look
like I was ready to field a line drive. The clueless toothy smile on
my face is quite ironic now, since my single season in Little League
turned out to be nothing short of a nightmare.

On the first day of Little League training, I went merrily up to
home plate and quickly learned that I was terrified that a kid my
age was now about to hurl an object with the density of a billiard
ball straight at me. I hunched over the plate, wiggling the bat back
and forth over my head, not because I was tensing my muscles in
preparation to swing the bat, but simply because I had seen Al
Kaline do it for years and figured I was supposed to do it, too. The
pitcher wound up and threw a meteor my way, and I immediately
jumped back about five feet as the ball smacked loudly into the
catcher's mitt, sending out an ominous cloud of dust that seemed
to say "This dust could have been your pulverized head, man."
My teammates laughed derisively and I suddenly felt like I wanted
to quit the team.

"Feig, what are you doing?" yelled the coach. "Stay in the batter's box."

I looked at him and nodded dumbly. Figuring that maybe it
was simply the shock of the first pitch that spooked me, I stepped
back in, hunched over, and wiggled my bat over my head again,
albeit this time with a little less enthusiasm.

The pitcher wound up and fired another rocket in my direction. Long-dormant primitive survival sensors deep inside my brain, which had once saved my caveman ancestors from saber-toothed tigers and flying rocks, lit up and screamed at me that I was in mortal danger. I once again leapt out of the box, and thus began a monthlong battle between the coach and myself to keep me from jumping away from the plate.

"Feig! Stay in there!"

"Feig! Lean in on that ball. It's not gonna bite you!"

"Feig! Goddamn it, stay in the goddamn batter's box!"

Now, look. I'm the first to admit when I'm being a big baby, but I don't think I was in the wrong on this one. I mean, this wasn't the major leagues. Kids were always making mistakes, and none of the ten-year-olds I knew were truly in control of anything their bodies did. So why would a kid, just by virtue of the fact that he had the title "pitcher" in front of his name, be any less apt to have a moment of bad aim and accidentally drill a hard ball into my head? He wouldn't, as far as I was concerned. But according to my coach, this never happened.

"Look, Feig, these guys are *trained* pitchers. I work with them day in and day out on their control. They can hit any spot they aim at. That's their job. And so the only thing they're going to hit when they pitch to you is the catcher's mitt, since there's no danger of them hitting your bat when you're running away from the plate like a little girl."

Correct me if I'm wrong, Coach, but I seem to recall seeing a lot of major league players being hit by pitches. The image of a ball caroming off a batter's helmet, the player then slumping lifelessly to the ground and subsequently being carried off the field on a stretcher to a round of pity applause from the crowd, had been burned into my brain many times via the local sportscaster on our evening news, who would always preface the clip with the phrase "Some scary footage from Tiger Stadium tonight." And now that I was standing at the plate feeling that ball whiz by, emitting much the same whistling sound I always imagined an African tribesman's spear would make nanoseconds before it pierced my chest, I had the distinct feeling that I was being conned by a guy who didn't really like me.

"Do I *have* to bat?" I would plead. "Can't I let someone *else* do it for me? I don't mind."

The coach sighed and gave me a long, searching look. I could tell he wanted more than anything to just buy me a dress and pom-poms and let me cheer the team on from the sidelines, but because his job was to provide all of us with athletic training and help our self-esteem, he quickly regrouped.

"Okay, Feig, here's what I want you to do. When you go home tonight, get your dad to go out onto the driveway with you. Get a bunch of tennis balls and stand against your garage door. Then have your dad throw the tennis balls at you as hard as he can while you dodge out of the way. You'll get used to it in no time and then you'll see it's not such a big deal. I did the same thing with my boy last season."

The pity I felt for his son at that moment was immense. The thought of this grown man putting his poor kid up against a garage door and then cathartically hurling tennis balls at him seemed more like something that should merit a visit from Child Services than self-congratulation. I'd hate to see what happened if his kid ever told him he was afraid of guns.

With the horror of his sadistic tennis-ball scheme fresh in my mind, combined with a fear that somehow he'd call my dad and actually convince him to do it, I vowed to stand my ground in the batter's box for the next pitch. I got in my stance and actually forced myself to lean into the plate, attempting to disconnect my danger sensors for the next few seconds. The pitcher sized me up as I forced myself to envision fluffy clouds, soft feather pillows, and oversize Nerf balls lazily drifting into my bat. The pitcher went into his windup and threw a screaming fastball that curved toward me like a guided missile and promptly hit me like a bullet right in my butt. Before I could even react in pain, the coach rushed over and grabbed me and started rubbing my butt vigorously, as if he were sure I was going to burst out crying and somehow his therapeutic touch could stop it.

"Okay, okay, you're all right, you're all right," he said quickly with a tone that had absolutely no concern for my well-being and everything to do with avoiding a potential lawsuit. The irony was that it actually didn't hurt that much, since the ball had hit me right in the fleshiest part of my butt cheek. But the fact that a grown man was now rubbing my hinder with a big fake reassuring smile on his face made me wish the ball had hit me in the head and knocked me unconscious.

Amazingly enough, my encounter with the baseball, coupled with the creepy feeling I got from the coach's manhandling of my ass, actually did slightly lessen my fear of being pitched to. Which was unfortunate because now that I could stay in the batter's box, there was no real excuse for the fact that I couldn't hit a ball with a bat any more than I could tear a telephone book in half with my bare hands.

Once the season began and our actual games started, I quickly realized that I hated everything about Little League. It was hot and depressing to stand out in the sun that long, I couldn't catch a ball to save my life, I constantly swung the bat too hard and would always miss and spin around and fall over like a ten-year-old Bowery drunk, and even the fun of chanting "Hey, batter batter, hey, batter batter, *swing*!" and "Cheer cheer cheer, the pitcher's full of beer / That's not all, the catcher's full of al-co-hol" couldn't make those endless games go by any quicker or easier. My teammates clearly hated me because to them I represented nothing more than a guaranteed error or an automatic out. I *wanted* out and all I could see was a season's worth of tedium and humiliation stretching ahead of me like miles of unpaved road. At night, I would look at those early pictures of me in my uniform posing in the living room with my big I-have-no-idea-what-I'm-getting-myself-into smile and think, What a dope.

As my mother and I were heading to my third regular season game, I looked up at the sky and decided that the few fluffy white clouds amidst the sea of sunny blue were indicators that a massive rainstorm was on its way to wash out our game, so there was really no sense in driving the three blocks to the diamond to check with my coach to see if the game was going to be called. My mother, who hated sitting in the hard sun-baked bleachers, who hated having to listen to the complaints of my teammates' mothers whenever I would leave one of them stranded on second base, and who hated having to watch me play Little League as much as I hated playing it, agreed with me that the weather looked ominous. And so the two of us merrily headed off to the local mall to eat Coney Island hot dogs and shop for clothes. This led to my missing the next three games as my mother and I became very adept at weather prediction, psychically foretelling impending storms out of clear blue skies. Our predictions never seemed to pan out, but I was more than happy to admit my mistake as I merrily sipped an Orange Julius and proudly wore my Little League uniform as I walked around an air-conditioned mall instead of standing on a humidity- and humiliation-soaked baseball diamond.

Unfortunately, all good things do come to an end and my good thing ended when the coach called my father to find out where I had been for the past four games. My dad, unaware that we had not been attending, gave both my mother and me a stern talking-to about the evils of avoiding hard work and about the importance of seeing things to which you had committed yourself through to the end, whether you liked them or not. We both nodded in shame, embarrassed at having been caught but mostly depressed that more bleachers and painful moments of nonathleticism were in our respective futures.

When I returned to my team for the next game, one of my teammates asked me where I'd been for all the games I'd missed.

"Oh, my mom made me go shopping," I said with a shrug. The kid stared at me as if I'd just told him I'd been out kissing guys.

"Your mom made you go *shopping?*" he said incredulously.

I felt trouble a-brewin' and knew I had to blame the whole thing on my mother. "Yeah, you know," I said with a Kabuki-like eye gesture that was supposed to say "You know how goofy moms can be."

The kid immediately called over to the rest of the team. "Hey, you guys, Feig missed all those games to go *shopping,*" at which point the whole team came over and started laughing and shoving me around.

"Oh my God, Feig. You're such a fag."

"Did you buy a dress, Fag Newton?"

"I bet the homo bought a purse."

Ah, the camaraderie of your teammates.

It wasn't until the final third of the season that something actually respectable happened to me. By that point, I had become the clown prince of our team, my skills in the field and at the plate so woefully inadequate that I almost became the team's mascot, much the same way that a group of nice, cool guys will take the school's retarded kid under their wing out of one part compassion and five parts amusement at his uncontrollable antics. I had dropped so many fly balls and tripped over so many bases and ducked away from so many line drives that I think the guys felt it was a little like having the San Diego Chicken on their team. If they didn't expect too much out of me except laughs, then they were usually satisfied. I had become the Designated Boob.

And that's why it was so surprising to everyone that during this one game, by a string of miracles, I had actually made it to third base. It had not come without a price. I had gotten to first base after being hit by a pitch in my upper thigh, then had advanced to second only after a line drive nearly took my head off, then stumbled my way onto third off a hit my teammates and the parents in the stands made me abundantly aware I could have easily run to home plate on. As I stood on third base, with the coach standing five feet away yelling, "Now, pay attention to everything I say—if I tell you to run, then you'd better run," the enthusiastic Paul Feig who months earlier had put on his uniform for the first time and dreamed of being the Most Valuable Player for the Clinton Township Little League Association slowly started to come back to life. It was the realization that I could possibly score a run without having to do anything other than sprint to home plate that made me think I should actually try and enjoy this moment. And so I went into my best one-foot-on-the-bag/the-other-foot-ready-to-spring-down-the-line pose, arms and fingers extended east and west, tensed and ready for action. I had no idea exactly when I should run if the ball were to be hit, but I figured that if I did indeed pay attention to everything the coach said, I might actually be able to do something competent for the first time in my baseball career.

It was only then that I noticed the kid on the other team who was covering third base standing next to me. Simply put, as I glanced over at him, I noticed that he had the biggest booger I'd ever seen hanging out of his nose. There were always kids when I was growing up who had no idea if they had something coming out of their noses or milk at the edges of their mouths or spit strings between their lips when they talked. From an early age I had categorized several of my friends by their particular bodily oddities and would plan my time with them accordingly. Spit constantly flew out of George's mouth when he talked, so I avoided having lunch with him. Brian always had terrible milk breath and so I would save my talks with him for when we were riding our bikes so that the wind would carry away what his toothbrush obviously couldn't. Scott had the world's dirtiest fingernails and so I would make sure not to trade any snack items with him. But now this kid, well . . . he had a booger hanging that was big enough to be categorized as a chandelier.

As he stared intently at the player at home plate, he would chant the standard "hey batter batter." But as he did it, the booger would swing either toward him or away from him, depending on whether he was expelling breath or drawing it in. It was hypnotizing, like car-crash carnage that you don't want to look at but can't for the life of you look away from. I started wondering if I should tell the kid about it. Would he be embarrassed? Would he thank me? Or would he just get mad and fling it at me, ten years old being the age where the thought of *not* flinging a booger at somebody else was as foreign as checking to see if a booger's there in the first place.

As I stared at the horror that was dangling from his nostril, I heard a *crack*. I looked up just in time to see the catcher stare up into the sky, scramble toward the backstop, and trip over his mask, which he had just flung to the ground. Before I could process it, I heard the coach yell into my ear.

"Run!"

I looked at him, confused. The ball was going straight up into the air, not out into the field as I knew it was supposed to. I didn't really understand much about foul balls or foul tips or foul anything, since my mind would wander off to thoughts of Marcia Brady whenever the coach would brief us on the rules of the game. The coach glared back at me and screamed a hot blast of dad breath into my face as he pointed wildly toward home plate.

"Run, goddamn it, Feig! RUN!!!"

And so I did. I had no idea what I was running to or what to expect when I got there but I ran. I heard the parents in the stands screaming, I heard my teammates screaming, I heard the other team screaming. I didn't know what anyone was saying, but I assumed they were all yelling at me for doing something wrong. I had heard those kinds of shouts all season, exclamations that usually had the words *what the hell are you doing?* somewhere within them. Maybe I was running the wrong way. I had no idea. My mind was a blur. I saw the catcher scrambling around in the dirt. He grabbed ahold of the ball and looked over at the pitcher, who was now charging forward toward home plate. One thing seemed clear to me. I had to get to home plate before either one of them did. And so, in a barefaced panic, I tried to run even faster.

I've always had a problem with my legs and running. At our school's yearly Field Day, an event straight out of the *How to Torture the Nonathletic Handbook,* I would usually enter a running race and within the first ten feet of my initial sprint I would try to run so fast that my knees would buckle and I'd end up falling to the ground, belly flopping down and sprawling out like a bearskin rug. And this day, as I started to put on the speed, I felt my knees once again giving way. Fortunately, I was very close to the plate. As my knees started to go out and the diminishing distance between my hips and the ground made the fronts of my shoes start to dig deeper into the dirt with every stride, I saw the catcher toss the ball to the pitcher, who was as close to the plate as I was. As he caught the ball and started to turn toward me to tag me in the chest, my knees went out completely and I collapsed underneath his arm. My fall was so quick and completely out of the realm of what a competent player's body is supposed to do in a slide that the pitcher never dreamed of lowering his mitt to the level that I was now at. My arms and face slammed heavily onto the plate as my stomach bounced roughly into the dirt. I *oofed* loudly and felt like someone had hit me in the breadbasket with a two-by-four.

Silence.

I had no idea what had just happened and for a brief moment thought that maybe I was dead. But it was then I heard a word that had never been used in conjunction with anything I'd ever done on a baseball field.

"SAFE!"

I was certain that the umpire for some reason was telling the pitcher that his tag of me was "safe." But when I looked up, I saw the pitcher give me a dirty look and roll his eyes.

And then I heard an amazing sound.

The parents in the stands and all my teammates started cheering for me. I looked over and saw parents on their feet, the coach smiling and wiping his brow, and then all the kids from my team running over. I got up, my stomach aching and my face scratched from hitting the gravel that had covered home plate, and headed toward them. They surrounded me, cheering and smiling and laughing. They all fought to pat me on the back, on the arms, on the head. I had never seen this group of guys so happy to see me. It was such a foreign experience for me that I remember actually pushing their hands away. It was too strange. In some weird way, their boundless approval was almost as disturbing and frightening as their disapproval of me had been throughout the season. I saw that the only way I would ever get these guys' respect was to have success on a baseball field. That had I been thrown out at the plate or fallen earlier or not run at all, things would have been business as usual, with my now smiling teammates shaking their heads and muttering the customary "God, what a fag" under their collective breaths. My one random act, performed only because the coach had yelled at me to do something that I didn't understand and would never have done on my own, a robotic following of a command that entailed no skill on my part outside of running for my life so as to avoid getting yelled at, had all of a sudden brought me the respect of my peers. It didn't matter who I was at that moment, nor what I knew of this world. I was simply a guy who had mindlessly scored a run. It all seemed so hollow and shallow that I was overcome at the hypocrisy of it all.

Well . . .

Actually, that's not true. I loved it. Hey, what can I say? For once in my life since I joined the team, I wasn't being referred to as a fag or a homo or a girl or a pussy or a retard or anything else that you're not supposed to call other people. I was the kid who, even though it was for a very superficial reason, these guys all liked very much at this moment. And I've never forgotten how great that moment felt for my entire life.

After the game, as we drank our celebratory bottles of Faygo red pop, the conversation got around to the next season. Several of the better players on our team were talking about their plans for the future.

"I think I'm gonna try out for Pony League next season," said one of them. "The coach says my hitting is good enough now."

"Yeah," said another kid, "I'm gonna try out, too. I was thinking maybe I'll try out to be a pitcher."

I looked around at them, my newfound friends, and for the first time felt like baseball wasn't so bad. It now seemed as if my time on the team had actually been okay. I had gotten some confidence and felt kind of cool being able to say for the past few months, "I can't hang out today. I've got a baseball game."

"Yeah," I said, nodding thoughtfully as I looked around at them all, "I'm thinking about trying out for Pony League, too."

They all stared at me for a second, then the best player on the team raised his eyebrow and said, "Are you kidding, Feig? You're way too big of a fag to play Pony League."

And with this, they all started laughing at me, harder than they'd ever laughed at me before.

Oh, well, I thought, at least jocks are consistent.

At the end of the season, after our team banquet and after we had signed each other's programs and after the coach had given us all autographed Tiger baseballs and told us that we had been great players, I came home, took off my baseball cap, and hung it on the post of my bed so I could see it as I fell asleep. My nightmare season in Little League was over, and I knew there was no way I would be playing again next year. I felt relieved, and yet I felt proud that I had made it through the entire season, save for the four-game shopping odyssey my mother and I had taken. And as I stared at my baseball cap hanging next to my head, I realized that the season hadn't been such a nightmare after all. True, it hadn't been the least bit fun, and most of the time it had been downright painful, but it hadn't been a complete waste of time, either.

I mean, after all, at least I now knew for certain that I was too much of a fag to play Pony League.

Ah, who am I kidding? Little League sucks. It always did and it always will.

Sorry, Coach.

THE GYM CLASS ARCHIPELAGO, PART I: THE WORST GAME IN THE WORLD

There was one class that I never enjoyed, that I faced each day with stomach-twisting dread: gym class.

I must admit that I didn't mind gym class as much when I was in grade school because, back then, it was literally just running around. We pretty much played easy games like kickball and tumbled on foam mats and never really worked up a sweat. And for that reason we were allowed to do it all in our school clothes. I liked dressing nicely when I was a kid and wouldn't have been caught dead in a pair of Sears Toughskins jeans. No, I liked to wear dress pants, or "slacks," as my father always called them. I guess I just associated jeans and dressing badly with the kids I was afraid of, kids who were always punching each other's arms and shooting at squirrels with their BB guns. I figured that if I dressed nicer than them, I could avoid being like them, as if a bully gene were ticking inside me, ready to go off the minute I pulled on a pair of Wranglers and threw a rock at a bird. When I was in grade school, polyester was all the rage and my closet was filled with it. I always wore polyester bell-bottoms in a host of fashion-defying designs. They all had some amped-up plaid pattern on them that even the least discerning Scottish clan would reject and cuffs big enough to keep a wallet in. I've always thought that because of all the polyester we humans encased ourselves in back in the 1970s,

if a nuclear bomb had ever gone off, we might not have died but
we would have definitely all been laminated.

One interesting science fact I discovered in grade school was
that gym floors and polyester pants don't mix. Because I used to
love to run and fall down and slide, and the first time I wore my
polyester pants in gym, I ran and fell down and slid and my pants
melted onto my knees. Anytime I'd create the slightest amount of
friction between the floor and my dress slacks, they would immediately turn into a liquid. After an hour of gymnastics, my plaid
pants would look like a Jackson Pollock painting.

But, fortunately, melted pants was about as bad as it got, and
gym class wasn't too tough in elementary school.

When I got to junior high, however, I was confronted with
something that I found quite disturbing—gym clothes. You see,
being told I had to wear gym clothes in PE class meant I had to
change into them. And changing into them meant I had to go
into a locker room. And going into a locker room meant I had to
take *off* the clothes I wore to school and put *on* my gym attire. And
taking off my clothes and putting on my gym attire meant that I
had to do all of this in *front* of my classmates.

And this was not something that I wished to do. At all.

See, I was an only child, and so I never had to take my clothes
off in front of anybody. Even my parents. If clothing had to be
changed, I'd always disappear into the privacy of my room, close
the door, pull down my shades, and come back out after the trans-
action was complete. Even when I took a bath, I'd go into my
room, disrobe, wrap a towel around myself, and then saunter from
my bedroom to the bathroom as if my aluminum-sided house
were a Las Vegas health spa. And my parents were not allowed to
watch as I dropped the towel and entered the water, which was
covered with a thick layer of Mr. Bubble, my bathtime guardian
who made sure my in-tub nakedness would be hidden from any
prying eyes. I had the system all worked out. No one on this earth
would ever see me with more than 40 percent of my body ex-

posed at any one time. I even told myself that after I was married, a system would be worked out between my wife and me to insure that no full-frontal viewings of my manliness would ever occur.

And then suddenly, thanks to a guy named Mr. Wendell, our new gym teacher whose burly physique and gruff attitude told me that he would not agree with my theory that "sports are stupid," I was expected to show 100 percent of myself to a bunch of kids I had grown up with, I didn't know, or who didn't like me.

Where was Mr. Bubble when I needed him?

On the first day of class, Mr. Wendell told us that we had to bring in a pair of shorts, a T-shirt, sweat socks, and a towel, and that we would be changing into our gym clothes every day before class.

"Mr. Wendell," I asked timidly. "Do we *have* to change?"

My question was immediately met with a mixture of laughter, jokes, and insults.

"What's the matter, ya fag?" said Norman, having made the transition from normal kid to heinous bully a couple of summers ago. "Can't your parents afford to buy you clothes?"

"Yes," I said, trying to defend the honor of my family. "I was just wondering, that's all." Jerks, I thought. Didn't they know how traumatic this whole thing was going to be for me? Didn't they care how overly sensitive I was?

"Hey, Feig, maybe they'll let you wear a tutu."

Clearly, they *didn't* care.

I arrived in gym class the next day with a new pair of gym shorts, a freshly purchased T-shirt, the first pair of sweat socks I'd ever owned, and a brightly striped yellow and orange towel my mom used when she went to the beach. My classmates and I stood around with our gym clothes in hand, waiting to hear what we should do next. All the other guys' gym outfits looked very athletic and broken in. Had they all done this before? I wondered nervously. Had these guys actually played gym-type games outside of school? And in the proper attire? I guess the problem was that my best friends were mostly girls, and that while these guys were playing football and basketball, I had been sitting around the house with Mary, Sharon, and Stephanie playing Mystery Date and Art Linkletter's House Party.

"All right, ladies," said Mr. Wendell, sounding very much like Sergeant Carter from *Gomer Pyle, USMC.* "Follow me and we'll assign you all a locker."

Mr. Wendell took us into the locker room. It was scrotum-shrinkingly cold in there, and the cream-colored cinder-block walls and rows of dented brown lockers looked very much like the room in which I saw a drug-dealing football player get shot on a recent episode of *Starsky and Hutch.*

"All right, gents. This is the locker room. You'll be changing over in this area, where the lockers are. And get yourself a lock, too, since you'll be leaving your stuff here every night."

I couldn't figure out for the life of me why we would need to lock up our gym clothes. If somebody really wanted to steal my shorts, they were more than welcome to them.

"Now, over in this cage is where we keep all the equipment. You may only enter here with my permission," he said, as Norman and his cohorts made faces at each other that seemed to indicate they planned on going inside it *without* his permission at some time in the future. Why anybody would want floor hockey pucks and miniature traffic cones was beyond me. But, as I was about to find out, there were a *lot* of things about being a twelve-year-old boy that I didn't really understand.

"And over here are the showers."

Showers? For what? Washing the equipment?

"Each of you will be required to shower after every class. No exceptions."

I figured I must have died and gone to hell. I guessed that when I was looking down at my English book on the bus that morning, the bus must have exploded suddenly and now I was dead and didn't know it, as if I were in a *Twilight Zone* for kids. That could be the only excuse for someone's telling me I was going to have to bathe in public.

I looked into the shower room. It was big and cold. White tile. Lots of nozzles sticking out of the walls. A drain in the middle. And NO DIVIDERS. NO STALLS.

Why in the world would we have to shower? I wondered, too confused to panic. I take a shower every morning before I go to school. I shampoo and blow-dry my hair. I brush my teeth. I'm the cleanest seventh grader this school has ever seen. He can't possibly be talking to me.

"Do we *all* have to shower?" I asked Mr. Wendell.

"Of course you do, ya fag! What do you want to do? Stink all day?"

Again this came from Norman, a guy I once saw wear the same T-shirt with a faded KISS iron-on for one week straight. And now he was nailing *me* on the topic of hygiene.

"All students must shower after class, Mr. Feig. I don't think you'd want to sit next to yourself in math after you've played a few games of basketball." Why not? I wondered. The idea of breaking a sweat during a game of basketball was as foreign to me as putting horse shit on bread and eating it like a sandwich.

"All right, boys. Change into your gym clothes. We're gonna have a little fun on your first day."

I normally responded to the word *fun*. But since this was gym, the only fun thing I could imagine happening was class being canceled.

I guess I must have had an abnormal amount of hang-ups for a twelve-year-old, because no sooner were the words *change into your gym clothes* out of Mr. Wendell's mouth than all my classmates just dropped their pants and changed. None of them really seemed to care that they were standing around in front of each other in their underwear. I, however, immediately froze. I suddenly knew I couldn't undress in front of them and so figured that I would wait until they had finished and headed out into the gym before I would remove my stylish polyester slacks. And so, in order to stall, I sat down on the bench and immediately pretended to become very interested in my towel. I studied a small piece of the weaving as if it were an equation that had to be worked out. It was all I could think to do but it didn't float.

"Hey, Feig! Quit starin' at your faggy towel and get dressed!" Norman again.

"All right. I just thought I saw something on my towel."

"Yeah. Probably lice from your house."

Everyone laughed at Norman's joke. They always laughed at what he said. He never said one funny thing the entire time I knew him but to hear the response he always got from my peers, you'd think the guy was Oscar Wilde. But it was clear. I was going to have to put my modesty on hold and change in front of this group of alpha males. So, like that hippie who thought about making love to his girlfriend as he was tortured during basic training for Vietnam in the TV movie *Tribes,* I let my mind remove itself to somewhere more pleasant as I took off my pants.

And as soon as they were off, my face went white.

Because I had forgotten about something.

A few weeks earlier, my mother had gotten into a hobby called Cameo, which was the art of drawing designs and pictures on fabric and clothing with these special Cameo ink pens. And one of the first projects she undertook was to hijack a pair of my underwear and draw a big dark red butterfly right on the back.

And that was the pair of briefs I had absentmindedly worn to school this day.

I swallowed what felt like a pool ball. I was frozen. Did anyone see it? I wondered. My mind started to race, in full panic mode. Trying to think clearly, I reasoned that I should just turn around slowly and put my back against the—

"Oh my God! Feig shit his pants!!!"

I knew I could count on Norman and his keen powers of observation. I suddenly found myself wishing that the school would cave in and kill us all.

"What the hell is that?!" said another kid, staring at my ass incredulously.

I immediately made a feeble attempt to make light of the situation. "Oh boy, that's my mom's doing. Ha ha ha. She sort of branded me."

They didn't hear a word I said. The whole class was moving toward me, staring at the butterfly on the back of my underwear, all of them with stunned, incredulous looks on their faces.

"My mom's pretty weird. Ha ha ha." I tried to defuse the situation but to no avail. What the hell is their problem? I thought, angry and frustrated. Why can't they just let it go? Who cares what I'm wearing? I'd seen them wear stupid stuff lots of times. Even Norman had once worn a T-shirt that had "Afternoon Delight" written across the front of it. But there I was, looking at this approaching sea of dumbfounded faces, their mouths hanging open, their eyebrows tight and furrowed. They just kept moving in closer, staring at the back of my Cameo-bedecked briefs, trying to figure out what they were looking at. I wanted to turn around and run but I just couldn't move.

As the famous bumper sticker says, "If you can read this, you're too close." Well, now they were too close. And they could indeed read it.

"Oh my God. It's a *butterfly!* FAAAAAAAAAAAAGGGGGGGG!!!!"

All hell broke loose. There couldn't have been more commotion if someone had lobbed a live grenade into the room. I really wanted to die, and I was trying to figure out how I was going to take my mother and her Cameo pens with me.

"FAG!"

"FAAAAG!"

"FEIG'S A FAG! FEIG'S A FAG!"

They had come unhinged. Apparently they'd never seen deco-

rative underwear and the sight of it had turned them into the kids
from *Lord of the Flies*.

"What the hell's going on in here?!"

Mr. Wendell entered angrily. I figured I was saved.

"Feig's got a butterfly on his underwear!" said Norman, pointing at my ass like he was ratting out a shipping container filled
with illegal aliens.

"He does?" said Mr. Wendell, raising an eyebrow. "Let's see it,
Feig."

So much for being saved.

Mr. Wendell leaned over and took a good close look at my
mother's handiwork.

"A butterfly? That's lovely, Feig. Was it always there or did it
used to be a cocoon?"

And with that, the room erupted again.

"FEIG'S A FAG! FEIG'S A FAG! FEIG'S A FAG!"

That's right. Just lynch me, boys. I was starting not to care anymore.

"All right, guys, all right," Mr. Wendell said in a laughing tone,
as if he were thinking, Aah, I wish *I* were a lad again so I could
join in on the taunting of this sensitive outcast. "Enough of this,"
he said with a smirk. "Get dressed and get into the gym." He started
to head out the doorway, then stopped and turned back to me.
"Oh, and Feig? You can flutter out with the rest of them."

All the guys burst into laughter and high fives.

Thanks, Mr. Wendell. You're really an inspiration to us all.

So, everyone finished changing, throwing out various taunts at
me for good measure. It was now becoming a means of peer acceptance to get a "good one" off at my expense. Even people I
thought were my friends were bending their brains trying to come
up with a humorous underwear quip.

"Hey, Feig, uh . . . nice *butt*-erfly."

"Does your dad have one on his underwear, too? I . . . um . . .
I bet he does."

"I bet that butterfly . . . uh . . . wishes that it . . . was . . . uh . . . that it didn't have to smell your butt all day."

My underwear had turned the locker room into a comedy-writing workshop. I couldn't be prouder.

I was the last to finish changing. I seriously thought about just leaving and probably would have if I didn't think that Mr. Wendell and the class would have hunted me down and dragged me in front of the entire school in my butterfly underwear. I closed my locker, barely having enough strength to do it. This episode had really taken it out of me and so I tried desperately to think of anything to make myself feel better. Wendell had said we were going to do something fun. Maybe we were going to get to watch a movie about sports or something else I didn't care about, and then I could just sit in the dark and let the rest of this already terrible hour play itself out with no further incident.

I entered the gym.

"FAG!" went up a loud chorus.

I trudged over and sat down with the group as I wondered if I could convince my parents to transfer me to an all-girls' school.

"All right, everybody," said Mr. Wendell, addressing the class. "Being that this is the first official day of gym, I thought we'd do something a little different. The game I'm going to let you guys play is a treat, and we'll play it every Friday *if* you've done well all week. And only if you've all done your best."

For as long as I can remember, my mother had been obsessed with "treats." To her, the only way to get through life was to have treats to look forward to. The strain from a tough day at school or a bad guitar lesson would always be salved by my mother suggesting that she and I should "go get a treat," which was usually some sort of dessert item like ice cream or cookies or something else that people really shouldn't be eating in the middle of the day. And so when I heard Mr. Wendell use the word *treat*, my automatic response was that it was going to be something good.

"The name of this game is . . . Killer."

It was *not* going to be something good.

"The object of the game," said Mr. Wendell as he paced in front of us, "is to be the last man left standing on the floor." In my book, anything whose description includes the phrase "last man left standing" is not something that should ever be used in conjunction with the word *treat*. But then again, I'm not a gym teacher.

"Aw, man, this is a great game!" said Norman, punching one of his friends in the arm. "I play it with my brother all the time!" Thoughts of Norman's brother, whom I envisioned as a drooling giant who left a path of oafish destruction wherever he walked, flashed through my head as Mr. Wendell continued.

"What you will be using to get your opponents out of the game are playground balls." With that, Mr. Wendell dumped about twenty of the dark red objects out of a large canvas bag. They bounced onto the floor noisily and rolled off in all directions. These were the same type of balls we'd used when we played kickball in grade school, but the ones we used back then were huge, the size of large pumpkins. These balls that Mr. Wendell had produced were small ones. Except for one big ball, which I later came to know affectionately as "Fat Man," these balls were no bigger than cantaloupes. Very *small* cantaloupes. I'd seen playground balls this size before but had always assumed they were factory rejects that had no real purpose. And maybe they were, but clearly Mr. Wendell had found a new and, I imagined, much more sadistic second life for them.

"Okay, in order to play Killer, you will be divided into two teams. Each team will take one side of the gym. Then, when I blow the whistle, you will throw the balls across the gym at the other team without crossing the center line. If you are hit by a ball, you're out. If you catch a ball, the person who threw the ball is out. Got it?"

Unfortunately, I did. And I realized that this was the last game in the world I wanted to play.

"These balls are too big," said Norman as he picked one up and stared at it with disdain. "When my brother and I play, we use tennis balls. They really hurt." Yes, I thought, that really does sound like more fun. Maybe if we're really good, one week Mr. Wendell will let us use golf balls and Chinese throwing stars.

"All right, girls, grab a ball and choose a side," said Mr. Wendell, clapping his hands together much the same way I imagine sweatshop owners do when they want their underpaid workers to sew faster.

Everyone scrambled to get a ball and then ran enthusiastically to opposite sides of the gym. Wishing I could just walk to the end of the gym where the door was and then continue walking through the door and out of the school and back to the safety of my bed, I sighed and wandered over to the side closest to me. As I approached, my classmates readjusted sides. I looked up and saw that almost everyone had gone onto the team opposite me. And they all had bloodthirsty looks in their eyes.

"Hey, Butterfly? You're dead!"

Oh great, I thought. This is a real treat. I was about to be the star of my gym class's production of "The Lottery."

"All right, you clowns, you can't all be on the same side," yelled Mr. Wendell, looking like he was trying not to chuckle. "Even up the teams. Now, get moving!"

No one moved, so Wendell had to walk out and manually separate us into equal groups.

"Aaw . . . I don't want to be on *Fag's* team!" complained Karl Scott, a short, pudgy cohort of Norman's.

It was at this moment that I had to reflect on the question "Exactly why do we *have* gym class in the first place?" Was it supposed to build morale? Self-esteem? To make us more confident about our bodies, our minds, and our abilities? That's what my father always told me, but if that was the case, then my school district was failing goddamned miserably.

So the teams were set and we squared off, waiting for the war to begin. I looked around at the four walls that surrounded us. Each was covered with retractable bleachers, long slabs of dark brown wood, horizontal prison bars holding me hostage. I looked over at the opposing team and saw nothing but intense looks of angry determination aimed directly at me. Looking to my own team for support, I saw pretty much the same expressions. It was clear. Everyone in this gym wanted to see me dead. I guess putting a butterfly on your underpants was right up there with defiling the American flag.

I had only one strategy in my head for this game they called Killer and that was: *get out*. As bad as the game sounded, I had to remember that these were only rubber balls. Not big enough for the thrower to grasp like a baseball or anything. I'd already survived Little League at this point and had gotten used to having baseballs thrown my way. These glorified Four-Square balls would probably just get lobbed lazily around the gym and if I did get hit, so what? It would be a symbolic gesture that might help release some of these guys' animosity toward me and then I'd be finished with this class and free to move to Oregon, where I could specialize in arts and crafts with my fellow societal escapees.

Mr. Wendell walked out onto the floor, whistle in mouth. He took a deep breath, ready to blow. The boys all tightened their grips on the balls. Hate radiated from their eyes as they looked toward me. My stomach started to hurt. Maybe this wasn't going to be as harmless as I imagined.

The whistle blew.

And I descended into hell.

BLAM! A ball drilled into the ground right next to me as I saw the first round of ammo heading my way at the speed of light. My only reaction was to hit the floor. Just as I did, I heard this first volley whistle over my head. BOOM BOOM BOOM! The balls hit the bleacher-covered wall. The noise was incredible. The hollow wood being hit by the now solid-seeming balls made a sound like a sonic boom. A sound I could feel in my heart. I suddenly realized that these "harmless" balls were actually lethal weapons, veritable cannonballs, when thrown by my classmates. On top of that, I was convinced that a few balls from this first strike came from my own teammates. If competitive sports were supposed to inspire teamwork, then my butterfly underwear had apparently inspired this group of fun-loving lads into a lynch mob.

I knew one thing. I had to keep moving. Fast. The balls were coming in at a blinding rate. I ran back and forth with a sort of high-stepping circus-horse gait, arms and legs flailing wildly. I'm sure I looked like a cross between Jerry Lewis and a member of the Silly Walk Society with ice cubes down his pants, but I couldn't worry about vanity at that moment. Keep moving. Keep moving. That's all my brain could tell me to do. Life hadn't prepared me for this type of evasive action. The worst bind I ever had to physically get out of before this was quickening my step to avoid an occasional swat on the behind from my father. But now, I suddenly found myself on Omaha Beach.

BOOM! The next volley came in. I dodged the attack. A few of my "comrades" fell. They had been hit. Ha. I had survived the initial surge. Maybe I would be okay. BOOM! Another hit. BOOM! BOOM! Now the balls were coming in separately. BOOM! Oh my God! That one almost took my head off! BOOM! I tasted rubber on that one. BOOM!

I noticed that the most impacted area was wherever I ran to. And my teammates knew this also. Every time I would run over to their part of the floor, they would yell "Get away from us!" and take off for safer ground. And always the volley of balls followed me. I never stopped moving. I ducked and bobbed and weaved whether something was being thrown at me or not. Just make yourself a hard target, I thought. Run serpentine. Do anything. Just *keep moving.*

BOOM! I'm sure I was just a blur of limbs to the opposition but they kept trying nonetheless. BOOM! BOOM! BOOOOOOOOM!

As the number of players on their team decreased from hits accredited to our side, more of them were able to get their hands on ammo. And that meant that the rounds were coming in faster and faster. Keep moving. I felt like I was going to puke. BOOM! I was in a frenzy, trapped like the ballerina in the red shoes in my spastic stay-alive dance. Every time I looked around, I noticed that more and more of my teammates were gone, taken out by the Playground Balls of Death. And because of this, I was quickly on my way to becoming one of the last players left, an honor I definitely *didn't* want. Something had to be done. I quickly went over the rules of the game in my head. I knew I could get out if I was hit. BOOM!!! Forget that. I could also be thrown out if I threw a ball and somebody caught it. That's it! I thought. I'll get *myself* out.

As I continued my survival dance, I tried to focus my attention on the ammo situation. Were there any balls around? No. BOOM! One hit over my head but the impact was so great that it just flew back across the gym to the other team. Well, I thought, now what? I've got to get my hands on a ball. BOOM! Oh man. This might not be such a great idea.

I started to notice that the balls weren't coming in as frequently as before. Was it possible that my oppressors were getting tired? Ha, the lightweights. I had too much adrenaline running through my veins to be tired now. I had the endurance of the *hunted*. I slowed my survival dance slightly in order to survey the situation. It was then that I remembered "Fat Man." The only big ball. I hadn't really noticed it in the beginning of the game, mainly because it was overlooked in favor of the more lethal "Little Boys." But now I saw that it was being lobbed around the floor in big harmless arcs. That was the one ball I could get, I thought. I ran over to the part of the floor that Fat Man was occupying. Karl Scott was throwing the large ball at our team and then letting it rebound back to him. I figured that once that ball hit the bleachers, its velocity would be decreased and I could then step in front of it and stop it from rebounding back across the gym. So, I ran in to get it. Karl Scott saw me coming.

"You're dead, ya big-nosed FAG!"

He heaved the ball and I ducked at the last minute. BOOM! Fat Man hit the wall and I went for the rebound. Unfortunately, my judgment was off and the ball glanced off my forehead before returning to Karl, filling the front of my hair with static electricity. Great. This wasn't working. BOOM! He threw again. And again I ducked and let it go by. I noticed out of the corner of my eye that the guys on the sidelines were now becoming interested in my plight. And this made Mr. Wendell take notice. I think he was surprised that I had lived this long. BOOM! Karl missed again. He was definitely getting frustrated now.

"Give up, ya fag. You know you're gonna get it."

From you, Karl? Not yet. Not without a fight. I was getting mad now. I think I'd heard the word *fag* one too many times this day.

Karl got a look of determination, wound up, and heaved the ball at me again, this time as hard as he could, delivering what he knew would be the Death Blow. The ball came straight toward my face. Suddenly, the world seemed to shift into slow motion. The ball was headed toward me, too fast to dodge, right on course to take my head off. I saw everyone on the sidelines. Their faces seemed to slowly transform from boredom to excitement at the prospect of "The Fag" getting pummeled. I saw Karl Scott's face over the top of the ball. He had a real smug smile, happy to be the one to bring the Butterfly Boy down. The ball kept approaching. This plan of mine had clearly not worked. Another miscalculation on a day filled with miscalculations.

Then, suddenly, everything went back into normal speed. The ball was whistling toward me, a few feet from impact. In a last futile act of self-preservation, I held my hands out in front of me and closed my eyes. I felt the ball break through my fingers, skid down my arms, and explode into my chest. Is this what it's like to be shot? I wondered. The force knocked me right off my feet. I slammed onto the ground, butt first, and hit my back against the wooden beams on the wall. A hot pain ran through my chest where the ball had hit. Everything was spinning from the shock.

Then, I heard something strange.

Silence. Absolute silence.

Then . . .

"OH *NO!*"

It was Karl Scott. He was mad about something. What?

I looked down and saw that the ball he threw was still lodged between my arms and chest. I had caught it. Karl was out. Because of me, Karl was OUT.

Oh my God, I thought, eyes wide. I did it!

I looked over on the sidelines and saw that all my teammates were staring at me with an equal amount of shock and confusion. No one could believe it, least of all myself. All right! They gotta respect me for this. I immediately pictured a scene in the locker room with all of them coming up to me and giving me a "We're sorry we misjudged you, you're really an okay guy" speech and then singing "For He's a Jolly Good Fellow." Maybe they'd even all get butterflies Cameoed on their underwear in a show of solidarity. Because, whether they wanted to admit it or not, I had just proven myself.

"You FAAAAAAAAAAAAAAAAAAAAAAAAAGGGGGGG!!!!!"

Karl Scott. Now the guy really hated me. And he was pissed. He started to run toward me as if he were going to do to me what the ball didn't. Fortunately, in his first humane act of the day, Mr. Wendell stopped him. Don't fool yourself, I thought. The guy probably just wants to leave you in so he can see you get killed properly.

BOOM BOOM! I was thrown quickly back into reality when two balls slammed into the ground on either side of me. I jumped up and started moving again. And when I looked around, I noticed one more horrible thing.

I was now the only one left on my team.

Five of the enemy remained, their eyes trained on me. Definitely not the position I had been looking to get into. I glanced down and noticed that I still had the giant ball in my arms. The five enemies moved in closer, right up to the center line, hunched over, stalking me like lions hunting a water buffalo. I knew I had to think fast. I still hadn't gotten to use my plan of letting someone catch a ball I had thrown, so I figured now was my chance. I took Fat Man and grasped him tightly. The five executioners kept moving in on me, closing in on the center line that separated us. They had a look of bloodlust in their eyes. It dawned on me that they were all part of Karl's "Rat Pack" and I guess they wanted to avenge their fallen leader. This is really stupid, I thought. It's a game with rubber balls, for God's sake. Let's just end it now and get a head start on working out some of the problems we'll encounter later in life. We can have an open discussion on human relationships, maybe hold a forum on how to start your own business and incorporate. I'll talk about anything right now. Just GET ME OUT OF HERE!

They moved closer.

Well, here goes, I figured. I'm gonna get myself out. I threw the ball high in the air, right toward Rick Jones. An easy catch, Rick. Just stick out your arms and you'll be the King of the Locker Room. The ball came down toward Rick. He watched it. He was holding a small ball. Drop it, Rick, I yelled in my head. Drop it and catch the ball I threw. Hurry up! Fat Man descended. It was gonna hit him! Oh, great. That's what I wanted, to find out the guy had no reflexes and have him get hit and be out and double the vendetta on my head. The ball was almost on top of him. CATCH IT, YOU ASS!

Rick sidestepped out of the way, casually, right at the last moment. The big ball bounced harmlessly away. Then Rick looked at me and shook his head, scary calm on his face.

"You ain't gettin' out that easy, Feig."

Great. That was just what I wanted to hear. Right after the words "Paul, could you make out with my great-grandmother?"

"Kill the Fag!" yelled Karl Scott. What a little jerk, I thought. I'm gonna steal his underwear and have my mother Cameo a whole bouquet of flowers on it if I ever get out of this alive.

"Kill the Fag. Kill the Fag. Kill the Fag."

It had turned into a chant by the guys on the sideline. Soft at first, then building as the number of participants increased. Voices united. It would have been inspiring if it hadn't been so offensive and directed at me.

"Kill the Fag. Kill the Fag. Kill the Fag."

Suddenly, I heard a whistle blow. It was Mr. Wendell. He was actually going to stop this. My persecution has ended! The man *finally* came through for me. He *does* have a heart.

"No borders, boys. The field is open."

Huh? What does *that* mean?!

We all looked over at him, unsure.

"That means you don't have to stay on your side of the center line. So, c'mon, get in there and let's finish this game up."

Oh, GREAT! Thank you, Mr. Wendell, you heartless prick, who's making his living off of my parents' tax dollars.

The time had come. Life as I knew it was about to end.

The five mouth-breathers surrounded me. I was dead. I looked over to the sidelines at my classmates, boys with whom I had grown up. I saw Mr. Wendell, the man put in charge of my physical development. I saw them all, the compassionless bunch. Would the sight of a trapped person, a cornered, defenseless animal, stir some sort of sympathy within them? Would it touch the very bottom of their humanity and make them realize that man cannot be pitted against his fellow man? That a nation divided must fall?

"KILL THE FAG!!!" they all shouted in unison.

There was nothing left to do. I officially hated these guys. I looked right at them.

"YEAH? WELL, FUCK *YOU* ALL, YOU FAAAAAAAAA-AAAGGGGSSSS!"

They were now a sea of blank faces as I stood there, panting, trying not to cry. They had lowered me to their level and it didn't feel good at all. I looked at the five assassins who surrounded me. Rick Jones stared at me, surprised, thrown, unsure at my outburst.

Then, out of nowhere, a smile broke across his face. He reached out slowly . . . and lightly touched me on the arm with the ball he was holding.

"You're out, Feig," he said kindly.

". . . really? . . ."

"Uh-huh."

I looked over at the group on the sidelines. Now I felt bad. Maybe I should apologi—

B-B-BLAM!!! The five surrounding balls exploded into my body. Everything went black.

When I came to, Mr. Wendell told me I'd be in detention for a week. For swearing.

THE GYM CLASS ARCHIPELAGO, PART II: DISTURBINGLY CLEAN

When I was an eight-year-old Cub Scout, we were taken on a trip to a local high school that had an Olympic-size swimming pool. I was excited about this since I enjoyed swimming. However, wanting to avoid having to put on my bathing suit in front of my fellow den members, I wore my swimming trunks under my pants. When we went into the locker room to change, I simply took off my pants, put them in the locker and headed for the pool. It was a genius plan for a kid who was terrified of getting naked in front of people. However, as I was about to exit the locker room, two older students from the high school who were in charge of the pool stopped me and announced to us Scouts, "Guys, before we can let you swim in the pool, we need to give you all a quick inspection."

What happened next is one of the most disturbing things I've ever been through. Over the years I've asked various medical and health care professionals why what happened to us occurred, and no one has yet been able to give me an answer; instead, they just look at me as if I were crazy. But I swear this happened.

The high school guys took positions in the doorway that led from the locker room into the pool area and had us line up. Then, as each one of us would get up to the front of the line, one of the guys would say, "All right, kid, bend over and crack a smile." And with that, we were each expected to pull our bathing suits down, bend over, and pull our butt cheeks open so the guys could visually inspect our rectums. They would peer at each kid's butthole for a second, then tell the kid he was okay to get in the pool. As I stood in line and watched each kid go through this, and when I, too, finally had to pull my bathing suit down onto my thighs and "crack" this proverbial "smile," it became the single most mentally scarring event of my young life. And because of it, I vowed never to swim in a public pool again.

What these guys were looking for, I had—and still have—*no* idea. At the time, I figured there must be some contagious disease that could only be detected by a full view of the innermost depths of our sphincters. But no doctor has ever confirmed this for me. And so now, I guess that either these guys were looking to see if we hadn't wiped ourselves properly, wanting to avoid having Cub Scout fecal residue floating around in the pool in which they themselves swam, or this was just one colossal prank they were pulling on Den Number Twelve.

It was with the sense memory of this event, the nightmarish remembrance of standing in the cold tile corridor wearing only my bathing suit and preparing to show off my dumper as my peers stood around me naked, that I entered our locker room on this, the first day that we were supposed to shower after gym class.

The bottom line was I simply did not want to get undressed in front of my classmates, especially after they had all just tried to kill me during dodgeball. While my fellow Cub Scouts had all been friends, my gym companions were mostly guys who didn't like me, and it was hard enough being around people like that with my clothes *on*. Take away my clothes and you might as well just grab a vegetable peeler and take the skin right off me, too. And while it's true that I had already undressed in front of them at the beginning of class during my embarrassing butterfly episode, I still didn't get "undressed." Being in your underwear in front of people is one thing—being *naked* in front of them is a whole other situation entirely. Even though my briefs were only a thin piece of cotton, practically transparent by clothing standards, they were still a covering. A symbol of civilization. Something that separates us from the monkeys. Take away our underwear and we all might as well be swinging from the trees, throwing around our feces, and eating lice out of each other's hair. No, underwear is the key to our place atop the food chain, and I wasn't about to give up that place in a junior-high locker room in front of a bunch of guys who called me a "fag" constantly. No way.

When class ended, we all ran into the locker room. At least, they all ran. I walked. Slowly. I knew I had nothing to look forward to. I really didn't sweat *that* much, I rationalized. Maybe Mr. Wendell would let me slide on the whole shower scene. I tried to conjure up the image of him giving me an understanding smile and saying, "You know what, Feig? I know you had a tough time today and that you're a little uncomfortable with all this showering business. Why don't you just get dressed and head to your next class, okay?" However, it was easier trying to imagine myself being voted "Sexiest Kid of the Year" than to believe Mr. Wendell would show any sort of humanity. And so, like a condemned man, I headed to my locker.

Everyone was busy stripping off their gym clothes, laughing and joking and tossing dirty socks around. I couldn't get over what a lack of modesty these guys had. This was just another moment in another day for them. If you told them to take off their clothes, they'd take off their clothes without thinking twice. I assumed if you told them to go run around the school naked, they'd probably do that, too. What was wrong with me? I wondered. Why was I so weird about all this? Was my mother to blame? Once when I was small, the story goes, I ran out into the street naked after a bath and my mother yelled at me. Maybe I had somehow stored that moment in my mind and now associated nakedness with punishment. Could be. Probably not, though. I think I just didn't like the idea of letting my nuts hang out in front of these guys.

I got to my locker and received my usual array of taunts.

"Feig, you're such a fag I can't believe it."

Thanks, Norman. A little locker-room morale. As I sat down and started untying my shoes, I heard someone singing "Please Mr. Postman," which was the Carpenters' big hit at the time.

"You know, the Beatles were the first ones to do that song. The Carpenters just remade it, that's all," said Dwayne. Dwayne always had some unknown fact on anything you were talking about and was constantly eager to share it. Only years later did I realize that most of what Dwayne told us was wrong.

"They did *not*," said Norman.

"Yes, they did," said Dwayne. "My sister's even got the album."

"But the song says that she's waiting for a letter from her boyfriend."

"Well, they sang it."

I *knew* what was coming. If I'd had a million dollars to bet, I would have put it all on Norman's next sentence.

"Then the Beatles were fags."

Bingo. Another fine example of Norman's Socratic logic hard at work. Man, did I dislike that guy. Fortunately, before the aggravating conversation could go any further, Mr. Wendell entered and clapped his hands loudly, the sound echoing through the locker room like gunshots.

"All right, boys. You've got classes to get to. Hit the showers."

Hit the showers. To this day, those words still strike terror into my heart.

Well, everyone did just that. They hit the showers. They yanked their underwear off the same way you would remove a Band-Aid from the hairy part of your arm, and then they headed for the showers. I actually lost my fear for a minute because I was so amazed at the spectacle before me. Kids I had known for years were now marching in front of me naked. Stark buck naked. It was such a bizarre moment that I was practically hypnotized. For one thing, they now all seemed much more harmless. I remembered on *The Brady Bunch,* when Marcia had to take her driver's test Mr. Brady told her she would be less intimidated by her examiner if she pictured him sitting there in his underwear. But he never said anything about what would happen if she imagined him sitting there *naked.* I can't speak for Marcia, but I personally found it to be quite empowering. I suddenly felt as if I could actually beat these guys up. With my clothes on, I was much less vulnerable than they were. I felt as if I were wearing a suit of armor. I felt invincible.

Karl Scott walked toward me. His towel was dragging on the ground behind him as he headed down the aisle, completely naked. *This* was the kid I was terrified of, I marveled. This was the bully who had been tormenting me ever since the previous year when we had a crafts class together. It was Karl who was the first to inform me that I had a big nose and for some reason had vowed daily to beat me up because of it. It was his fault that I was so insecure about my looks and that I was afraid to go to an arts class I really liked. I was over a foot taller than he was and yet I was scared of him, this harmless little pile of flesh. He was actually rather pathetic-looking now without his clothes on. Just a little runt.

So why did he hold such power over me? If I tried, I could probably beat him up. In fact, I was sure I could. One good shove and it'd be all over. It'd be so easy. One day, when he was making my life miserable, why not just say, "You know what, Scott? Fuck you," and then simply punch him right in the face? I felt like I could do it if he was naked. I could do it right that moment, I realized. I'd already caught his ball and got him out. This was the perfect chance. If I waited until later, I might never do it. Because he was so much more intimidating with his clothes on.

But why? I asked myself, feeling like I was on the verge of a life-changing epiphany.

I guess it all had to do with attitude: pretend to be tough and you are. Well, Karl Scott certainly had it down to an art. It made me start to wonder what life must be like for Karl. Why he acts that way, why he feels he has to be a bully. Maybe his father is very abusive, I thought. Or dead. Maybe Karl had to assume the role of leader in his family. Has had to become a man before he's even grown up. And being short was his major obstacle in life. He's had to overcompensate his attitude to make up for his altitude. As I thought about all this and watched him walk toward me, I suddenly felt sorry for the guy. I really did. Maybe he wasn't such a bad guy after all. There might be a wonderful person under all that aggression that's just dying to get out. Maybe, like Charlie Brown's sickly Christmas tree, all Karl needed was a little love and understanding. As he walked past me toward the showers, our eyes met. I looked deep into his soul, trying to see the boy inside the man.

"What are you starin' at, Feig, ya ball-catchin' faggot?" he said. "Wanna suck my dick?"

Clothes or no clothes, the kid was still an asshole. And scary as hell.

Karl proceeded to inform me yet again how he was going to kick my ass after school for getting him out in Killer, and I tried to avert my eyes away from him. It was then that I turned and saw something very strange. Something to do with Norman. Something I had never seen before.

Norman was uncircumcised.

However, back then, I didn't know what *uncircumcised* meant. I just figured the guy was deformed. His penis looked like a cigar with a twist of hair at the end, the same kind of curlicue they do with the top of a Dairy Queen ice cream sundae. I was horrified, but I couldn't stop looking at it. Fortunately, Karl had moved on, and Norman's attention was on something stuck to his foot, so he didn't see me staring. My mind reeled with explanations as to why everyone else's penis had a head on it and Norman's didn't. I immediately opted for the "decapitation" theory. I figured that Norman was goofing off in wood shop and for some reason unzipped his pants and accidentally cut off the top of his dog on the circular saw. What else could have happened? To me, there was no other logical explanation for something that looked like half a penis.

"Hey, Feig. Are you just gonna sit there enjoying the human spectacle or are you gonna take your foul mouth into that shower?" Mr. Wendell snapped me back to the real world, and all my musings about my naked classmates and their genitals weren't going to save me from the fact that there was a shower nozzle out there that had my name on it.

I didn't know what to do. I was trapped. I was going to have to get naked and take a shower. That is, unless I could just stall until everyone else had left, then wet my hair a bit and leave, giving the illusion of having showered. It was then that I saw my plan would never work. Mr. Wendell had stationed himself at the shower door with a clipboard and was checking off each student's name as he headed in. My stomach sank. There was no escape, and now I was faced with the unsettling realization that Mr. Wendell was going to stand there and *watch* us shower. Things were getting worse by the second.

"Feig, get moving!" shouted Mr. Wendell. "Now!"

I watched as the rest of my class headed into the shower. But now they weren't walking toward it. They were *running* toward it. They were actually looking forward to getting in there. As they all entered the tiled, steam-filled room, I heard their voices and laughter echo. Then, I heard something very bizarre.

They went wild.

From inside the shower room, I heard splashing and yelling and laughing and screaming and running and punching and it sounded like a riot was taking place. I waited for Mr. Wendell to start yelling at them to quiet down. But he didn't. I looked up and, to my horror, I saw that the guy was standing there staring in at my classmates with a big heartwarmed grin on his face. He shook his head and chuckled as if to say, "Ah, the good ol' days. I wish I were in there with them." Was this why grown men taught gym? Did they like gym class so much when they went to school that

they vowed to do whatever they could to stay around it for the rest
of their lives? He really seemed to be enjoying the scene in front
of him. I don't even think he had checked off any names yet. I
looked around. There has to be a way out of here, I thought.
Maybe if I just threw on my clothes and bolted—

"Feig! I told you. You already got one week of detention. Unless you want two, get *moving!*"

Well, the time had come. There was nothing else I could do. It
was time to disrobe. I took off my shorts, then realized I hadn't
taken off my shoes, so I had to sit there with my shorts around my
knees as I struggled to unlace my sneakers. And, of course, I
pulled the wrong end of my shoelaces, causing the lace to become
one giant knot. So I had to lift my foot onto the bench in order
to undo the knot but I couldn't get my foot up because my shorts
prevented my legs from separating wide enough to complete such
a move and I almost fell off the bench and I really wanted to die.
The only appropriate music to accompany me at that moment
would have been an oompah band doing a Bavarian version of
"The Stripper."

Finally, I got down to my butterfly underwear. The moment of
truth had arrived. I was now going to have to take it off. The
problem was, I truly couldn't bring myself to do it. I had never
been naked in public before. Not totally. And I didn't see how in
the next few seconds I could be without my underwear. It didn't
seem possible. It was against everything I stood for. As we go
through our everyday lives, a lot may happen to us and we may
experience a lot of trauma, but we always have the physical and
mental support of our underwear to keep us going. It's the one
thing that keeps us together. With it, we feel complete, we feel
contained, we feel protected. Whether we're conscious of it or
not, we always know that our underwear is there for us, support-
ing us. If you've ever walked around without it, you know what I
mean. Those occasions when my family would go on a camping
trip and I wouldn't pack enough underwear and just couldn't stand

to wear the same pair another day and so I'd have to walk around with no underwear on under my pants—those were the times I felt terrible. I'd always end up doing that readjustive hitchstep as I walked, trying to get everything back in place without having to actually stick my hands down my pants and put things back in order manually. It would affect my mood. I would be physically uncomfortable. It was as if Mother Nature had pulled some key linchpin out of my body, and my whole existence just fell apart. That's what it was like for me to not have my underwear on. And that was when I had other clothes on over my underwearless mid-section. But now I was expected to take off my underwear and be absolutely, positively, no-holds-barred BUCK naked. It was at that moment I knew that I definitely couldn't do it.

"Feig! This is the last time I'm gonna tell you. Drop that underwear and get in this shower!"

I tried to but I just couldn't. I felt faint. I couldn't bring my hands to grasp the waistband and pull my underwear down. I felt that if I did, my skin would give way and my organs would spill out all over the locker room floor. I started hoping it would happen so Wendell would feel guilty that he made me do this. The loud, echoing horseplay increased in intensity from inside the shower room. It sounded like a war. The whole scene was surreal. I started to realize that if I didn't go in and shower now, my class-mates would start coming back to their lockers, having finished their showers, and it seemed far worse to have to drop my under-wear in front of them as they were getting dressed than it did to simply appear in front of them already sans briefs. *Just pull them down,* I yelled inside my head.

My hands truly wouldn't move. It was against all my better judgment. Trying to get naked in a locker room at my junior high school was in direct opposition to my basic code of survival. Some people's code was, "Don't go down without a fight." Others' was "Never trust anyone over thirty." Mine was, *"Don't get naked in public."* To be forced into this was a violation of my rights as a member of the human race. I'll take this all the way up to the Supreme Court, I thought. This can't be constitutional. As a matter of fact, I'm gonna get dressed right now and go find my congressman—

"GODDAMN IT, FEIG! I SAID GET IN THAT SHOWER NOW OR I'M GONNA *THROW YOU IN!!!*"

The next thing I knew, I was standing there with my underwear in my hand. Stark naked. I don't know what happened. My mind disconnected. Mr. Wendell had come at me with death in his eyes. It was the same look and tone that my father had the time I stole money out of my mother's purse.

The realization that I was naked sunk in. My body suddenly went into panicked overdrive. I guess I figured that if I moved quickly, I would have the appearance of being dressed. I threw my underwear into the locker and grabbed my towel. The brightly striped one. It was folded and I didn't bother to unfold it. I just held the one-foot-by-one-foot square of terry cloth in front of my genitals and headed toward the shower. I didn't allow my mind to speculate on what would transpire in the next few minutes. I just moved.

"Well, finally," Mr. Wendell said with a shake of his head. "His Highness is ready to grace us with his presence."

It was bad enough having to endure Mr. Wendell's taunts fully dressed. But naked, it was like throwing a bucket of salt water on a freshly skinned rabbit.

I walked up to the entrance to the shower room. Against the wall was a bar where we were supposed to hang our towels. However, the bar was right next to the open doorway so that it caught the full force of the spray coming out from the showers, thereby rendering the area absolutely useless, unless its purpose was to predampen our towels. I took a deep breath and peered into the shower room.

I saw a sight I will never forget.

There, before my very eyes, in this white tiled room that had water spraying out of the walls, were all the boys I had grown up with, been tormented by, and at one time or another wished injured, engaged in a naked pubescent frenzy. Twenty or more wet, bare bodies running wild, jumping up and down, sprinting back and forth, pushing and shoving each other, sliding on their butts and stomachs, wallowing like a bunch of Greeks at an olive-oil orgy. It was what I imagined a riot during the ancient Junior Olympics might have looked like. The guys were playing a game of hockey with a bar of soap, kicking it with their bare feet and chasing it around the floor, smashing into one another as they tried to gain possession of it. Or at least that was their excuse for going as berserk as they were. As I watched this spectacle in front me, I realized that these guys, who had each accused me of being a homosexual about once every five seconds, were now engaged in what was truly the gayest event I'd ever witnessed before or since. Talk about the jackass pots calling the beleaguered kettle black. How could I possibly walk into this festival of preteen testosterone?

"Well, Feig, you've made it this far," said Mr. Wendell with a smirk. "You'd might as well go on in."

What could I do? I was naked. That didn't put me in much of a position to argue. The next thing I knew, I was hanging my towel, my final line of defense, on the soaked bar. Wendell had done it. I was naked. Absolutely naked. It wasn't a feeling of freedom. It wasn't a feeling of release. It was a feeling of being totally and utterly exposed. I didn't know what to think. I was numb. I was now more vulnerable than I had ever been in my life.

Like a POW who's been broken by his captors, I figured I might as well do what Mr. Wendell had said. I might as well go in and take a shower. At this point, I felt like I had nothing else to lose.

I slowly entered the shower room. The last thing I wanted was for the homoerotic hockey team to notice I was in there. I was going to do this as quickly and as painlessly as possible. All I'm required to do is get wet, I said to myself. Mr. Wendell didn't say anything about lathering up or washing your hair or anything like that. And if he was thinking about forcing the issue, he could forget it. This was about as far as I was going to be pushed. I was defeated, but not without a few final kernels of self-respect left. I looked around for the nearest showerhead. My classmates were too involved in their raucous "hockey game" to notice me. The sound inside the shower room was incredible. Every yell and scream was amplified ten times by the echoey acoustics of the tile. An insult hurled a minute before still echoed around the room. I saw a shower spout in the wall next to the door. Just run under it and leave, I told myself. It's as easy as that. I looked at the doorway. There was Mr. Wendell. Standing there. Watching me. The guy was staring directly at me, leaning against the doorway, observing my every move. Say what you will, this man really seemed to take his job seriously.

I stood under the water for a second. It was unpleasantly cold. *Refreshing* would not be the word I'd use to describe this shower. Uncomfortable, at best. Soul-crushing, at worst. So, I let the water hit me for a few seconds and then figured that was it. If I left now, I could be dressed and out of there before they had even finished the first period of their game. I got out from under the water and headed for the doorway.

"Just a minute, Feig," Mr. Wendell said loudly, alerting everyone in the shower to my presence. "I need you boys to stay in here a minute. There's something I've got to do."

Before I could even begin to feel angst over why Mr. Wendell wasn't letting us out of the showers, I realized that the room had gone completely silent.

Something was terribly wrong.

I felt something hit my foot. I looked down. It was the bar of soap from the hockey game. I froze and heard laughter. Evil laughter. I slowly turned toward the sound. Behind me, I saw a terrifying sight. The entire class was standing there in a group, staring at me with demented smiles on their faces. They were hunched low, arms tensed and set, ready to pounce.

. . . oh, no . . .

I looked back at Mr. Wendell. He had a smile on his face. An "uh-oh, watch out for those kooky guys" look. He apparently knew what was up. I didn't. But I was about to find out. And it was far worse than ANYTHING I could have imagined.

My classmates all yelled at the top of their lungs in unison: "DOG PILE!!!!"

And with that, they all came running at me, the whole bare naked bunch of them, their wieners flopping and their faces wild and sadistic. I looked quickly at Mr. Wendell for some sort of support or protection, but there was none to be found. The man had a big grin on his face, barely able to contain his excitement over what was about to happen to me. When I turned my eyes back to the approaching mob, it was too late. All I had time to see was the first volley of them leap through the air toward me. The next thing I knew, I was slammed into the tile floor as what seemed like a thousand naked twelve-year-olds dog-piled on top of me. All I felt was wet flesh everywhere and the impacts of other idiots slamming down on top of the pile, quickly making me part of the floor. More and more bodies piled on top of me. It felt like they must have gotten every boy in the school out of class to help in my moment of hell. I knew what a gazelle must feel as it's being killed by a pack of lions. When I had been caught in the middle of a dog pile in elementary school, my main concern was not being able to breathe. I used to go wild trying to get out from under everyone and into the fresh air. But in the shower room, caught naked under a mountain of naked bodies, my mind just went dead. I was literally in shock.

"All right, boys," I heard Mr. Wendell say with a chuckle. "That's enough. Everybody up."

One at a time, they all started to get off me, laughing and congratulating each other on a job well done. When they were all off,

I stood up slowly, sore, bruised, and broken. They had crushed my spirit, along with my rib cage. I no longer cared that I was naked. I don't even think I realized I was anymore. All I could do was stand there and think about the fact that this was merely the first day of gym class. Nine more months of preteen locker-room torture awaited me. And then the entire eighth grade after that. And then four more years in high school after *that*.

Raise the white flag. I surrender.

However, as in all tragedies, just when I thought nothing worse could happen, it did.

"Boys," said Mr. Wendell, "before you can towel off and get dressed, I need to give you a little visual hygiene check."

Mr. Wendell looked directly at me as my jaw dropped to the floor.

"Feig, you're first. Bend over and crack a smile."

I woke up in the nurse's office.

CAN BUY ME LOVE

The whole time I was in school, from kindergarten all the way through graduation, I can't remember a time when I didn't have a crush on some girl.

But I never had fleeting, casual crushes. I had terminal, obsessive crushes. The kind that would last all school year and occasionally flow into the next. The kind that make you sit up at night and stare out windows and walk around in Hallmark stores. The kind that make you misty watching romantic movies, wishing that it was you and Beth or Tina or Julie and not that good-looking movie-star couple who were walking down the beach at sunset, totally and passionately in love. I have a feeling I spent more class periods staring longingly at girls who didn't know I existed and wishing they were mine than any other kid in the history of the educational system.

Or at least it felt that way to me.

One of my biggest crushes was on a girl named Yvonne. We were in the eighth grade together, and she sat across from me in homeroom. Our class was laid out with two groups of thirty desks facing each other on opposite sides of the large room, creating an open area in the middle where our teacher lectured from—sort of an educational theater-in-the-round. Because of this, I had a di-

rect view of Yvonne each day as she sat forty feet away from me,
completely unaware of my existence.

She looked like Veronica Lake with black hair. My mother had
made me watch *Sullivan's Travels* that summer on the afternoon
movie, and I thought that Veronica Lake was the most beautiful
woman I'd ever seen, even though she only existed in black and
white. Even when my mother told me that Veronica Lake was
dead, I still couldn't stop thinking about her. And on the first day
of eighth grade, when I saw Yvonne for the first time, I felt as if
she had been sent to me from afar, that perhaps Miss Lake had
come back to Earth in this form when she heard that the gangly
kid with the John Denver haircut had been dreaming about her
every night. Yvonne had the same kind of long straight hair as
Miss Lake and always had it partially covering her face. Her eyes
were very big and exotic-looking. Like the eyes of an Indian
princess, I thought poetically. And I would wish for hours on end
that those eyes could be staring longingly into mine.

Unfortunately, her eyes were usually staring at our homeroom
teacher, Mr. Parks. He was a handsome young guy with a neatly
cropped beard like Kenny Loggins's, and I was convinced that she
had a huge crush on him. Mr. Parks would always bring his guitar
to class and sing sappy 1960s love songs under the guise of opening us up to the music of his generation. But I knew he was just
doing it to steal Yvonne away from me. I was sure of it. It didn't
matter, though. Even the way she looked while she sat and watched
Mr. Parks with passion in her eyes made me love her all the more.
She always wore short skirts and sat at an angle, extending her exposed legs out into the aisle while resting her cheek on her hand.
The effect was stunning and only strengthened my resolve to make
her my girlfriend with each passing day.

I'm not really sure if I had any idea what it would be like to
have a girlfriend back then. I knew I wanted one, but beyond that
the image was murky and undefined. I guess more than anything

I wanted a girlfriend so that she would walk around with me and hold my hand and I could point to her when I was with my friends and say, "Hey, check it out, you guys. That's my girlfriend." But how I would make this happen without actually physically having to talk to her was the unknown part. Because there was no way I could simply walk up to her and start chatting. That was far too terrifying a prospect. No, a sneaky little plan was needed. How could I make her come over and throw her arms around me with a minimum amount of risk on my part? How could I make her realize that out of all the guys in our school, I was the one she should fall in love with—the shy kid with the plaid dress pants and the romantic thoughts who sat silently across from her, staring at her longingly instead of listening to his teacher and learning things he might really need to know later in life?

Well, there was only one way that I could think of, and that was to buy her off.

I was going to give Yvonne a present.

You know . . . bribe her into it.

The idea was based on the time I gave Pam McGovern a forty-five record of "I Honestly Love You" by Olivia Newton-John. She was my sophisticated seventh-grade science lab partner whom I *also* had a crush on, and she had told me one day that it was her favorite song. So, that night, I went to the mall and bought her a copy. The next day, sweating profusely, I gave her the record. She gasped and kissed me on the cheek, and I was on cloud nine for the rest of the day, head over heels in love. It was this feeling that prompted me to do what I consider to be one of the dumbest things I've ever done. I wrote her a syrupy note thanking her for the kiss. I left it in her science book the next day. The day after that she didn't mention the note, but she was never quite as friendly to me. She moved her chair farther away from me than usual and I kept catching her looking at me weirdly. And that same day, Kevin

Phelps threw gum in my hair. The note had been a bad idea, but the bottom line was that the actual gift had done what it was supposed to do.

And now I was going to try to repeat history.

I went home that night and tried to think of something I could give Yvonne. Something special. Something that would scream "Look what a great boyfriend I'd make." I looked around my room, but all I could see were dragster models, magic tricks, and hand puppets. Not exactly items that made girls want to kiss you. The problem was I had no way of knowing what Yvonne liked or needed. All my friends were too chicken to go over to her and do any investigating for me. And without the proper reconnaissance, the wrong gift could be a disaster, an accidental "Gift of the Magi" that could possibly drive her away from me and end our affair before it had even started. And so, figuring I needed to approach this from a woman's point of view, I decided to consult my mom.

"Mom," I said, approaching her timidly, "I'm . . . uh . . . I'm in love with this girl who's . . . uh . . . kinda my girlfriend and . . . um . . . I wanted to give her a present, but I don't know what to get her."

My mother had a very surprised look on her face. I knew that she was aware of my crush on my next-door neighbor Mary, but beyond that I don't think she even thought I interacted with girls at school.

"Oh, Paul, that's so sweet," she said in a tone that made me feel kind of creepy. "What kind of things does she like?"

That was a stumper. I felt like saying "If I knew what she liked, I wouldn't be asking you in the first place." But feeling that this was my only chance at doing things right with Yvonne, I decided to suck it up and navigate my way through this weird moment with my mother.

"Well, she's really into dressing up. She always wears nice clothes to school." That *was* true, even though it was information that could be gleaned by anybody with a pair of eyes and wasn't necessarily the intimate knowledge of a beau. But my mother didn't care. I could see that she was already getting an idea.

"I have *just* the thing," she said, getting up.

Feeling a bit guilty that I had fooled my mother into thinking I had a girlfriend who actually liked me—or at least knew my name—I followed her into her bedroom to see this perfect gift. She opened up her jewelry box on the dresser and pulled out a dark gold necklace. It was an exotic piece of jewelry that looked like a bunch of miniature boat chains that had been welded together and then driven over with a steam roller. Looking back, I think it was copper or bronze, but at the time I entertained the thought that it was solid gold. It wasn't a very pretty piece of jewelry by any means, but it was substantial.

"This belonged to my mother. She gave it to me when I was a little girl."

Geez, this is great, I thought. Yvonne'll want to *marry* me if I give her something *this* good. My mom looked at the necklace a little sadly, because my grandma had just died. But this made me feel happy because I knew the necklace would now stay in the family. Yvonne and my mother could have long talks comparing their childhoods and swapping stories about all the things that happened to them while they were wearing the necklace.

"You sure you don't mind?" I asked her, reaching out for the necklace. It was even heavier than it looked.

"No. Besides, it's your first girlfriend," she said with a smile. "And I don't have a daughter anyway, so this is the next best thing."

That made me want to cry. I started thinking that maybe I should just give Yvonne a copy of "I Honestly Love You." But the song was no longer a hit, and the necklace *did* seem like the perfect gift. And when Yvonne found out how valuable it was, she'd be putty in my hands. I didn't know what I'd do with her once she *was* putty, but that wasn't a concern yet. First things first.

I didn't sleep much that night. I tossed and turned, imagining what Yvonne would do when I delivered my mother's heirloom necklace. I kept drifting into dreams that would alternate between Yvonne's giving me a soul kiss and Yvonne's laughing in my face. By the time I got to homeroom that morning, I was a wreck.

Until I looked across the room.

There she was. My love. Sitting the way she always did. Short skirt, legs crossed, out to the side. And today she had a mysterious black beret on, looking quite French. Just when I thought she couldn't get more beautiful, I said to myself, newly excited about my plan.

My stomach started to hurt. I felt like I had to go to the bathroom. This could only mean that it was time to go into action.

But how? I hadn't actually thought about how I would deliver the present.

The task seemed easy enough. Get the necklace from point A (me) to point B (Yvonne). Logistically, it made perfect sense. But emotionally, it couldn't be done. I ran over my options in my head:

Option #1: I could walk the necklace over myself but that would mean I would actually have to talk to her.

Option #2: I could sneak over and put it in her coat pocket, but she'd never know it was from me and think it was from Mr. Parks and then he'd profit off of my mother's priceless childhood heirloom.

Option #3: I could drop it on her desk wrapped in a note, but my dad had always told me to never write notes to girls. "You should never write down anything that somebody could hold you to legally." I didn't know what kind of lawsuit my dad thought I'd get into in eighth grade, but I figured he must know better than I did.

And so, I realized I had only one other option.

Option #4: Have the necklace delivered.

The problem now became which one of my friends would

even consider going up to a girl. None that I could think of off-hand. We were all about even when it came to the amount of female-phobia surging through our veins. No, it would have to be somebody outside my circle of underdeveloped peers.

I looked around and immediately saw the answer.

Chris Nubellski.

Chris was the most polite kid I knew, which is unusual for an eighth grader. At that age, everyone is pretty much socially retarded. But Chris was just this friendly thirteen-year-old father figure who seemed out of sync with his age. He was the only kid I didn't worry about introducing to my mother. With other kids, you always had to worry about whether they were going to be rude or clam up or make fun of your mom's hair or burp or fart in front of her. But the one time I brought Chris over to my house, before we went to see *Young Frankenstein,* he was the most sincerely polite kid my mom had ever met. And so, he was the perfect candidate to act as my delivery service.

I went over to Chris and told him my predicament. Once before I had mentioned to him that I had a crush on Yvonne, so my request for his help came as no surprise to him.

"I'd be happy to, Paul," he said in his usual brotherly tone. And before I had time to think, he grabbed the necklace out of my hand, immediately leaped up, and headed over to Yvonne's side of the room. I wasn't expecting him to deliver it that very second and so was completely unprepared emotionally. I wanted to stop him but he was already halfway to her. In a panic, I hurried back to my desk so that I could hide behind my math book. As soon as I hit the chair, Chris bent over to Yvonne, handed her the necklace, said something to her, and pointed right at me. My heart stopped. My stomach imploded. Everything around Yvonne went black, as if I were looking at her through a long tunnel. All I could see was Yvonne, in slow motion, turning her head to look at me. I started to feel dizzy. All I could think of was that I wished I hadn't done this. I wished I could have somehow magically transported Chris back and erased the last few seconds of my life. In my suspended perception of time, Yvonne's head was still swiveling to look at me. What would I do when our eyes met? Should I wave? Smile? Act cool? Pucker up? Throw up? My brain was spinning. Maybe I'll just run out of the room. No time. Her eyes were almost at mine. And what if she's so happy about the necklace that she runs across the room and kisses me right here? That would be great. Everyone would see it and it would secure my place in the Junior High Hall of Fame. But I've never kissed a girl before. And now maybe I'd have to do it right in front of Mr. Parks and everybody. It was all happening too fast. I should have thought this through more. Oh, God. She's gonna know I exist now. Somebody help me.

The moment of truth was here.

Her eyes hit mine. My body went numb. She gave me a puzzled look that said "Who the hell are you?" I think my legs fell off. My face immobile, I quickly looked into my math book and stayed there. The whole hour I could feel her gaze burning through the top of my head. I wanted to look up at her, but my neck wouldn't bend. All the sounds in the room became loud and fragmented, like they do right before you doze off in study hall. I felt like there was an enormous spotlight on me. Everyone in the room had to know exactly what was going on in my head at that moment, I thought. I've gotta look up at her, I've gotta look up at her.

But I never did.

The hour somehow passed. I didn't hear a word Mr. Parks said the entire time. Everything in the room sounded like a foreign language to me. And all I kept thinking was how I wished I hadn't done this.

The thing is, if you're a kid and you have a crush on a girl and you never do anything about it, I think you ultimately enjoy it more. You can enjoy the thoughts of what might have happened with her and what you would have done with her and how cool you would have been with her, when in reality, you know you never would have done any of the things you thought about. You would have ended up talking to her and not having much in common and finding out that she had friends that you couldn't stand and a big brother who didn't like you and that you could never muster up the nerve to even hold her hand, let alone kiss her. She'd think you were a goofball and that you were boring and that your friends were immature and she'd start looking around at other guys and then you'd start to feel all jealous, even though you really didn't want her to be your girlfriend anymore. And you'd end up not talking to her after a few days and then you'd have to spend the rest of your junior-high and high-school career avoiding her in the hallway and answering the question "Hey, weren't you and Yvonne going together for a while?"

"Well, yeah, but we broke up."

"What the hell's wrong with you? She's a fox."

You know what's wrong with me. I'm a loser, that's what.

Well, Yvonne never did talk to me or thank me for the necklace or give me the time of day after that, and I avoided her more diligently than I avoided the bullies who wanted to beat me up. My romance had ended before it even started. Which was fine with me, because I started listening in class again and actually ended up learning stuff.

Once, however, a couple of months later, some friends and I put together a band for a class project and played an extremely terrible rendition of "Sgt. Pepper's Lonely Hearts Club Band" during homeroom. During it, I looked out at the class and saw that Yvonne was staring at me. Trying to be cool, I made an "oh, brother, these guys are bad and if I had some better musicians up here with me I'd really wail on this guitar" face at her. She gave me a smile and an expectant look that made my heart skip a beat and realize why guys are in bands. But then Mr. Parks asked me if I wanted to cut loose and jam on my guitar and I realized that I couldn't and Rick McBane jumped up on stage and took my guitar and played an incredible version of the guitar solo from

Chicago's "25 Or 6 To 4." The class rocked out and I saw that Yvonne's eyes were filled with passion for Rick. Of course. And that was the last time she ever looked at me.

The next year, when I got to high school, I heard that Yvonne and her family had moved away and no one knew where they went.

And my mother never asked me what happened to her necklace.

I guess when you give an eighth grader an heirloom for his girlfriend, you've just got to figure that you're not going to get it back.

RESUSCI-ANNIE

I heard a story once, when I was around eight years old, about how Frank Zappa was so outrageous that at one of his concerts he passed an empty cup around the audience and told each of the crowd members to spit into it. They did, and when the cup was full, it was brought back up onto the stage and Frank Zappa drank the whole thing.

I don't know if that story was true and I tend to doubt that it was, especially since Frank Zappa was famous for not taking drugs and, let's face it, only a person on drugs could even conceive of doing something like that, let alone seeing it through to completion.

But the story affected me profoundly. I had nightmares for years after that, fever dreams in which I was onstage with Frank, and when the spit cup would come back up to him after making its rounds through the audience, full and warm and sloshing over the sides, Frank would hand it to me and say, "Here, you drink it tonight. I'm not feeling so hot." And then the band would force me to guzzle it down in one long gulp.

A nightmare for anyone, to be sure. But for me, the thought was immobilizing.

When I was a kid, I was germ conscious. *Really* germ conscious. But I'm not sure if it was actual germs I was conscious of or if it was really just the thought of other people's spit that made me feel like passing out.

You see, much of childhood is set up as one big germ- and spit-spreading activity. And it seemed as if all of my grade-school peers were more than willing to put their mouths on whatever it was that I or anyone else happened to be consuming at any given moment during the day. Other kids just didn't seem to care about germs or spit—or dirt or bugs or worms or anything else that made my skin crawl, for that matter. Which always left me feeling more like a miniature version of the prissy Dr. Smith from *Lost in Space,* shrieking in horror at the sight of an attacking Cyclops or space biker, than someone who had anything in common with the kids in my neighborhood. The problem was, no matter how hard I tried, I just couldn't force myself *not* to obsess about my revulsion toward anything that came out of, or resided inside of, anyone else's mouth. And this made it quite difficult to be a kid, because it seemed like whenever I had a bottle of pop (or "soda," as you non-Midwesterners call it) at any point from age four to fourteen, it was guaranteed that within seconds of opening it, some kid I knew would appear behind me and utter these dreaded words:

"Hey, can I have a drink?"

Every time. And then I was stuck. Because if I dared to say no, it was sure to provoke a thoughtful and understanding response of "C'mon, ya baby. I'm not gonna drink it all."

"Yeah, but you're gonna get your *mouth* all over it." Or at least, that's what I *wanted* to say. But instead, in my true nonconfrontational fashion, I'd always relent.

"Uh . . . okay. Here."

I mean, what other option did I have? What else could I do without sounding like an oversensitive only child in serious need of an ass-kicking? Unless I was prepared to dig into the old coffee can I kept my extra allowance in and buy every kid who came up to me their own bottle, I had to give in or suffer the consequences.

But it really made me mad. And it made me want to cry. Because I was always so happy and the world was always a much nicer place when I would buy myself a bottle of pop. My mother had her rum balls, which she would eat whenever she felt as if the day had dealt her too much hardship. And me? Well, there was nothing I liked more than a good soul-soothing bottle of liquid candy.

The circumstances were always the same. It would be a warm afternoon. I'd be walking home from grade school, tired and worn out from a full day of crushes and failures and overreactions. I'd approach the old drugstore, where I usually bought a 3 Musketeers bar or some oversize Sweet Tarts or a few long strands of Bubs Daddy Grape Bubble Gum, the flavor that tasted so good when I chewed it and yet had the power to turn my stomach when smelled on the breath of others. Feeling like a snack, I'd check my pockets and discover a dollar bill that my mom would occasionally give me on the days when she was overcome with love for her only son, money she had specially earmarked as "buy yourself a little treat if those boys are mean to you again" cash. I'd smile warmly as I pulled out the dollar, thinking about my mom. What a nice thing to do, I'd muse. At least *she* likes me. I mean, she never calls me Fig Newton or Pig Newton or Paul Fag. At least not to my face. And so, dollar in hand, I'd head into the store. Since it was usually warm and humid outside, I'd make up my mind to get a bottle of 7-UP. Or maybe a Dr Pepper. But not a Coke. Because Coke would stunt my growth and rot my teeth and make me question authority in a caffeine- and cocaine-induced stupor. Or so my mom always said. And so, I'd settle on a Squirt. I'd grab an ice-cold bottle out of the refrigerator and go up to the counter. There would be nice old Mr. Ken. I never knew his full name, but I always liked him, even though many weeks later he'd falsely accuse me of shoplifting. What a jerk he turned out to be. But on this day, he was still good ol' Mr. Ken. I'd pay for the bottle, say "thank you," and head outside. As I walked, I'd twist off the top. The bottle would give me a friendly hiss that seemed to say, "Oh, friend, are you going to enjoy me." I'd take a deep breath, releasing all the tensions of the day, raise the bottle to my lips, tilt my head back and take a drink, enjoying life to its fullest. The world seemed to melt away. I'd forgotten that Karl Scott tried to beat me up in math class and that I'd gotten yelled at by one of the playground ladies for jumping off the swing. What did they care if I broke my leg? They never came to my rescue when someone was trying to push me off the top of the monkey bars or strangling me with the tetherball cord. No, no, let it go, Paul, I'd think to myself. You've got your Squirt. Enjoy it, drink it slow, and maybe you can make it last all day. And life for that one moment was good.

That is, until the dream would be shattered when Norman would suddenly walk out of the bushes and want to backwash into my bottle.

So, I'd reluctantly give him my Squirt and he'd put his mouth on it and take a sloppy swig and I'd feel defiled as I'd watch him gulp down my once pleasure-producing soft drink. My thoughts would be torn between hoping he choked on the pop and figuring out how I could possibly salvage what was left in the bottle. Maybe I could pour out the top inch of spit-contaminated liquid, then thoroughly wipe down the mouth of the bottle with my shirttail to remove the memory of his mouth. I would actually start to feel there might be a possible second life for my pop when suddenly the nightmare would worsen.

Another kid would invariably walk up.

"Hey, Norman, can I have a drink?"

"It's okay with me, but it's Paul's pop. Ask him."

What was I gonna say? "No, I don't mind Norman's saliva but yours is a no-go." Why did all these kids have to drink out of the same bottle anyway? Couldn't they go and buy their own? Didn't it bother them that they were drinking out of something that two people had already contaminated? There's no way *I'd* do it, so why

would *they?* Was I that much weirder than everyone else? Was I
that much smarter? Or was I just an expert at making big deals out
of nothing?

Whatever the answer and no matter what anyone said, I was *not*
swapping spit with *anyone,* especially a bunch of guys I didn't even
really like.

So Norman's friend would grab the bottle and take a drink and
get his stupid mouth all over it and then a gang of Cub Scouts
who were friends of the kid currently drinking would show up
and take their turns and after an eternity I'd get the bottle back.
The top would be coated with everything our grade school served
for lunch that day and the few inches of liquid left at the bottom
of the bottle would have about the same viscosity as old motor oil.
I'd look at it and feel queasy and feel like crying but instead would
try to sound casual and say, "You guys can have the rest. I'm not
thirsty anymore."

"No way. I'm not drinking that. It's all backwash."

Yeah, YOURS! What started out as a pleasant, tension-relieving
interlude with a bottle of pop had once again turned into yet another in a long line of torturous moments that made up what
were supposed to be my carefree days of youth.

Self-imposed torture, granted. But torture nonetheless.

Well, it was a couple of years later into this neurotic little world
of mine, when I was in junior high school, that something happened during gym class that was to prove one of the most traumatic events of the spit-and-germ-avoiding segment of my childhood.

Simply put, I met a girl. And that girl's name was . . . Resusci-
Annie.

"Annie," as I've affectionately come to know her, wasn't a girl
in the standard person-who's-actually-alive sense. No, Annie was
a mannequin, a life-size doll with a rubber head, a mouth, a
working windpipe, a set of lungs, and a body that was in possession of neither arms nor legs. Resusci-Annie, Queen of the Latex
Torso Women, was something invented by paramedics and CPR

instructors to be used for the teaching of the uninitiated in the
fine art of mouth-to-mouth resuscitation.

Annie also had one other thing going for her. . . .

She was terrifying.

The first traumatic thing about Annie was that she looked like
a dead person. Her face was white and rubbery, her eyes were
closed, her mouth was loosely open, exposing a disturbing set of
rubber teeth, and she had a full mane of greasy, matted hair on top
of her head. She hardly looked like someone anybody had a
chance of saving. I'd throw a blanket over her face and start con-
tacting next of kin if I saw her lying in the street. But as far as the
emergency health care community was concerned, Annie had one
purpose in this world and that was to be revived over and over
again by anyone and everyone trying to master the very practical
skills of lifesaving. A group, I'm ashamed to admit, I had no desire
to join. If anyone was thinking of having a medical emergency
around me back then, they'd better have made sure their life insurance was paid up, because I'd be about as useful to them as
earplugs at a whispering contest.

Mr. Wendell told us to gather in the center of the gym as we
came out of the locker room. As we walked over, we saw Resusci-
Annie lying on the floor.

"Whoa, cool, a dead person," said Norman, as if the sight of an
actual armless and legless corpse would be something one could
consider "cool." We gathered around and stared at Annie.

I had recently been taken to my first open-casket funeral by my
parents and had gone up and viewed the body of the deceased. I
didn't really know the man who had died, but I was amazed at
how alive he actually looked lying there. Although it's a cliché, the
guy truly looked like he was sleeping, as if his eyes might pop
open at any moment and he'd yell at me to "Stop staring, you little big-nosed bastard." Looking back on it, seeing a dead body like
that should have been a traumatic experience, but with the sad
organ music playing and flowers everywhere and people quietly

crying, I was surprised at how well I had handled the whole thing. It seemed very natural. All part of life's process. I had thought dead people would look different. I thought they'd be scary. I thought they'd give me nightmares.

In short, I thought they'd look a lot like . . . well . . . like Resusci-Annie did that day. And as I stood there, staring at her lying on the dirty floor of my school's gymnasium, my fear of dead people immediately came rushing back like the Johnstown Flood.

Just then, a very large policeman with a big red drinker's face and a handlebar mustache entered the gym and walked up to us.

"Hello, gentlemen. My name is Sergeant Korn." He said it loud and proud, like a guy who knew that since he was a cop, nobody was going to laugh at his goofy name. "As part of an organized effort to teach people in our community about emergency medical procedures, I'm here today to demonstrate to you the proper way to administer the life saving technique of mouth-to-mouth resuscitation." He droned on for several minutes about how this procedure could be used to revive a drowning victim or a choking victim or a victim of any number of other accidents and maladies that would send me running for the hills if someone around me actually fell victim to them. So I wasn't exactly sure what I was supposed to get out of all this. However, if learning mouth-to-mouth meant it would keep us from having to play flag football or floor hockey or having to embark on yet another pointless attempt to do enough sit-ups to try to qualify for the much-unwanted President's Physical Fitness Award, then I was all for it.

"And now, with the help of my good friend Resusci-Annie here," Sergeant Korn said, gesturing grandly and then chuckling at his allegedly cute comment, "I'm going to show you the correct way to administer the 'Kiss of Life.'" And then, accompanied by an aria of grunts and groans, he awkwardly got down on his knees next to Annie. He stuck his fingers into her mouth, telling us that before we did anything, we were supposed to make sure that there were no "objects" blocking the victim's throat. So, I wondered, before you saved someone, you were supposed to stick your fingers into his or her mouth and fish around for gum or a toothpick? Forget that. If a person was dumb enough to drown while chewing on a wad of Bubble Yum, then it's not really my fault if he or she dies.

Sergeant Korn pinched Annie's deathly white nose, put his hand under her neck to "open the throat," took a deep breath, put his mouth on top of Annie's, and blew. Annie's chest rose and fell. Sergeant Korn watched it, his face a bit redder than it had been a few seconds ago, then took another deep breath, put his mouth back on Annie's, and blew again. Again her chest rose and fell. I immediately started to feel a bit nauseous. Even though we were watching a very clinical procedure, it had the feeling of something that we really shouldn't be seeing. Maybe it was the image of an overweight cop on his hands and knees blowing into the mouth of an oversize doll and making his already uncomfortably red face even redder that made it feel more like I was watching a very low-quality porn film than a lifesaving demonstration. Unsettling images of Sergeant Korn's private life with Mrs. Korn started to flood into my head. Fortunately, before I was able to ruminate on these mental pictures for too long, Sergeant Korn looked up and breathlessly said, "Resusci-Annie . . . now has enough air . . . to start breathing on her own again." He took a few more deep breaths to compose himself. "And I can now feel good that I just saved a life." And then he struggled to stand up again, improperly equipped as his body was for kneeling and bending, let alone chasing bad guys. How this man with the physique of a sumo wrestler got to be a cop was beyond my comprehension. But then again, this was small-town Michigan. Guys of this body type were as common a sight in one's life as cars whose lower halves were completely eaten away by rust. However, hearing him pant and try to catch his breath, I had a momentary flash that Sergeant Korn might keel over and that one of us would then be expected to put our newfound Kiss of Life knowledge to the test.

Well, I knew one thing for sure: that "one of us" wouldn't be me.

"Easy to revive a person, isn't it?" said Sergeant Korn as he adjusted his belt and pants, his red face glowing like a shiny new fire truck.

Sure. Easy as pie, I thought. Can we leave before Mr. Wendell makes us play Killer again?

To be honest, I wasn't really sure why Mr. Wendell was showing us this in the first place. I guarantee that if I was lying on the ground unconscious and in need of revival, not one of my classmates would turn me into their Resusci-Danny. "I'm not gonna kiss him," I could hear them saying. "I ain't a homo." *Emergency*'s Gage and DeSoto these guys were not.

So, Sergeant Korn had shown us what he came to show us and I figured that was it. But it wasn't. No, my friends, my nightmare was only beginning. Mr. Wendell stepped forward.

"All right, you guys. Line up. You're all gonna take a turn."

Huh? Excuse me? I'm sorry, I must not have heard you correctly. It sounded like you said that we were all going to take a turn giving mouth-to-mouth resuscitation to that doll that Sergeant Korn had just had his grown man's mouth all over. That couldn't be right. It would be completely unsanitary. That is, unless you have a bunch of freshly boiled and sterilized Resusci-Annies in the back, enough for each of us to have one of our own.

I looked over at Mr. Wendell and saw him produce a bottle of rubbing alcohol and a rag. He dumped some alcohol onto the rag and wiped Sergeant Korn's spit off of Annie's mouth. My stomach dropped into my Keds. A wave of panic overtook me. My natural instincts kicked in and I immediately started for the locker room.

"Feig! Where do you think you're going?" yelled Mr. Wendell.

"I have to get something out of my locker."

"It can wait. Get back here and line up."

My eyes zoomed in on Annie's mouth. White and cold and open and now dripping with an indeterminate mixture of Sergeant Korn's spit and alcohol. My head started to spin.

"I said get in line, Feig."

My mind raced. This couldn't be happening. But it was. My fellow classmates were starting to line up in front of Annie. There had to be some way out of this. It just wasn't possible that I was going to have to put my mouth on that thing. Especially after other guys in my class were about to do it, too. Something had to be done.

"Mr. Wendell, I think it's against my religion to do stuff like this."

"Feig, I don't care if you're the pope. You're *doing* this, so get in line."

I couldn't move. I couldn't think. Visions of germs swimming en masse in a sea of spit sloshed through my brain. And as my panic rendered me stationary, my fellow classmates just kept lining up like lemmings. All my stalling was very quickly placing me at the back of the line. And yet I truly couldn't move. I tried to engage in a logical discourse with myself. Maybe being at the back of the line would be a good thing, I thought, since class might end before I got up to Annie and I wouldn't have to do it. But then I noticed that the line was moving at a pretty fast clip. Kids were reviving Annie one after another. Reality was starting to sink in.

There was no way around it. I was eventually going to have to give Annie the Kiss of Life.

I watched kid after kid kneel down in front of her. I saw her chest rise and fall a couple of times, then saw the kid walk away wiping his mouth and then saw more alcohol dumped on the rag that was now soaked with spit and disinfectant brought down to wipe off Annie's face. I was really starting to feel sick. And this was before I realized that with all the air going in and out of Annie's chest, there was a whole reservoir of lung germs inside my future Resusci-girlfriend just waiting to infect my body. I felt like a trapped animal, as I had so many times in this emotional gulag we called gym class. I had to get out of there but I knew I couldn't. I was stuck, doomed, and now the last in line. More and more spit was being deposited on Annie by the second. Instead of having to revive her, I could accomplish the same effect by walking around the room and licking the inside of everyone's mouth, including Sergeant Korn's.

I was getting closer. And now I noticed that the kid directly in front of me was Doug Blaychek, our school's most infamous mentally retarded kid. He was a nice enough guy if you met him in the hallway, but he had extremely large and droopy lips that constantly seemed to be soaked with saliva. I'd always been unsettled by the sight of his spit-covered mouth, but until this moment the odds had been nonexistent that I'd ever have direct contact with it. But that was all about to change.

Doug turned and gave me a big, wet smile. I forced one back at him. My life started to flash in front of my eyes.

Four more people to go. I thought about running out of the gym and making a dash for home, but for all I knew, Sergeant Korn would chase me down and make me *date* Resusci-Annie.

It was Doug's turn. He kneeled down and bent over Annie. He took a loud, deep breath as if he were preparing to jump into the ocean to dive for pearls and put his mouth onto her face. I saw his back rise and fall several times as he tried to revive the lifeless rubber doll on the floor. However, it looked like Doug was actually trying to inflate her, and after a few moments, Sergeant Korn put his hand on Doug's shoulder and said loudly, as if Doug were deaf, "Okay, that's fine, young man. You saved her."

Doug stood up and threw his arms in the air as if he had just won the hundred-yard dash at the Special Olympics. As he moved away, I looked down.

There she was. Annie. Her face was soaked. I didn't know what

part of that "soaked" was spit and what part was alcohol, and I
didn't care. It was a mess. And there was now officially *no way* I
was going to do this. Mr. Wendell slapped the rag on Annie's
mouth and haphazardly pulled it across. Was that how he disin-
fected her every time? Annie's face must now be a festering
cesspool of disease and death.

"All right, Feig. You're up."

I just stood there, staring at Annie. Maybe if I throw up all over
it, I won't have to do it, I thought. No, I'm sure they'd just make
me do it anyway.

"C'mon, Feig. What is it with you? Get moving!" barked Mr.
Wendell.

"Yeah, c'mon, ya fag! Do it already!" yelled Norman. Sure, it
was easy for him to say. Norman would probably wring out Mr.
Wendell's spit rag into a Dixie Riddle Cup and drink it for a quarter. My mind reeled. I had to do something and I had to do it
immediately. But what? Think fast, I told myself.

Then it hit me.

Faint.

I coughed violently and fell over. There was immediate commotion. I hadn't been sure if they would buy my sudden and con-
venient fainting spell or not, but I guess that the perception of me
as someone who was prissy enough to faint at the thought of giving mouth-to-mouth resuscitation was enough to convince them.
As they all gathered around, I wasn't sure if I should be insulted by
this or not. But at that moment, all I cared about was how close I
was to getting out of having to ingest a tidal wave of my peers'
saliva.

"I'LL SAVE HIM!"

It was Doug the retarded kid. New panic set in as I heard him
stomp toward me to deliver his newly learned Kiss of Life. I was
nanoseconds away from blowing my cover by screaming and running away when Mr. Wendell saved me by quickly grabbing Doug

by the arm. "No, Blaychek," said Mr. Wendell, "we don't know if he needs mouth-to-mouth."

I was starting to feel pretty good about myself. I had done it. I had substituted a brief moment of colossal disgust for a nice lay-down and a shot at becoming the center of attention. And not only was I going to get out of Annie duty, but I'd probably get to go home early. It was only second period, so I'd be able to watch *The Price Is Right* and eat lunch in the safety of my own living room. I could practically taste the SpaghettiOs.

"He coughed really loud before he fell down," said Norman. Good, I thought, you were paying attention. Maybe now you'll leave me alone when you realize this is probably just a delayed re-action to your drinking all my Squirt years ago.

Sergeant Korn stepped forward and looked me over. "You said he coughed?" he asked, sounding tense and official.

"Uh huh."

"Then he must have choked. Everybody step back."

And with that, Sergeant Korn stuck his fingers in my mouth, pinched my nose, and kissed me.

I was home sick for three days.

THE WORLD AND
MR. CHICKEN

I was a huge chicken when I was a kid.

It's hard to say why, exactly. I mean, most kids are scared of one thing or another, but I just seemed to be afraid of absolutely everything. And when you're afraid of everything, you're going to be afraid of some pretty embarrassing stuff.

Loud noises always scared me. Up until about the age of six, I always reacted to a thunderstorm in the same way: I'd clamp my hands over my ears and refuse to take them off until the thunder stopped, the storm clouds cleared, and the sun came back out. The loud rumbles and claps of thunder sounded to me as if the earth were exploding and about to fall apart, and I guess I figured that if I could keep the sound out of my head, I could somehow make myself exempt from the world's destruction. My parents' anecdote about the thunder being the by-product of bowling angels was of little comfort, making the sound even more off-putting because of the image their explanation conjured up—hundred-foot-tall giants in white robes with enormous, feather-covered wings growing out of their backs throwing balls the size of elephants down a lane made of roiling black clouds, knocking down pins that would crash on top of each other like the unsettling footage of falling trees I had seen on a *National Geographic* special about lumberjacks. My fear that these gigantic bowling pins might break through the clouds and fall on top of my house, killing us all, made me angry at these recreation-loving angels who were so self-absorbed that they had no idea how much they were traumatizing a kid who was forced to go to Sunday school every week just to learn about how wonderful they were supposed to be. If it was thundering during a meal and my parents wanted me to eat, one of them would have to feed me by hand because my palms would not leave my ears even if I was on the verge of starvation. I'd put my arms up and elbows out to the sides and clamp my hands so solidly onto the sides of my skull that the Jaws of Life couldn't pry them off. I looked like a human loving cup, the living booby prize for my poor parents, who were quickly discovering that their only child was a neurotic mess.

My first experience in a movie theater went from fun to frightening when my mother took me to a double feature that saw a Winnie the Pooh cartoon inexplicably programmed on the same bill with the Rat Pack's Roaring Twenties bootlegger musical *Robin and the 7 Hoods*. Sammy Davis Jr. sang, jumped up on a bar, danced a few steps, then pulled out a tommy gun and started firing wildly. As a trucker might say, I was "off like the bride's panties" and cowering in the lobby before Sammy finished his first verse.

Circuses scared the hell out of me, both because performers always seemed to be shooting off giant cannons all the time and because the disturbing antics of the creepy clowns usually involved blowing something up or hitting each other with exploding sticks that would crack loudly like gunshots. As the kids around me were cheering and laughing at these allegedly comedic exploits, I would be fleeing for the parking lot like an extra in a Godzilla movie.

Those clowns also played into another of my major fears: I was afraid of anyone in a costume. A trip to see Santa might as well have been a trip to sit on Hitler's lap for all the trauma it would cause me. Once, when I was four, my mother and I were in a

Sears and someone wearing an enormous Easter Bunny costume headed my way to present me with a chocolate Easter egg. I was petrified by this nightmarish six-foot-tall bipedal pink fake-fur monster with human-sized arms and legs and a soulless, impassive face heading toward me. It waved halfheartedly as it held a piece of candy out in an evil attempt to lure me into its clutches. Fearing for my life, I pulled open the bottom drawer of a display case and stuck my head inside, the same way an ostrich buries its head in the sand. This caused much hilarity among the surrounding adults, and the chorus of grown-up laughter I heard echoing from within that drawer only added to the horror of the moment. Over the next several years, I would run away in terror from a guy in a gorilla suit whose job it was to wave customers into a car wash, a giant Uncle Sam on stilts, a midget dressed like a leprechaun, an astronaut, the Detroit Tigers mascot, Ronald McDonald, Big Bird, Bozo the Clown, and every Mickey Mouse, Minnie Mouse, Donald Duck, Pluto, Chip and Dale, Uncle Scrooge, and Goofy who walked the streets at Disneyland. Add to this an irrational fear of small dogs that saw me on more than one occasion fleeing in terror from our neighbor's four-inch-high miniature dachshund as if I were being chased by the Hound of the Baskervilles and a chronic case of germ phobia, and it's pretty apparent that I was—what some of the less politically correct among us might call—a first-class pussy.

Even though I tried to conquer my fears as I went through grade school and junior high, convincing myself that loud noises could be cool when they came in the form of firecrackers blowing up model cars and Led Zeppelin albums turned up full blast, and teaching myself that people in costumes are usually only present when an event is supposed to be "fun," I would still succumb to a fear of anything unknown.

Especially if the unknown meant I was potentially going to get my ass kicked.

One of the biggest unknowns I feared was high school.

In the weeks before I became a freshman, I was terrified. But it wasn't because of the theory that being afraid of high school is really a fear of starting at the bottom of the social ladder again. Granted, it's true that by the end of junior high you're one of the "big kids," the upperclassmen/elder statesmen of middle school, and then once you arrive in high school, you're back down in the depths of uncool again, a lowly freshman ready to be humiliated by the older students. But that wasn't the cause of my fear. Depression, yes, but not fear. No, the fear came from something I prefer to label "High School Folklore."

A lot of my more irrational fears as a kid came from the fact that my next-door neighbor Mary and her older sisters used to love to scare the crap out of me. They'd always tell me horror stories about things that would happen if I did something or other. They're the ones who, when we were all at the beach, put the fear of God in me that I might spontaneously combust because "it happened to this kid over on Moravian Drive after he stayed out in the sun too long." They made me paranoid for years about a mythical "sewing bee" that reportedly flew into kids' bedrooms and sewed their mouths and nostrils shut in the middle of the night so that they'd smother to death. And to this day, I'm still afraid to put my cold hands in hot water because they told me if I did, my fingers would fall off. Looking back, I know that they were merely having fun with my perpetual fears and my chronic gullibility. And in the weeks before I was to enter high school, their minds reeled at the opportunity to ruin something I was actually starting to look forward to.

One summer evening, I was sitting with them in the ditch in their front yard talking about stuff our parents told us not to talk about. It was in that same ditch, when I was six, that they explicitly explained to me what sex was, resulting in a strange fever dream that night in which I was lying on the ground naked in a dark room as a life-size nude Barbie doll was slowly lowered down on top of me. But as we sat in the ditch that summer evening and listened to seventeen-year-old Becky, the eldest girl in their family, explain to us what hermaphrodites were, she suddenly looked at me and said, "So, Fig Newton, you're starting high school next month, huh?"

"Yeah," I said proudly.

"You better be careful. They don't like freshmen very much."

A hot flush immediately went up the back of my neck.

"They don't?" I asked, trying unsuccessfully not to sound worried.

"Nope," said Becky, giving me a very sober look. "You should see what they do to freshmen. Sometimes, if you're walking down the hall, a bunch of seniors will grab you, drag you into the bathroom, and give you a swirly."

I looked at Sharon and Mary, who were listening to Becky, wide-eyed.

"What's a swirly?" I said, even *less* successful in my attempt not to sound terrified.

"It's when they stick your head in the toilet and flush it. Last year, some kid drowned. The year before, another kid got sucked down. They found him in the sewer. Long and skinny and dead."

I felt faint. "Really?"

"Yeah. But that's nothing," Becky continued, leaning forward toward me to heighten the impact of her warnings. "A lot of times, what they'll do is grab a freshman, drag him into the bathroom, and make him eat drugs."

I was now officially in a panic. My dad had just the other night given me the world's most sobering talk about drugs after he and I came across a picture of a hippie shooting up heroin in an anti-drug ad in *National Geographic*. My father had sighed a scary, disapproving sigh, pointed at the picture, looked me right in the eye, and said, "You see that kid? That kid is the stupidest kid you'll ever see. And you know why he's so stupid? Because what you see him doing, right there, is throwing his life away. Right down the toilet." My father then launched into a one-hour lecture, telling me that if I took drugs, any drugs—if I decided it'd be fun to "get all *doped* up"—I'd turn into a vegetable. Immediately. And all of a sudden, there I was in the ditch hearing that a group of crazed seniors were going to put me in a coma the minute I entered the school on my first day.

I came home very upset.

"Mom! I'm not going to high school. No way!"

"Of course you are. What are you talking about?"

"I'm just not going. Forget it!"

"Why not?" my mother asked, concerned. Whenever I was upset, my mother would immediately become twice as upset, whether she knew what I was upset about or not.

"Because they're gonna make me eat *drugs.*"

"Who is?"

"Seniors. They hate freshmen. This kid was walking down the hall last year and a bunch of seniors jumped him and stuck his head in the toilet and made him eat drugs!"

"Where did you hear this?"

"From some kids who go to the school." I figured my fear would seem more valid if I didn't tell her that Becky had been my source. After all, I was trying to get out of having to go to high school, not simply looking to be told that I was overreacting again.

"Oh, my goodness," my mother said, extremely concerned. "I'll call the school tomorrow."

"Okay," I said, pouty. I knew things would be okay if my mom was going to "make a call."

The next day, my mom told me that she had talked to Mr. Walker, the principal of the high school. Apparently, she tracked down the poor guy's home phone number and bothered him during his summer vacation because of my paranoia.

"I spoke to the principal today," she said, looking a bit embarrassed. Clearly he had convinced her that her son was crazy. "He said he wasn't aware that any of this toilet and drug business was going on but that he'd look into it. He told me to tell you not to worry, though. He said it was probably just a story."

Between my mother's face and my reading between the lines of what the principal said, I immediately felt like the dumbest kid in the world. I started imagining the conversation that must have taken place between my mother and the principal.

"Mr. Walker, my son says that the older boys in your school force the younger ones to eat drugs."

"Um . . . *who* is your son?"

"Paul Feig."

"Feig? I don't seem to recall the name."

"Well, he's not in high school yet. He starts next month."

"Oh, well . . . I think he's just been told some wild stories by some students having a little fun with him."

"So, you don't think it actually happens?"

"I sincerely doubt it, Mrs. Feig. If the kids have any drugs, I really doubt they're going to waste them on your son."

And then he probably hung up and mentally filed the name "Paul Feig" in the Whining Little Idiots folder.

That night, we had a very loud thunderstorm, and as I lay in bed and listened to the thunder claps rattle my bedroom window I started to hate myself for having spent my life up to that point being such a wuss.

When I got to high school the next month, still nervous and on guard, just in case Becky was right and I was going to be jumped, dunked, and turned into an addict, I found that high school wasn't the jungle I was imagining it would be. More than anything, it just looked like junior high all over again, except that the girls were more mature and a lot of guys who were older than me had mustaches. And after a few days of being looked through like the Invisible Man by sophomores, juniors, and seniors, all of whom were having more fun than I was, I found myself with a new and actually legitimate fear—the fear of being completely ignored. I suddenly wished that even one of the older kids in my school would find me noticeable enough to merit a swirly or a forced meal of their stash.

Because, after all, if people are sticking your head in a toilet or shoving drugs down your throat, at least they're paying attention to you.

NOW YOU SEE IT, NOW YOU DON'T

My father has spent his whole life collecting jokes. From his years as a young man frequenting nightclubs with names like the Elmwood and the Top Hat across the Detroit River in Canada to his time as a father and community leader attending his weekly Kiwanis Club meetings with his lodge brothers, whenever he would hear a good joke, he would write it down and memorize it. At family functions or at dinner parties with my parents' friends, ten minutes would seldom pass before my father launched into one of his "stories."

My father was a great joke teller. He really had impeccable timing and could always land a punch line effectively. His jokes always received a hearty response and over the years I found myself wishing that I, too, could entertain a group of my peers as effectively as my father entertained his.

And so, when I finally got the chance, I jumped at it.

I was in ninth grade and saw a poster in the hall one day announcing that my school's yearly talent show was gearing up and that auditions were going to be held the following week. I had attended the Chippewa Valley High Talent Show the previous year to see my next door neighbor, Craig, perform. He had bought a small Moog synthesizer and composed an original electronic mini-symphony entitled "Synthesis." His performance of it consisted of him putting on a suit, platform shoes, and Elton John glasses, plugging his keyboard into the school's sound system, and then turning it up full blast to show off every sound effect that the good folks at the Moog Corporation had seen fit to include in this starter's package. I was in awe at the spectacle of someone I knew being on stage in front of such a large audience. And even though most of the people in the crowd were gritting their teeth and smiling politely while small children covered their ears in pain as Craig and his Moog assaulted them aurally, the effect was enough to make me vow that I, too, would one day be mounting that stage and taking part in this yearly cavalcade of teenage talent. Especially when I saw that at the end of the evening, a panel of judges voted for a winner, who was then awarded the staggering amount of fifty dollars cash on top of the honor of being voted that year's most talented performer. To beat out everyone else and win the adoration of my peers was the most exciting and validating thing I could imagine happening to me.

And so, as I stood there staring at the poster for the talent show auditions, I was filled with excitement. The key to my acceptance by the entire school was right in front of me. And all I had to do was reach out and grab it.

The only problem was what I would actually do that could be considered "talent."

When I got home that day, I looked around my room to see what inspired me. I had been playing the guitar ever since I was eight and had actually won a classical guitar competition in Kalamazoo, Michigan, the year before (it was only me and one other kid), but, having seen how many people had done musical acts in the previous year's talent show, I knew that I wouldn't stand a chance of winning against any of the girls from the swing choir who chose to croon out torch songs and usually ended up placing first, second, and third. No, in order to have any chance at victory, I would have to offer a viable alternative to the singers and musicians who made up the Chippewa Valley High talent pool.

It was then that the answer came to me   I had to do my magic act.

In true geek fashion, I had been into magic for years and had spent almost all my earnings from working at my father's store on semiprofessional magic tricks and equipment. Knowing the success I'd had in the past entertaining the octogenarians at the various nursing and retirement homes where I'd been performing since I was eight, I figured that translating this success to an audience full of high school students and their parents couldn't be too huge of a leap. And so I pulled out my magic trunk and started going through my tricks, trying to determine which combination of them would create an act worthy of a fifty-dollar win and the respect of my schoolmates.

I spent the afternoon assembling what I felt to be a strong routine and was feeling pretty good about myself. I would start with the Color-Changing Shoelace trick, followed by a few of my sure-fire show stoppers, which included the Silk Tube—a clear plastic section of pipe into which three different colored silk handkerchiefs would be stuffed and then blown out the other end to reveal themselves mysteriously tied together—and the Color-Changing Records—a cardboard record sleeve into which three black forty-fives would be placed and then removed to reveal that they had miraculously changed colors. Color changing was a big part of the affordable magic available to us nerds of the world back then. Sawing women in half and making tigers disappear were strictly for those who had the money and the storage space. I would then end my act with a prestidigitacious double whammy: the Hippity Hop Rabbits, followed by my always popular Drum O' Plenty— a large "empty" silver tube that, once paper had been secured over both ends to transform it into a drum, became a cornucopia of silk handkerchiefs and colored streamers once the magic words were spoken and the paper was broken.

I tried out my act on my parents, who had seen my magic routine in its various forms for the better part of six years. After I was finished, my father furrowed his brow and said, "If you really want to win that talent show, you've got to do more than just magic. You've got to *entertain* those people."

My first instinct was to be horribly insulted at this, but I decided to hear the man out. After all, my father had actually entertained people in his time, unlike me, who had simply held the interest of a roomful of retirees who were happy to watch me as an alternative to sitting in their rooms and staring into space.

"Well, what should I do?" I asked him, trying not to sound defensive.

"You've gotta make them laugh," he said, sitting back. "You've gotta tell them some jokes."

I decided to give in to my father's advice and work with him on my act.

Over the course of my fourteen years on Earth, I had always been a little frightened of my father. He was never mean to me or unduly harsh, but the fact that he owned a store and spent most of his time being in charge of other people gave him an aura of toughness that was always a bit off-putting to me. He was the very definition of a no-nonsense guy. In my mother, I found nonjudgmental acceptance and encouragement of every whim I had, whether it made sense or not. But my father was always the sober rule-maker, the one who would get mad when I appeared in the living room wearing an expensive Pierre Cardin three-piece wool suit on my ten-year-old body, a body whose growth would render the suit unwearable within months, or sigh in frustration at the news that I had used all of my grandmother's inheritance money to purchase an electric guitar, because the acoustic guitar that I wasn't that good at playing "wasn't good enough to play rock 'n' roll on." My mother was my enabler and my father was my disapprover and, of course, I always chose my mother's accepting ways over my father's practicality. But now, sitting in his den with him, as he leafed through the pages and pages of nightclub jokes he had stored up over the past thirty years, I felt closer to him than I had ever felt in my life. Simply put, he and I were bonding over comedy.

"Okay, here's a good one to open with," he said as he brought over a three-by-five index card out of the kitchen recipe box that made up his "joke file." He told me the joke, an acceptably off-color anecdote about an elephant eating cabbages in a garden, and I listened, laughed, and then memorized every pause and inflection he put into his delivery. I knew I was learning from the master, or at least the only joke master I had access to, and I treated him with the proper amount of respect and deference. Over the course of the next two hours, he and I mapped out a running patter for my magic act that would have made Myron Cohen proud. True, these were nightclub jokes whose comedic expiration date had passed about ten years prior, but to me it didn't matter. I now had a full-fledged routine that I felt at least stood a fighting chance against the "Moonlight Sonata"s and the "I Got a Name"s that the music department would be throwing my way.

The following week, using a mod 1960s white and yellow plastic stool in the shape of an hourglass as a magic table—a stool that had stood next to the hamper in our bathroom for the past six years—I auditioned my comedy/magic act at the talent show tryouts. And, much to my delight, even though my auditioners sat and watched my routine stone-faced, I was accepted and put on the bill.

Overwhelmed, I spent the next week rehearsing and honing my delivery. Every morning I would awaken with the nervous realization that in just a few days, instead of lying in my bedroom, unobserved by the outside world, I would be up on a stage in front of hundreds of people trying to entertain them and hoping to win fifty dollars by out-talenting my fellow student performers. The idea that I could be under sheets and blankets in the privacy of my own bed at one moment during the day and then a few hours later be up on stage in front of hundreds of strangers, my every word and movement completely exposed and vulnerable to rejection by the masses, was both terrifying and enticing. I had alternating visions of doing my act and either being triumphantly hoisted aloft on the shoulders of my adoring fans or being pelted with tomatoes and rotten eggs, like a bad opera singer in an old Abbott and Costello comedy.

By the time the day of the talent show rolled around, I was both terrified and out of my mind with excitement.

That night, as I waited backstage, I heard performer after performer get up and launch into ballad after sad ballad, each indulging their artistic teenage depression with songs like "Eleanor Rigby" and "Send in the Clowns." I would occasionally peek out at the audience from the edge of the stage. The show was being held in our cafetorium, which, as the name implied, was half cafeteria, half auditorium. The auditorium part was simply a crude stage that had been built into one of the walls so that if the lunch tables were rolled away and butt-numbing folding chairs brought in, the room could function as if it were a theater, albeit one out of a Third World country. The place was filled to capacity with parents and relatives of the performers, as well as all the students whose acts weren't accepted into the show, there to see just how crappy the rest of us really were and how unfairly their own artistic skills had been rejected. Since my spot on the program wasn't until second from last, I had a lot of time to get nervous and watch all the female performers, who made up the lion's share of the bill, alternately crying on each other's shoulders as they dealt with massive bouts of insecurity and hugging each other in support, even though it was clear that each one of them wanted the other to lose in order to secure her place in the coveted fifty-dollar spot. They weren't hugging me, though, an unknown freshman dressed in a knock-off version of a pricey denim squares leisure suit, which was not made up of actual fashionable denim squares sewn together but of one single sheet of low-quality denim pinched and stitched to appear as an amalgamation of high-priced blue jeans patches. I was the lowest of the low in their books—a com-

mon variety performer, a populist plate-spinner whose only goal
was to entertain the groundlings, not to move or enthrall or introduce an audience to new heights of art and emotion via the
miracle of music. I was merely light entertainment to them, a diversion needed by the stage crew to fill time as they pulled a baby
grand piano on stage in preparation for a soul-wrenching performance of Carole King's "It's Too Late." I stood and politely held
my ground, smiling at them supportively as I went over my 1950s
cabaret jokes in my head. I mentally ran through my magician's
checklist, making sure I had loaded the secret compartment in
my Drum O' Plenty correctly, putting the single-color silks on
top of the more elaborate floral print scarves I had taken from
my mother's fancy underwear drawer, so that the multicolored
extravaganzas would come out last and amaze my audience with
their supposed beauty.

My heart was practically pounding out of my chest by the time
the evening's emcee, Ms. Owens, the music teacher, got up to introduce me to the crowd. My tricks were all crammed onto the
top of my bathroom-stool magic table as I stood nervously waiting. As the curtains parted and the bright spotlights hit and immediately blinded me, my head filled with visions of myself
picking up the stool to move it to centerstage and causing everything to fall off and crash destructively onto the floor. I could
sense the crowd sitting in front of me, waiting to see what I would
add to the already overlong proceedings, and I cautiously pulled
my yellow and white plastic makeshift magic table out to the performance area. It shuddered and shook threateningly as I slid it
across the wooden stage floor, and the five feet I pulled it seemed
to consume several hours of time. Satisfied that I was in the right
spot, I looked up and stared out at the invisible crowd. I could
only see the outlines of their heads, but from their silence and lack
of movement, I knew the time had come to try to entertain them.

I took a deep, nervous breath and began.

"Ladies and gentlemen, a lot of things that we see in the world are not really what they appear to be. This reminds me of a story . . ."

A graceless way to launch into a joke, to be sure. But I had stated my premise and was now about to elaborate upon it. Nobody at Toastmasters International could take me to task for that, I don't think. I continued.

"There was a woman who owned a cabbage patch, which sat on top of a hill in her backyard. Well, one night, an elephant escaped from a circus that was passing through her town and, being hungry, this elephant wandered into the woman's cabbage patch and started eating. The woman looked out her window and saw the elephant on top of the hill silhouetted by the moonlight, so that it was hard to tell which end of the elephant was which. The woman called the police and said, 'Officer, there's an elephant in my cabbage patch and he's pulling my cabbages out of the ground with his *tail*.' 'Really?' said the officer. 'And what's he doing with them after he pulls them out?' "

I paused dramatically, as my father had taught me to do, and then headed into the punch line.

" 'Officer,' the woman said, 'if I told you, you'd never believe me.' "

I waited for the laughs that my father had guaranteed would come.

They didn't.

There was nothing but total and utter silence.

I stared out at the crowd in shock. Sweat immediately popped out of every open pore in my body. How could my father do this to me? I thought. Did he know that this joke was going to tank? Was this some filial revenge he'd been waiting to take on me for all the times my mother and I had gone against his wishes and bought something he considered to be ridiculous? Or had all my father's friends and relatives simply been humoring him all these years, laughing at his jokes so as not to hurt his feelings, and I was now finding that I had such a bad sense of humor that I wasn't able to distinguish an authentic belly laugh from a well-intentioned pity laugh? Whichever it was, I knew I was quickly seeing fifty bucks and my reputation in the school fly right out the cafetorium window.

I stood frozen.

And then, after a few seconds of silence, I heard something strange. From somewhere in the middle of the audience, I heard a teenage girl's voice.

"Oh," she said.

It was an "oh" similar to the "uh-oh" I would always hear someone in the audience say during reruns of *I Love Lucy* or *The Brady Bunch*. Whenever Lucy was about to put a vase on her head that we in the audience knew was going to get stuck or whenever Bobby Brady poured an entire king-size box of laundry soap into the washing machine that we all knew was going to flood the house with suds, some woman in the studio audience, whether laugh track or living, would always go "*uh*-oh" as the reality of what she was seeing on the screen dawned on her.

As soon as this "oh" was uttered, a wave of laughter swept through the audience. At first, I thought they were laughing at the "oh," but then I realized the laugh was not a derisive one that reveled in my failure, but the sincere laugh of an audience who needed a few moments to realize that a kid had just told them a story about a woman who thought she saw an elephant shoving cabbages up its ass. The laugh was long and loud, and I immediately felt like Johnny Carson. Every insecure gene in my body transformed into superconfident strands of comedy magician DNA. As I pulled out my Color-Changing Shoelaces and made them do their thing, the audience laughed when they were supposed to laugh, gasped when they were supposed to gasp, and applauded when I had always hoped they would applaud.

The rest of my performance was a blur. Every one of my father's old-time jokes worked, every one of my store-bought tricks worked, and even the fancy silk scarves my mother let me produce from the Drum O' Plenty worked, receiving the proper amount of oohs and aahs. By the time I got to my final cornball departing line, "Like the mother cow said when her baby boy calf fell off the tall cliff, 'A little bull goes a long way,'" I could do no wrong. The audience burst into whistles and applause as I waved to them in what felt like slow motion. I was Elvis. I was Sinatra. I was the Beatles. And I never felt cooler in my life.

I ended up winning first place, even though the girl who came out and sang after me also brought the house down. Her very adult rendition of "I Don't Know How to Love Him" definitely moved the audience, but I think, at the end of the day, the judges were so tired of hearing kids sing that they gave me the prize out of gratitude for any kind of nonmusical diversion. I didn't care what the reasons were. I simply knew that I had hit a home run on stage that night, and now I had fifty dollars and the admiration of all my peers and their parents to prove it.

That night, I couldn't sleep. All I could do was replay my performance in my head. My mother had brought along our clunky portable cassette recorder and taped my act, but she made the mistake of having my uncle Ferd hold the recorder in his lap, so that all I could hear on the tape was the faint sound of my voice telling jokes from what sounded like the inside of a toilet and my uncle breathing, laughing, and clearing his throat. This was fine with me, however, because my memory of the event was much better than the tape could relate. On the tape, my voice and delivery sounded halting and tentative, my joke delivery rushed, and the laughs of the audience not as all-encompassing. But I knew what I had heard and I knew what I had felt, and I slept with the envelope that contained the fifty dollars and had the words FIRST PRIZE written on it in green felt-tip marker under my pillow, so that I could touch it during the night and reassure myself that I had actually won and not dreamed the whole thing. My body felt more tingly than it did the night after Pam McGovern kissed me on the cheek for giving her that copy of "I Honestly Love You." I slept the sleep of kings that night.

In the morning, I awoke to the sounds of singing birds. It was Saturday and I was supposed to go in to work at my father's store, as I had done every Saturday for the past six years. Normally I dreaded it. But today I couldn't wait. I wanted to tell everybody about my triumph and bask in their approval and work side by side with my father, the man who helped me have the best evening of my life.

As I got on my green Schwinn ten-speed and pedaled off for his store, I was lighter than air. The victory of the previous night hadn't lost any of its luster. If anything, it had grown. I knew I could now buy fifty dollars' worth of new tricks and expand my routine. I started thinking about my shining future in show biz, about how I would take my act out on the road, how I would per-form on *The Tonight Show* and travel to all the state fairs in the country and possibly end up with my own variety show. If Doug Henning could do it, why couldn't I? After all, I was funnier than he was. And as long as my father had jokes in his joke file, I would have an unbeatable, show-stopping act.

As I rode along through the undeveloped section of our neigh-borhood, which was made up of overgrown fields and deep drain-age ditches, I was whistling a happy tune. I truly don't think I've ever felt happier in my entire life than I did as I rode along that day, with the sun shining and the sound of an audience's applause and approval playing on a loop in my head. As I coasted down the incline toward the main avenue my father's store was on, I heard a car coming up behind me. I pulled my bike closer to the shoulder of the road and considered whether I should give the people in the car a little "good morning" wave, just to share my good mood with the world. It was then that the car pulled up next to me and before I could turn to look at it . . .

THWACK!!!

A huge, softball-sized glob of paper towel that had been soaked in ice water hit me full force in the side of the face. The impact was so hard that it knocked me clean off the side of my bike. My green ten-speed and I crashed onto the asphalt and then tumbled violently down into the drainage ditch, landing in an algae-thickened pool of stagnant water.

As I lay there in the ditch, my clothes soaking up the scummy pond of drainage, my face pounding and throbbing from the projectile's impact, I was completely stunned. It felt as if I had been hit in the side of the head with a baseball bat. I had no idea who threw it or what car they were driving. I didn't even hear anyone laugh or shout or see them drive away. I only knew that it hurt like hell and it had knocked every ounce of happiness out of me.

After a few minutes, I got up and pulled my bike out of the muck. The bike that I had so diligently washed and polished each week was now dirty and scraped. The front wheel was bent and the seat had torn on the side from its impact with the asphalt. Dazed, I clambered back up to the road and started walking my bike back to my house to change my clothes. As I walked, all I felt like doing was crying. The win at the talent show now seemed more like a burden than a triumph. Was the person in the car who threw the paper at me one of the other competitors? Was it one of their boyfriends or brothers? Was I now a marked man? Was this the other side of success, suffering the revenge of those you've defeated? After all, in order to win and succeed, a lot more people have to lose and not succeed. I had won the talent show and the fifty dollars, but it was now starting to feel like my victory, like most other things in life, carried an unpleasant price tag.

Or maybe they were simply some random jackasses knocking kids off bikes with ice water–soaked balls of paper towel. Either way, I felt like the universe had decided to knock me down a notch, making me pay a painful price for feeling so good about myself.

When I got to my dad's store later that day, I had a huge red welt on the side of my face. This became more of a topic of conversation than my win at the talent show. People whom my dad had told about my victory congratulated me and I thanked them. I tried to get my excitement back again, but the moment had passed. I put the fifty dollars in the bank on Monday and ended up spending it not on more magic tricks but on fixing my bike and a record-buying spree at Peaches. I figured that listening to records in the privacy of my own room was something that would at least allow me to hide from the outside world and hopefully not upset anybody enough for them to come after me with more balls of water-soaked Bounty.

I continued doing magic in retirement homes, worked on my comedy patter, and eventually bought some new tricks with the money I made working at my dad's store. I performed again the next year in the talent show, but this time safely out of competition, coming back as the previous year's winner to entertain the audience as the judges tallied up their scores. My dad had helped me put together a whole new set of jokes and my act got another great reception. As I stood there soaking up the crowd's applause, I felt good that I was only entertaining people and not trying to defeat any of my fellow performers.

After all, the fifty dollars I won had long been spent, and winning the talent show hadn't made me any more popular with the people whom I thought I wanted to impress. But doing my act made me happy. My dad and I had found something we truly enjoyed doing together, and it was the first time in my life that I actually thought of the guy as not just my dad but my friend. And so, I figured, that had to be more important than trying to convince an audience that I was more talented than the swing choir's Kerry Reynolds singing "Seasons in the Sun."

But I still always looked to see who was driving up behind me whenever I rode my bike. I mean, being friends with your dad and feeling good about yourself are all well and good, but taking a wet paper towel in the side of the face is something you should always strive to avoid.

'TIS THE SEASON TO AVOID DATING

There was a couple in my freshman class, Cathy and Dan, who were more mature than the rest of us. Or at least I thought they were more mature than the rest of us because . . . well . . . they made out with each other all the time.

In school.

In *public*.

The idea of knowing a girl who liked me so much that she'd make out with me in front of other people simply blew my mind. Just the thought of getting a girl to kiss my fourteen-year-old acned face in the privacy of her bedroom or a backyard fort or even a tent in her driveway seemed about as attainable as my childhood dream of being able to fly by flapping my arms. Patty Collins may have misguidedly wanted to kiss me when we were six, but now that I was actually old enough to do it, I simply couldn't imagine putting my face that close to a girl's and not having her scream in terror. And if she did let me get that close to her, I figured a quick peck on the lips would be about the most I could hope for. Or handle, for that matter. I liked the idea of holding hands with a girl as I walked down the hall and of kissing her good-bye in front of the open door to her next class, with my fellow students seeing this as they thought to themselves, Wow, Paul's really cool. He's got a girlfriend and she's kissing him in front of us. She must find that ring of pimples around his mouth really sexy. But the idea of making out heavily with a girl, in public or otherwise, was both terrifying and off-putting.

It was also something I became more and more obsessed with as I watched Cathy and Dan engage in their public displays of affection.

Cathy was a very tall girl. She was Italian and had shortish black hair that had been styled into one of those ubiquitous Dorothy Hamill cuts, with a subtle touch of curling-iron work around the bangs. She had a pretty face and a large mouth with full lips and big teeth. She wasn't skinny but seemed shapely in a six-foot-tall-girl kind of way. She had a very natural beauty about her and never really wore makeup, outside of lip gloss. Back in high school, I thought lip gloss was the sexiest thing a girl could wear. I couldn't envision a day in the future when girls would no longer put it on. Pretty girls, at least. On the wrong girl, lip gloss just didn't seem to work. If a girl was weird-looking or had thin lips, the gloss simply gave the illusion that she hadn't wiped her mouth in a while. Girls like this would end up looking more like my friend George, who was a nice guy but who always had shiny wet lips and perpetual strings of white spit at the corners of his mouth that would stretch and hang on for dear life whenever he talked. The faux moisture that lip gloss provided had to be used with care, since its usage walked a constant razor's edge between good and evil. Lip gloss was a privilege, not a right. But on Cathy, it just made her beauty complete.

Cathy had a pretty smile and was always friendly. In many ways, she didn't really jibe with my concept of the kind of girl who would make out in public. That distinction was usually saved for the burnouts who populated the back of our school bus: tough girls in tight jeans and halter tops, the kind who fastened roach clips into their hair that had leather strings with a bead and pink feather hanging at the end. These were the girls who would wear long leather coats and black gangster hats, short rabbit-fur jackets

and tube tops, girls who could be heard throughout the day yelling to each other, "Hey, Sandi, toss me a ciggy butt" and "Fuck
you, Sheila, you slut!" They would occasionally show up in school
pregnant and still look like they could and would kick your ass if
you gave them a sidelong glance. To me, these were the kind of
girls who made out in public. Girls like Cathy laughed at your
jokes and actually cheered at pep rallies. You could introduce
them to your mother and borrow chemistry notes from them.
Simply put, Cathy was an enigma. And her enigmatic qualities
were causing her to have a starring role in my sweaty little pubescent dreams more and more frequently.

My growing obsession with Cathy made me feel guilty. I'd
known Dan since middle school and he was an extremely nice
guy. Like Cathy, he also wasn't the type of person I envisioned
spending his days indulging his libido in front of his peers. That
was the job of the freak guys who hung out in the auto shop or
on the smoking patio. They were the guys with dirty hair and
wispy mustaches, who smelled like cigarettes and pot and gasoline
and who would occasionally throw one of the burnout girls over
their shoulders and run around the school slapping her butt as she
screamed and laughed until the principal yelled at them to knock
it off. Dan was on the football team and was a very handsome,
clean-cut guy with perfect hair, big teeth, and a perpetual tan—
a Michigan ski bum, the type who always wore a form-fitting,
brightly colored ski jacket with a bouquet of lift tickets sprouting
from the zipper tab. Dan was one of the most polite guys I knew,
almost as polite as Chris Nubellski, and I never once saw him look
sad in the entire four years we were in high school together. But I
guess I'd be constantly happy, too, if I looked like he did and was
making out with Cathy all the time.

Cathy and Dan seemed to have everything in common. There
was a picture of them in my freshman yearbook from a class ski
trip. They're standing hand in hand at the base of the ski lift, smiling broadly and looking as natural in the wintry sport setting as

my friends and I looked at a *Star Trek* convention. I avoided that ski trip like the plague, having been taken skiing once by my church youth group—a trip that saw me screaming down the side of a mountain after an attempt at "snowplowing" failed. My downhill odyssey ended only after I smashed into a ski rack and sent twenty pairs of skis coasting down the beginners' slope behind the lodge. Any fantasies about having Cathy as my girlfriend were always derailed by the thought of taking her skiing: her schussing gracefully down the diamond run as I did my best Ray Bolger impression on the bunny hill before colliding face first with a tree. No, deep down I knew we didn't have a lot in common and, in true high-school fashion, that only made me desire her attentions more.

Sometime around November of my sophomore year, after a grade and a half of watching the two of them in perpetual liplock, I realized that I was seeing Cathy and Dan together less and less. They were still friendly with each other, but I didn't notice a lot of making out going on. And finally, on the first Tuesday of December, my friend Tom brought me the news I had waited so long to hear.

"Hey, guess what? Dan and Cathy broke up."

"Really?" I said, completely thrown. "Why?"

"I don't know. I guess they got bored."

"Are they mad at each other?" I asked.

"I don't think so. I heard they're still friends."

My mind raced. The Christmas Dance was coming up in a few weeks and I really wanted to go. I had never taken a girl to a dance. Not for lack of trying, though. In junior high, I took my next-door neighbor Mary to a school dance, but when we got there, they wouldn't let us in because Mary wasn't a student at my school. She was attending the Catholic school at the end of our street and, for some reason, it seemed my junior high had a policy against letting religious outsiders dance in our cafeteria. I was outraged as only a twelve-year-old can be and immediately saw us as two star-crossed, martyred lovers, caught in a world that neither understood our love nor would allow it. In reality, I guess I was more upset at the thought that I had been cheated out of my first official excuse to slow-dance with a girl. Not to mention the fact that my mother had bought me a spicy new blue-and-white-checked leisure suit and red turtleneck sweater that I was sure would make me a hit with all the other girls at the dance and drive Mary into a jealous rage. But I had been denied all of those pleasures, and now, with the Christmas Dance looming and Cathy a free agent, I saw my chance to set the record straight.

I spent the next few days doing reconnaissance. Step one was to start talking to Cathy. This wasn't a big leap for me because she was in several of my classes and we had a passing acquaintance with one another. She thought it was funny when I would do Steve Martin routines, which I would always pass off as my own. It was the year before Steve Martin broke big and nobody in my school had ever heard of him. I was able to get away with my plagiarism all the way until my junior year, when Steve Martin's song "King Tut" became a hit. After that, my former admirers turned against me and every time I would make a joke, they would ask, "Is that joke yours or did you steal it from Steve Martin, too?" I was scared straight from intellectual property theft after that but, at the time I was trying to get in with Cathy, I was still living comfortably off of Mr. Martin's repertoire.

"I'm so *mad* at my *mother*," I performed for Cathy, making sure to keep my tone just searching enough to seem like I was improvising the routine on the spot. "I mean, she calls me up the other day and says she needs to borrow fifty dollars so she can buy some *food*." I put the proper disdainful emphasis on the word *food* in order to exactly replicate Mr. Martin's delivery. The fact that the joke was only funny because Steve Martin was rich and yet I was only a sophomore with a couple of dollars in my pocket didn't seem to ruin the routine for Cathy. She laughed at my unoriginal antics as I went in for the kill. "So, I decided I'm gonna make her work it off by moving my barbells up to the attic."

Cathy laughed again, covering her mouth. "Oh, Paul, you're so funny. Did you just make that up?"

I shrugged in a sly, yet vague, way that seemed to indicate "Hey, this stuff comes out of my head constantly," covering my tracks in case I was put on trial for theft by Steve Martin's estate. "Miss, did you actually *hear* Mr. Feig *say* that he had written the material in question *himself?*" "Well . . . um . . . not directly but—" "No further questions, your honor!"

"You're really clever," Cathy said in a warm tone.

I made a "thanks, I like you, too" face at her, then waited a few seconds. "Hey, I'm sorry that you and Dan broke up," I said, making the universal sad face of the empathetic supportive confidant.

"Oh, that's okay. We're still really good friends."

"Huh" was all I could reply. Things were looking promising.

Later that day, as I was heading out of my geometry class, I spotted Dan in the hallway. I quickened my step to catch up, then slowed down and feigned surprise as I came up next to him. "Oh, hey, Dan. I didn't see you there. How's it going?"

We exchanged a few pleasantries, and I shrewdly asked him what his skiing plans were for this winter, just to throw him off my scent. Then I came in for the kill.

"That's too bad that you and Cathy broke up."

"No, not really. We've been together for a while. We're just really good friends." I couldn't fathom how someone you'd spent over a year French-kissing could suddenly be just a "really good friend." But, then again, I was a newcomer in the *arte de l'amore.*

"Cathy's really great, isn't she?" I said, trying very hard to keep an objective tone.

"Yeah, she's the best. She really likes you, too. She's always talking about how funny you are," said Dan. He definitely threw me with that one. And, because I was fifteen years old, just hearing that Cathy liked me made me start to get a boner. I shifted my books to the front and continued.

"Really? She does?" My nonchalant tone had been put to the test with that one. My voice came off sounding as if I were trying to talk in a car that was driving down a very bumpy road.

"Yeah," said Dan with a friendly smile. "You should ask her on a date. I think she'd go out with you."

Boner ahoy! I pressed down on my books and tried to walk normally. This was unbelievable. Dan was pimping his ex-girlfriend out to me. It was all going so well that it made me wonder if I was being set up. I'd always remembered an episode of *My Three Sons* where Ernie started going out with his best pal's girlfriend. Uncle Charley got all scary when he found out and said, in a tone that sounded like he was going to punch Ernie, "A real man doesn't take another man's girl." Did Dan know that I was angling for Cathy? Was he laying a trap that would end with him and his football buddies going Uncle Charley on my ass? I had no way of knowing, but my fifteen-year-old libido was in too high of a gear for me to care.

In the cafeteria, I went over to Cathy, who was emptying the beef fritters from her hot lunch tray into the garbage can.

"Hey, Cathy, um . . . I was wondering . . . uh . . ." The reality of what I was about to do hit me at that very moment, but I had clearly reached the point of no return.

"What?" she said with a sweet look on her face.

"Um . . . do you want to go to the Christmas Dance with me?" Right around the word *want* I started to feel faint. I know the rest of the words came out of my mouth, but, just like when you've been driving and suddenly realize that you have no recollection of actually piloting the car, I couldn't remember finishing the sentence. It was only Cathy's face and response that made me realize I had actually gotten the full request out.

"Sure, Paul," she said with a smile. "I'd love to go."

I had done it! My weaselly little plan had worked. I had set a goal and seen it through. I had longed to be the guy making out with Cathy for a year and a half, and now I was well on the road to making it happen at the Christmas Dance. I was beyond happy. *And* I had a raging boner that was fortunately camouflaged by the garbage can.

I had entered a whole new world.

I spent the next few weeks getting nervous about the date. Cathy and I didn't talk any more than we normally did, but there was now a connection between us. She would always give me a smile and a big "Hi, Paul" when we would see each other in the hallway. On top of that, word started getting around. The same gossip machine that had disseminated the news of Cathy and Dan's breakup was now busily spreading the word of our unlikely Yuletide rendezvous.

"Man, you're going to the dance with *Cathy*?" was a phrase I heard out of several of my friends' mouths. I would always respond with a Hugh Hefner–esque "Hey, she *wanted* to go with me."

Even Dan came by to give me his blessing. "That's great that you're taking Cathy to the Christmas Dance. She's really happy about it."

It was a relief that he was taking this so well, but it also made me feel like a dork. The subtext of his words seemed to be "I'm glad Cathy's going with a guy who's such a nerd that I know nothing other than dancing will happen between them." I resented the imagined implication. As far as I was concerned, Cathy and I were going to spend a very romantic evening of slow-dancing, groping, and making out. An epic romance was about to blossom, and I knew I was mere days away from my new life as a guy who was very comfortable engaging in public displays of affection with a tall, pretty high-school girl.

The evening of the dance, my mother dropped me off at Cathy's house. The plan was for Cathy and me to drive to the dance with her friend Sandy and Sandy's boyfriend, Walter. Walter was seventeen and had a driver's license. I was a bit nervous about double-dating with a guy who was two years older than me. Since I was such an inexperienced dater, I didn't want my embarrassment to be compounded by some guy who "knew the ropes" watching me and judging my every move. But, realizing that being driven to the dance by a seventeen-year-old was far less painful than being driven by my fifty-five-year-old mother, I gave in.

"Have a great time at the dance," my mom said as I stepped out of the car, replete with a wide-lapeled velour jacket with my large shirt collar worn on the outside. I looked down, admiring my tight-fitting Angel's Flight slacks and black platform shoes. I look just like the guys on *Soul Train,* I thought to myself. My hand came up to check that my puka shell necklace, bought not in Hawaii but at Silverman's disco clothing store down at the local mall, was properly in place. I was ready for action.

"You look so cute," my mom called out from the car.

"Mom," I said in a whiny tone, turning the monosyllabic word into two syllables. Her use of the word *cute* had been a bone of contention between the two of us for the last few years, and she knew what I really wanted her to say.

"Oh, I'm sorry. You look *'cool,'"* she said in a mocking tone that foretold the fact that she would call me "cute" and not "cool" yet another day.

And with that, she took off down the road as we had agreed, so that neither Cathy nor her family would see that I had been driven over by my mother. I walked up to the front door of her house and rang the bell. My heart was beating quite fast. I had been imagining what this evening would be like, but now that I was staring down its cocked and loaded barrel, my nerves were really kicking in. However, everything was about to start happening more quickly than I was prepared for.

Her father answered the door. He was a normal-looking man with a mustache, a dad like most dads in the Midwest, the kind of

guy you could easily imagine being in a bowling league and enjoying the wide-eyed exploits of Dondi on the funnies page.

"Well, you must be Paul," he said in a casual tone that showed
he had greeted Cathy's dates several times before.

"Yes, sir. It's nice to meet you."

"C'mon in. Cathy's almost ready."

I entered their house. Cathy's mom was at the top of the stairs,
gazing down with a look that said she was trying to control her
giddiness about something.

"Cathy's almost ready," she said, not knowing that her husband
had just uttered the exact same three words to me seconds earlier.
Cathy's father gestured for me to sit on the couch. I complied.

"So," he said, sitting down heavily in his armchair, "I see they
don't make you wear ties to the Christmas Dance, huh?"

The thought of wearing a tie to a dance in 1977 was as foreign
as wearing pegged pants. "Oh, they only make you wear a tie to
the prom, I think."

"Wow, that's pretty nice. What I wouldn't give to not have to
wear a tie to work. You know, you're lucky you don't go to a
Catholic school. They make you wear ties with those uniforms."
He shook his head, his eyes getting the look of a man whose mind
was going back to unpleasant times. "They made me wear a tie to
school for years. Man, did I hate that."

It's always weird talking to someone else's parents because you
realize how different your life could have been if you had come
out of a different womb. I'm sure Cathy and her family had heard
her dad get spooky over his lifelong battle with neckwear many
times, but for me, a guy whose only goal was to French-kiss his
daughter, the man was starting to creep me out. But I forced myself to look at him sympathetically, just in case Cathy and I fell
madly in love and he was destined to become my father-in-law.

"Huh, that's too bad," I said, trying to sound empathetic.
"That must have gotten hot in the summer."

"Oh, Christ. Don't get me started on summer school."

Fortunately for me, Cathy's mom came down the stairs and saved me from having to journey any further into her husband's dysfunctional past. "She's *read-y*," her mom said in a singsongy voice that announced she had probably spent most of the afternoon helping Cathy prepare herself for this big evening.

I looked up at the top of the stairs. Her bedroom door was shut. There was definitely something exciting about the whole thing, as if I were on *Let's Make a Deal* and was about to find out if I'd picked the door with the new car behind it. Knowing how pretty Cathy was in school every day, my heart raced at the thought of how beautiful she was going to look after half a day of preparation.

The door opened. Cathy stepped out slowly with a shy look on her face, a look I had seen on the faces of brides in so many Westerns, when the innocent farm girl is first revealed in her wedding dress to her intended. In those movies, the cowboy always slowly takes off his hat in reverence to her unexpected beauty and whistles to himself, amazed. I stared up at her. Cathy looked down over the railing and gave me a coy little smile. Her expression bore the words *So . . . what do you think?*

So . . . what did I think?

Zonk, as Monty Hall would say.

She was terrifying. Whatever she and her mom had been up to all afternoon should not have occurred. Cathy's normally soft Dorothy Hamill hair had been sprayed up into a shape that is best described as a Nazi storm-trooper helmet. It hovered up and away from the edges of her scalp like a flying saucer, defying both gravity and attractiveness. Her face had been made up like a ventriloquist dummy's, with bright red cheeks and thick blue eye shadow that said less "I'm your dream girl" and more "I just got punched out in a bar fight." She was wearing an ill-advised dress that was very silk-esque and clingy, which instead of being enticing simply drew attention to the fact that Cathy had the slightest bit of a gut on her. I had only ever seen her wearing tight jeans in

school and suddenly realized the girdlelike qualities of tightly
packed denim. The tops of her arms, which had never before
been exposed to me, were now on display and revealed an over-
abundance of moles. She wore white pumps with a noncommittal heel that looked exactly like the shoes nurses used to wear in
hospital shows from the 1960s. And topping off her ensemble was
a loosely knit white shawl draped around her shoulders—the exact
same shawl I'd seen my eighty-something grandmother wear for
years.

If ever one could hear the sound of a libido dropping, the thud
of mine must have been deafening.

"Wow, Cathy," I said, forcing myself to sound like husbands I'd
heard on TV shows. "You look great."

Cathy gave me a shy smile and descended the stairs. Her mother
led her over and delivered her to me as if we were at the wedding
altar while her father took pictures of us. As we stood together
posing, clouds of Love's Baby Soft wafted off of Cathy and assaulted my nose like the green fingers of the plague that killed the
firstborn males of Egypt in *The Ten Commandments*. Cathy kept
giving me sweet, coy looks that I knew were supposed to be romantic. However, they only succeeded in unnerving me. Maybe I
wasn't cut out for this dating thing, I thought. Because looking at
Cathy right then, the last thing I wanted to do was make out with
her.

The doorbell rang and Cathy's friend Sandy came in with her
boyfriend, Walter. Cathy's parents knew Sandy quite well and so
there were big greetings all around. They had also apparently met
Walter several times and liked the guy, and so the air was suddenly
filled with familiarity that threw me into the outsider role of
standing off to the side and smiling as I forced myself to enjoy the
warm scene in front of me. Once additional pictures had been
taken with the four of us being placed into every conceivable
combination, we headed out the door and climbed into Walter's
car. We all waved good-bye to Cathy's parents and headed off. It

was such a *Leave It to Beaver* moment that I was completely unprepared for what was to follow.

The second Cathy's house was out of range, Sandy reached
under the driver's seat and pulled out a can of beer.

"Who wants a brew?" she asked with a big, evil smile.

"Allllll-riiiiiiiight!" Cathy said in the same cadence that Jimmie
"J.J." Walker from *Good Times* used to say his catch phrase of "Dy-
No-Mite."

Sandy cracked open the beer and took a small sip. She handed
it off to Walter, who took a slightly bigger sip. Walter then handed
the can over his shoulder to Cathy. Cathy took the beer, raised it
to her lips, and chugged down the entire can. I watched in amazement as she drank, pulling the beer so hard that trickles of it
leaked out of the sides of her mouth and ran down her jawbone
as if she were in a Mountain Dew commercial. She took the
empty can away from her mouth, gave an "oops, did I do that?"
look, and then burped. Sandy cracked up, Walter cracked up, and
I pretended to crack up even though I was completely and utterly
horrified. At this point in my life, I had only tasted beer once and
that was at a friend's house when we were twelve and retrieving a
beer for his lawn-cutting father. I had taken a small sip and
thought it tasted much like I imagined beef-flavored apple juice
that had gone bad might taste.

"Wow, you must have really been thirsty," I said, trying to
sound unaffected.

"I just wanted to get loose," Cathy said to Sandy.

What did that mean? Was she nervous? Uptight? Was there
something about her date with me that she had been dreading? I
was immediately insulted and I think my face gave me away. Cathy
saw this and quickly explained herself.

"I mean, these dances can be so boring and I thought we
should get ourselves more in the party mood." She gave me a
smile and called up to Sandy in the front seat. "You got another
one for Paul?"

"Yeah, right here," said Sandy, reaching under her seat.

"Oh, that's okay," I said, trying not to sound panicked. "I'll wait until later." Scenes from all those ABC *Afterschool Specials* about the evils of teenage drinking flooded my brain. I had just seen the TV movie *Sarah T.—Portrait of a Teenage Alcoholic* and was now scared that by the end of the evening, I, like Sarah T., would be getting drunk and killing a horse by riding it into traffic.

"Well, if you don't want it, I'll have it," said Cathy, who grabbed the can and cracked it open like a Shriner. She drank half of it, burped again, handed it back up to Sandy, and then turned to me, excited. "We're gonna have so much *fun* tonight!"

I forced a smile back. I was beginning to sweat in my velour jacket.

When we got to the school, the Commodores' "Brick House" was booming out of the cafetorium doors. Officially ready to party the night away, thanks to one and a half cans of Stroh's beer, Cathy grabbed my hand and pulled me out onto the dance floor. She immediately started dancing wildly, jumping and gyrating as if she were a featured dancer on *American Bandstand*. She was scanning the room as she danced, looking for friends and checking to see if Dan had come with anyone. I looked around and was thrown by the sight of everyone from my school dressed in their finest evening wear. You get so used to seeing your peers dressed like your peers that it's always surprising when they show up somewhere dressed like your parents.

"Hey, Cathy, what's goin' on?" yelled over one of her other friends. The girl, who was wearing a form-fitting Danskin leotard dress as if she were a cast member of *A Chorus Line,* made a face at Cathy whose meaning I could only decipher as "Who's the dork you're with?" Cathy made a big smiley face back at the girl that seemed to convey both "Shut up" and "I know, can you believe it?" The two girls laughed to each other across the dance floor, then Cathy turned back to me and gave me what I think was supposed to be a sexy look. Having never been the recipient of a sexy look in my fifteen years on earth, I had no idea how to interpret it. But it felt like something that was supposed to throw me off the scent of the exchange she knew I must have just witnessed. I wasn't sure how to take any of this because, being a newcomer to the dating scene, I had no idea if this was about me or just the kind of thing girls did with each other on dates. Girls always seemed to be laughing about something whenever they were with their friends, and I had been paranoid for years that every time they laughed, somehow they were laughing at me. I forced a smile back at her, and Cathy then started dancing even more wildly, whipping her head from side to side. I became hypnotized by the fact that her rock-hard flying-saucer-shaped hairdo was completely immune to the centrifugal force her actions were exerting upon it. You could have hit that hair with a wrecking ball and not made a dent in it.

As the song started to wind down, I noticed that Cathy's dancing seemed to lose its initial intensity. She was still gyrating in a sort of belly-dancer-meets-drunk-guy-at-the-accounting-department-Christmas-party way, but her face showed she was becoming preoccupied. By the time the song faded, she threw me a look and said, "I'll be right back." And with this, she walked very quickly out of the cafetorium.

Twenty minutes later, I was standing on the side of the dance floor talking to my friend Tom, whose date was off talking with some of her friends.

"Where's Cathy?" he asked.

"I don't know. I think she went to the bathroom or something."

"I wonder if she's talking to Dan," said Tom. "I haven't seen him in a while."

I hadn't even considered this possibility and quickly grew concerned. But my concern immediately turned into a hope that she *was* talking to him. In fact, part of me really wanted them to be professing their love and agreeing to get back together. I wasn't enjoying this date with Cathy very much, and any excuse to get to leave the dance and go home to watch *The Six Million Dollar Man* and drink root beer was a welcome thought.

I concocted a plan in which I would walk outside and discover Cathy and Dan making out and then play the sad, jilted cuckold as I walked home through the rain in my dress clothes while sad music played on the sound track. Looking forward to my new role as the Misunderstood Romantic, I headed out of the cafetorium to find Cathy. However, as I entered the trophy case–lined front lobby of our school, her friend Sandy ran up to me.

"Paul, Cathy's in the bathroom and she's really sick. She's throwing up and everything."

"What?" I asked, my mind reeling with horrific images of Cathy on her hands and knees in her dress heaving into a school toilet. "Does she have the flu?"

"No, it's because of the beer. I think it made her sick," Sandy said, looking upset.

I immediately lost sympathy for Cathy and my feelings of ambivalence about our date now turned into indignation. This is what she gets for downing a beer two minutes into our date, I thought to myself. If the idea of spending an evening with a nice guy like me was so hard to face that she had to turn to booze for moral support, then she can just heave all night for all I care. But, being a kid who was brought up to never make others feel bad about themselves, I forced a concerned look onto my face and said, "Oh, man, I hope she's okay."

"She's really upset," Sandy said with a look that showed she was worried I was going to be mad at Cathy. "She's crying and everything. She said she didn't want to ruin your evening."

Too late, I thought. When an outing to a dance sees one half of the couple hearing that the other half of the couple is puking up beer into a toilet a mere thirty minutes into the date, then I'd say the evening is about as far down the road to ruin as it can get. Unfortunately, hearing that Cathy was crying made it hard for me to act angry. I once again slipped into the role of the Concerned Guy.

"Oh, she shouldn't worry about that," I said kindly. "I just hope she's okay."

"She's fine. We got her cleaned up after she stopped barfing about five minutes ago. I'll see if she's ready to come out." And with this, Sandy disappeared into the bathroom.

I had no idea what I was supposed to do. The idea that Cathy had been vomiting put the final nail in the coffin of my make-out fantasies. The mere mention that she had to be "cleaned up" made me wish she would simply stay in the bathroom all night, since the thought of seeing Cathy with puke stains on her already less-than-enticing dress was making my stomach sore. Before I could formulate any sort of a plan, the bathroom door opened and a contrite-looking Cathy emerged. There were no stains on her dress, but her makeup had taken a hit. The blush on her cheeks had clearly been wiped clean and reapplied with even less competence than her mother had demonstrated. Her eye shadow had been repaired simply by doubling its already heavy dosage. But it was her mascara that had borne the brunt of her emotional and gastrointestinal outburst. The black from her eyelashes had run and commingled with her liner, giving her eyes a Norma Desmond–meets–Alice Cooper effect. She walked over to me, her eyes cast down at the floor.

"I'm so sorry, Paul," she said, looking like she might cry. "I understand if you don't want to talk to me."

What was I going to say? I really *didn't* want to talk to her, simply because I was terrified that I might smell the vomit on her breath. Her large mouth, which I had found so sexy in the past, had now become the focal point of my angst. I knew that vomit had come out of it very recently, and I couldn't be sure that bits of it weren't still floating around in there. I knew from the few horrible times I had vomited in my life, that the taste had stayed with me for hours. Therefore, no matter how sad and coy Cathy was going to act, she was one thing and one thing only in my mind: a person who had just puked.

"How are you feeling?" I asked, shifting my weight back a bit.

"I feel terrible," she said, stepping forward in order to get close to me. "I've completely ruined the evening."

I shifted my weight away from her again, inching my foot back discreetly. "No, it's not ruined. You just probably shouldn't have drank all that beer in the car."

She sighed heavily. I held my breath, afraid of what I might smell. "You're right. God, it was so stupid. You don't even drink, I can tell." She looked into my eyes as if I were some sort of wise man. Clearly the girl was a mess. All I could do was stare at her mouth and wonder just how many times she had thrown up and whether her hands had gripped the sides of the toilet bowl as she did.

"As long as you're okay, that's all that matters," I said with a forgiving smile, stepping back and putting my hands on my hips, as if I were her father. She sighed in relief to Sandy, then gave me a look that said she now thought I was a great guy and a potential boyfriend. "Slow Dancin' " came on inside the cafetorium. She looked toward the music, then gave me one of her now-familiar shy looks.

"Do you want to dance?" she asked, doe-eyed.

Good God, no, I thought. "Okay," I said.

She took my hand, gave me a romantic smile, and led me into the dance. Her friend Sandy gave me a grateful smile that showed she was happy that I didn't care about what had just happened in the bathroom. I smiled back, trying to figure out exactly how I could get the hell out of the rest of this date.

Cathy and I got onto the dance floor. She put her arms around my neck and pulled me close, in the standard death-grip slow-dance position that we as teenagers in the late 1970s were required to perform. Gone were the one-hand-on-waist-the-other-hand-up-and-out-to-the-side days of our parents. I had danced with my mother and aunts for years in this old-fashioned way and had dreamed about the time when I would finally get to put both my arms around a girl and pull her close, her arms around my neck, our foreheads touching, staring deeply into each other's eyes, moments away from a kiss neither one of us could stop. Now, Cathy's arms were around my neck, her face was inches from mine, and all I wanted to do was run. I gingerly put my hands on her waist and held her lightly, tilting my head back a bit, pretending to survey the room as I moved my nose out of breathing range.

"Wow, there sure are a lot of people here," I said in as non-romantic a tone as I could muster.

"I wish there weren't," she said quietly. "I wish it was just you and me."

I had lain awake at night for years dreaming of having a girl say something like that to me. I looked into Cathy's eyes. She smiled coyly and exhaled. I smelled a trace of vomit on her breath. I felt like I was going to faint.

"Oh, yeah, well, too bad it's not." I delivered the line much like a clerk in a complaint department would tell a customer that he understood her grievance but there was nothing he could do about it.

Cathy looked into my eyes and moved her head forward, getting very close to my face. I held my breath. "I'm so glad you asked me to the dance," she said sweetly.

"I'm glad you came with me," I said, contorting my neck into a question-mark shape in order to put the maximum distance possible between her mouth and my nose.

"We're going to have a great time." Cathy's smile started to transform into the flat-faced expression that people get just before they kiss someone. She moved her face toward mine. My neck had put my head as far back as it could go without dislodging it from the top of my spine. As Cathy moved her mouth toward mine, eyes closing to commence the kiss, I moved my head to the side and forward, effectively dodging her face and parking my ear next to hers. It was such a bold move that I didn't know if she was going to get mad and push me away or if she'd just assume I didn't know she wanted to kiss me and figure I was simply going into the heads–together slow–dance position. Cathy leaned her head against my cheek and sigh contentedly. All I could think of was how happy I was that her face was now behind me.

The dance went by slowly. I started pawning Cathy off on other guys she knew. I worried that she would figure out I was trying to get rid of her, but my nice-guy act was going so well that I had Cathy fooled into thinking I was being selfless.

"Are you sure you don't mind?" she would ask me before going onto the dance floor with any number of football players.

"No, no, you two should dance," I'd reply, as if I were her grandmother who was just happy to be sitting and watching the young people enjoy themselves. I hung around with the few guys I knew at the dance. None of my core group of fellow nerds had bothered to attend, knowing as I did that school dances were not the place where any of us felt at all comfortable. Coffee shops, movie theaters, and our bedrooms were our turf, and we never had to defend those places from cool guys.

As the dance ended, I wondered if Cathy and Sandy would forget that we were all supposed to go out to dinner. It was a tradition, I had been told, to go to the dance, then to take your date out for a nice meal in a fancy restaurant. When I say "fancy," I mean, of course, one of the several medieval-themed restaurants peppered between the fast-food chains and twenty-four-hour family restaurants that accounted for most of the eating-out experiences available to us noncoast dwellers. Within most small Midwestern communities, there is an equation that anything having to do with a king is somehow symbolic of the highest-quality meal a person can enjoy. Restaurants with names like Ye Olde King's Table and His Majesty's Court were the places where you took dates, celebrated birthdays, or proposed. I had made the four of us a reservation at The King's Inn, a huge dark-wood restaurant that incongruously had a statue of a giant ten-foot-high steer out in front. Much like a lobster tank in a seafood establishment, I guess the sight of a beefy heifer standing out in front of a restaurant was supposed to be the lure that would prove too tempting for any hungry driver to pass up. But tonight, with the image of the vomiting Cathy lodged in my head, driving past The King's Inn and heading home was my one and only wish.

Cathy, Sandy, Walter and I walked out of the dance toward Walter's car. Other dance attendees were loudly burning rubber with their cars, doing doughnuts and making the parking lot sound like a drag-racing strip. After Walter finished hooting and yelling "Burn it fuckin' out, baby!" to a souped-up Dodge Dart that was wearing out its back tires by gunning the engine with the brakes on and sending a huge cloud of black smoke into the atmosphere, I yawned and tested the waters.

"Man, I'm tired," I said, stretching my arms above my head in the most unsubtle portrayal of a sleepy guy ever attempted.

"Tired?" said Walter to me, as if the next thing out of his mouth was going to be an accusation of homosexuality. "I'm *starving*."

"Me too," said Cathy. "I've been thinking about a steak all night."

"Yeah, you must be hungry," said Sandy with a smirk. She then did an imitation of Cathy barfing. Cathy opened her mouth wide in shock, then punched Sandy on the arm.

"God, Sandy, shut up," she said, motioning toward me with her eyes, as if Sandy were reminding me of something I could possibly have forgotten.

They were hungry. Cathy wanted a steak. This evening was not going to end.

At dinner, in the dimly lit restaurant, Cathy ordered a large steak complete with onion rings and a baked potato with sour cream and chives. As if the idea of her having thrown up was not enough of a libido killer, watching her pound down this costly combination of bad breath–inducing foods was enough to send me to a monastery. As we ate, I could do little but look at her mouth, knowing that I was going to be expected to kiss that mouth good night in a very short time. Throughout dinner, Cathy and Sandy talked and laughed as Walter made "they're crazy" looks at me. I smiled and nodded and laughed along with them as I pretended to be enjoying myself. But all I could think of was getting back to the safety of my house and my much more familiar geek life. It was only after Cathy had ordered a piece of ricotta cheesecake that I was able to herd them out of the place.

As we left the restaurant, I made quite a show of taking some of the breath-freshening after-dinner mints out of the bowl next to the register, the same type of mints that news programs have since shown to be covered with urine from customers going to the bathroom, not washing their hands, and then using their piss-soaked fingers to grope around in the mint bowl. Fortunately, I did not know this fun fact back then and saw these mints as the only line of defense between me and Cathy's barf-steak-onion-ring-and-cheesecake-tainted mouth.

"Anybody want a mint?" I asked casually.

"No thanks," said Cathy. "I don't eat candy."

No, just everything else, I thought.

As we drove along in Walter's car, Sandy turned to Cathy and me in the backseat and said, "Hey, you guys, let's go park out at the beach." Panic flashed through my brain as I realized this evening was supposed to continue and that its continuation would consist of nothing but going face to face with Cathy. It was officially Make-Out Time.

"Oh, man, I've gotta get home," I said, abandoning any attempts to try to sound remotely cool.

"Really? It's only 11:25," said Cathy, looking at her watch. "I don't have to be home until midnight."

"Oh, I'm sorry," I said, trying to sound disappointed, "but my dad said I have to be home by 11:30. He's weird about stuff like that."

I saw Walter and Sandy exchange a look in the front seat that indicated whatever nerdy things they had been thinking about me throughout the evening were now confirmed. And at this point, I didn't care. I just wanted out of that car.

Walter drove me back to my house and pulled up in our driveway. My stomach was in knots the whole way home, since Cathy kept throwing looks at me that said she wanted me to kiss her. I had been able to hold her off, even as Sandy was kissing Walter as he drove. On top of everything else, their mobile necking made me feel like I was in one of those driver's training films I had to show to upperclassmen during my A/V hour. I just knew that Walter and Sandy's kissing was going to lead us right into the path of an oncoming train as the narrator says, "Was it really *worth* it?" The whole time Cathy was staring at the side of my face, trying to get me to turn toward her and dive in. Between nervously watching the road whenever I knew Walter was distracted and pretending to be fascinated with every business sign along the boulevard on which we were driving, I was a mess by the time we reached my house.

"Well, thanks for the ride, Walter," I said jovially, as if he were my Little League coach dropping me off after a game. I turned to Cathy and she gave me a smile that said, "Now it's time for you to kiss me."

D Day had arrived.

Up in the front seat, I saw Walter and Sandy start making out. How people could just start making out in front of other people perplexed me. When I had seen Cathy and Dan doing it for the last year and a half, it looked cool to me. I guess I hadn't ever considered all that went into making out—the exchange of spit, the physiology of pressing your face against that of another living human being, the consequences of your partner's food intake, the

matter of germs and contagion. Not to mention that kissing and
making out were supposed to be highly personal activities, performed out of love and affection for your partner and not to be
used as some status symbol to lord over those less fortunate or
more discreet than you. Displays of affection were supposed to be
private matters, not spectator sports. And now, with Sandy and
Walter making out in the front seat like two primal beings whose
libidos made them unable to sense my utter discomfort with the
entire situation, I started to feel mad. I looked at the front of my
house and, through a space between where our curtains came together, I could see my father sitting in his chair watching television in his pajamas. This was the time of night that he and I
usually watched *Benny Hill* reruns on the local VHF station, chan-
nel 50. I saw my father laugh and knew that Benny was probably
hitting his little bald sidekick on top of the head, something that
never failed to crack my father up. I turned and looked at Cathy,
who had shifted herself closer to me but had leaned back against
the seat so that she was braced for me to lean in and kiss her
heavily. A montage of the evening ran through my brain—the
beer, the vomit, the stinky dinner, and the mocking laughter between Cathy and her dancing friend—as I prepared myself for
what I knew I had to do. It felt like a gateway moment to me, the
door through which I would pass to leave my childhood forever.
Once you'd kissed a girl—*really* kissed a girl—you left your innocence behind, I thought. You'd no longer be able to enjoy simply
holding hands, you'd no longer feel a hot flush at getting kissed on
the cheek, you'd no longer feel your heart pound uncontrollably
as you danced the box step with a girl at a wedding. Only physical acts beyond openmouthed kissing would provide you any
thrill. No, I was standing on a cliff looking down into the darkness of adult pleasures, and peer pressure was forcing me to jump
off. I wasn't sure if I could do it.

   But I knew that if I didn't, I'd always be judged for it.

And I knew that if I blew this opportunity, I might always feel that I'd made a big mistake.

And just like that, it was decided. I was going in, whether I really wanted to or not.

I took a deep breath, tried to put my visions of the inside of Cathy's mouth out of mind, and slowly leaned forward to kiss her. That is, in my mind I was slowly leaning forward. In reality, I lunged forward very rapidly. I immediately made contact with Cathy's lower lip and the better part of her chin. I tasted what I knew had to be makeup and quickly dragged my lips upward. In doing so, I got an even bigger blast of pancake base. With my mouth now directly on top of hers, I felt her tongue start to move in toward mine. In a panic, I quickly thrust my tongue at hers and firmly pushed it back into her mouth like a Hong Kong subway worker shoving riders into a packed rush-hour train. Finding my tongue was now inside her oral cavity, I realized I had absolutely no idea what I was supposed to do in there. I had heard one of my teachers use the phrase "tongue wrestling" once when he yelled at two burnouts to stop necking. And I recently overheard a jock say he was going to stick his tongue down his girlfriend's throat. So I did some quick math and figured that I'd better move my tongue around and try to engage something. My tongue snapped upward and immediately hit her teeth. Feeling the sharpness of them pressing down on my taste buds, I pulled my tongue back so that the tip of it was now pressed against her front incisors. Not knowing what else to do, I proceeded to run my tongue sideways across her upper teeth, then down and back the opposite way across all her lower teeth, then back up and across again until I had completely licked the front of every tooth in her mouth, turning my first French kiss into a full-fledged dental-cleaning session.

I quickly pulled away and looked at Cathy. She had a look of surprise on her face that I could only interpret one of two ways— it was either the best kiss she'd ever had or the absolute worst. Her eyes had a look of shock that was impossible to read. The only thing I knew for certain was that for me the kiss had been the most disturbing moment of my life up until that point. I fumbled out a "good night," halfheartedly thanked Walter again for driving, and quickly made my way into the house. I entered the living room as my dad was laughing at the fast-motion antics of Benny as he was chased around by several girls in bikinis.

"How was your date?" he asked.

I quickly moved past him and headed down the hallway. "Fine," I called back and ran into the bathroom. I closed the door, grabbed my toothbrush, and proceeded to brush my teeth and tongue vigorously for the next fifteen minutes.

I went into my room and looked around at it sadly. My posters of Steve Martin looked back at me, his smiling face the same as it had been before I left for my date. I stared at Steve's mouth and lips as I changed into my pajamas. Did Steve French-kiss? Had he made out? Did he have sex? Would a person ever be able to be funny again, to be happy again, if they did any of this? I didn't know, but at that moment, I didn't think any of it could be possible.

I went out into the living room and sat on the couch. *Benny Hill* was just ending, and I felt a wave of sadness wash over me, realizing that I had missed what would have been a fun evening watching TV with my father for a misguided desire to make out with a girl, an activity I was now sure I was not cut out for. My dad looked at me with a concerned expression.

"Are you okay?" he asked.

"Yeah, I'm fine," I said. From the look on his face as he studied me, I could tell he knew something had gone wrong. I looked at the TV and grew more depressed as I saw the final producer's credit flash on the screen as Benny and the bikini girls disappeared from the frame and the picture faded to black. The evening was over. I had blown it.

"I was gonna go to bed," my dad said, shifting in his seat. "But

I was looking through the *TV Guide* and it says they're going to show some Laurel and Hardy shorts next. You mind if I stay up and watch them?"

I looked at my dad, who gave me a fatherly smile. At that moment, the thought of watching Laurel and Hardy shorts with him was the only thing in the world I wanted to do.

"Yeah," I said, "that'd be cool."

And as we sat there watching Stan and Ollie trying to move a piano up a very long flight of stairs and laughed our heads off, I remember feeling extremely happy that I was only fifteen years old and wouldn't have to French-kiss anyone anytime soon if I didn't really want to.

.

HAIL TO THE BUS DRIVER

I've never liked to judge people, especially when it comes to their jobs. We've all done terrible things for a paycheck at one point or another. And our reasons for doing so usually have more to do with that annoying need to eat every day and have a roof over our heads than with any burning desire to start a lifelong career as, say, a clerk in a dry cleaning store or a busboy at a children's pizza restaurant. We live in a capitalist society and, like it or not, we all have to pay the bills somehow. And so, to anyone who is struggling to make ends meet in a less than exciting career, my heart and admiration go out to you. But, having said that . . .

Anyone who would voluntarily take a job as a school bus driver has to be either a masochist or just plain out of his or her mind.

Even as a kid whose idea of the perfect job was to be a waiter at a Farrell's ice cream restaurant (home of the Zoo and the Pig's Trough), I would look at the shell-shocked unfortunates piloting those black-and-yellow, smoke-belching behemoths and think, Oh my God, I would *never* do that. No other career in the history of mankind ever invited so much disrespect and downright hatred as that of school bus driver.

Or, at least, this was the case in *my* neighborhood.

I'm not exactly sure why so many of the kids who lived around me hated our bus drivers so much. I guess the main reason was that bus drivers were the people who transported us to the one place on this planet where none of us wanted to go. If you were driving us to the amusement park, you'd be our best friend in the world. But once an adult, no matter how nice or cool or friendly he or she was, sat behind that giant black steering wheel, switched on that rickety little fan, and started grinding those gears for the express purpose of taking us somewhere to learn things, then he or she might as well have been Mussolini as far as the gang on my bus was concerned.

My neighborhood was quite famous throughout the school district, if not the entire state of Michigan, for our bus etiquette nihilism. The Wendell Avenue route was an assignment that immediately struck terror into the hearts of experienced bus drivers. I used to imagine that they'd all sit around in their break room and trade their personal horror stories with one another like old sailors after years on the sea. Young, inexperienced newcomers would be warned of their impending peril by the older seasoned salts, with stories that always began, "It started out as a morning just like any other . . ."

The strangest thing about all this rolling rebellion I witnessed over the years was that the guys on my bus were never the ones who misbehaved. The torturing and tormenting of our drivers was the sole work of girls—more specifically, the burnouts or "freak chicks." In retrospect, I guess it really wasn't that surprising. During my ninth-through-twelfth-grade tour of academic duty, I learned the hard way that high school girls who decided they didn't want to play by the rules could be far more terrifying than even the toughest high school guys. This was because these girls had the ability to get completely out of control. They could scream and yell and hurl insults with cruel unbounded energy and nobody ever really tried to stop them. Who in their right mind would? Society isn't set up for this kind of thing. Guys, no matter what age they are, have all been taught to be nice to girls, and, on a deeper psychological level, all men are essentially terrified of women—or at least of women who clearly don't like them. And a woman who is looking to make trouble can very easily destroy a man's psyche with an insult regarding his physical appearance or by the simple act of laughing at him. Teenage girls looking to rebel throw out the Geneva Convention–approved rules of engagement and do things that guys who are the worst of enemies would never dream of doing to one another. Any unfortunate male teacher who dared to attempt to control a group of anarchistic girls would find himself having either his nose, ears, hair, skin, stomach, ass, breath, or any combo of the aforementioned items referred to as either "big," "gross," "dorky," "hairy," "ugly," "fat," "stink-ass," or "retarded" by his female adversaries. If he was strong enough to survive this first onslaught, the inevitable accusation of his having a "small dick" and being "a fag" was usually enough to finish him off. And any female teachers who tried to step into the fray were simply written off as turncoats and dismissed with a venomous "Get away from me, bitch," which would stun the usually mousy teacher long enough to allow the marauding girls to head off down the hallway in search of an illegal place to smoke their cigarettes. No, girls who wanted to be mean pulled out all the stops, and heaven help you if they aimed their guns in your direction. And the freak girls on my bus always had their sights aimed directly at the driver's seat.

We always seemed to get Viking-esque women as our drivers, types that my father would refer to as "sturdy" and "no nonsense." They were the kind of ladies who had small, compact beehive hairdos and wore electric blue Team Cobra racing windbreakers over their polyester blouses and green Kmart stretch pants, women you knew were married to garbage men, truckers, and janitors, and for some reason always wore earrings and red lipstick on the job. I was always aware that they were probably somebody's grandmother and could never figure out why a family would ever let a loved one take part in this horrible profession. But then again, I'm sure they simply saw it as "the perfect job for Mom, now that the kids are all grown up and out of the house." Perhaps in Mayberry, but not in Mount Clemens.

Mrs. Black was our most recurring victim. Every year she would emerge and drive us around for a few months. Then, someone would usually throw gum in her hair or hook the tail of her shirt to the bottom of her driver's seat, so that when she stood up to yell at us she'd rip her blouse, and after that she'd be gone again for the rest of the year. We figured she would either go crying to her husband, who would forbid her from returning to work until the district put some sort of "prison guards on those buses to keep those damn animals in line," or else just check back into the psychiatric ward for her yearly batch of reconstructive mental therapy. However she refreshed herself, her faith in the youth of today must have been strong, because come the first day of the next school year, there she'd be behind the wheel with a new plastic seat cushion under her ample bottom and a freshly lipsticked smile on her face. But her eyes were her weakness, always showing the riders she was about one illegally smoked rear-of-the-bus cigarette away from snapping back into unemployment. And for the freak girls on my bus route, there was a great pleasure in knowing that the beginning of the school year meant a new chance to break an old record for driving Mrs. Black back to her husband.

One year, they tried to put her out of commission on her very first morning back. It was when the first "boom box" portable radios had been introduced on the market. The burnout girls got on the bus carrying one. Mrs. Black gave them a "let's put our old problems behind us and start anew" smile and greeted them warmly.

"Good morning. I hope you girls had a pleasant summer," she said in a singsongy voice that already had tremors of strain in it.

"We did until we saw your face," countered Sue Clark in a tone that made me glad the insult wasn't hurled my way.

But Mrs. Black just gave them an "oh, those kids" chuckle and put the bus into gear. My friend George and I exchanged an impressed look. Maybe Mrs. Black was going to be all right this year. She seemed to have shaken that one off pretty well. But, in retrospect, I guess anyone can absorb an initial blow gracefully.

Once we were on the main road, the familiar smell of cigarette smoke began to waft up to the front. I immediately saw Mrs. Black's eyes pop up into the long mirror over her visor that helped her overlook her rolling domain.

"Girls, you know this from last year. No smoking on the bus. Now, put out the cigarettes, please."

Nothing but evil laughter from the back. A more frightening and unsettling sound does not exist. Because when teenage girls laugh like that, you can bet they're not laughing with you. They're laughing *at* you. Their laughter went on a little too long and a crack started to show in Mrs. Black's armor.

"C'mon, ladies, I said put those cigarettes *out.*"

The only response from the back of the bus was the sound of their portable radio turning on. "Black Betty," a very popular song among freak girls back then, performed by a band called Ram Jam, blasted out of the radio and up to the front of the bus. *"Whoa-oh, black Betty, bam a lam! Whoa-oh, black Betty, bam a lam . . ."*

"Turn that radio off!" shouted Mrs. Black, thrown by this new weapon in the girls' arsenal.

The girls all started clapping and dancing in their seats and singing along. These girls were out for blood. I think there was money riding on the prospect of getting rid of Mrs. Black on the first day of school. Girls who were not helping the cause were quickly enlisted.

"C'mon, Bev, get into it," urged Sue's extremely loud friend Rhonda to another freak girl across the aisle.

"Whoa-oh, black Betty, bam a lam! She really makes me high, bam a lam . . ."

"I told you girls to turn that radio OFF!"

"What?" yelled Sue, hand to her ear.

"I said to TURN THAT RADIO OFF!!!"

"What? I can't hear you. The radio's too loud."

I have to admit, that one made me laugh a bit. But not Mrs. Black. Her resistance was quickly disappearing, months of mental preparations crumbling like stale cookies. The next thing we knew, she sharply pulled the bus off the road and slammed on the brakes. We all flew forward, almost knocking our teeth out on the seat backs in front of us.

"God, kill us, why don't ya?!" Rhonda yelled indignantly.

"I want you girls to turn that radio off and put out those cigarettes right now," Mrs. Black said in a controlled tone, never turning around or getting up from her driver's seat. I saw her eyes make contact with Sue's eyes via the mirror over the front windshield. This would be a mental crossroads for Mrs. Black, I realized. She had never taken this sort of authoritarian chance so quickly before. Compliance would make her a rock. Rebellion would send her back to Mr. Black. We all held our breath and waited. "Girls? Did you hear me?"

Sue Clark was silent as she locked eyes with Mrs. Black in the mirror. Sue's stare was hard to read. Had Mrs. Black actually caught her off guard and infiltrated this year's rebellion before it could become effective? The silence in the bus was thick with anticipation.

Sue finally took a long drag of her cigarette, fixed a soul-piercing stare at Mrs. Black, and uttered the following words: "Why don't you just drive the bus, you old cunt."

CRACK! You could actually hear Mrs. Black's mind snap. Her eyes sunk into her head, her shoulders trembled, and the next thing we knew, she literally flew out of the driver's seat. I've never seen anyone over fifty pull a move like that before or since. Within seconds she was down the aisle and in the back of the bus. All the freak girls started laughing and screaming as Mrs. Black went nuts.

She started pulling cigarettes out of girls' mouths and trying to grab the radio. The girls kept screaming and tossing the radio back and forth, subjecting a frothing Mrs. Black to a desperate game of Monkey in the Middle. Mrs. Black was screaming, too, but no one could make out what she was saying. It was some unholy mix of religious references and imagery with a hearty dose of what I can only interpret, looking back on it now, as speaking in tongues. We kept hearing the word *Jesus* but couldn't put it in context.

After what seemed like minutes of sheer pandemonium, suddenly Mrs. Black had the radio. The advantage had shifted and it was quickly reflected in the screams of the freak girls. Laughter had been replaced with indignation as the radio continued to blast.

"Hey, that's my radio, fat ass!"

"Whoa-oh, black Betty, bam a lam!"

"That's personal property, you whore!"

"Black Betty had a child, bam a lam!"

"Give it back, you fuckin' witch—"

SMASH! Mrs. Black, in a feat of unbounded strength, had cocked her arm back like a major-league sidearm pitcher and smashed the radio into a metal partition between the windows, shattering the boom box into an explosion of debris. Plastic shards flew everywhere as we all ducked. The freak girls screamed in terror. Ram Jam and "Black Betty" evaporated as Mrs. Black hurled the broken remains of the radio out the window.

Silence.

Mrs. Black stood breathing heavily. Occasional cars zoomed by us on the main road, shaking the bus slightly.

More silence. Only the sound of Mrs. Black's breathing could be heard. After what seemed like a few years, she took a deep breath and looked at Sue Clark.

"When I say turn down that radio, I expect you to turn it down."

Her voice was perfectly calm. We were truly terrified. She turned and started to walk slowly to the front of the bus. Zoom. Another car passed. The bus shook again.

Silence. No one dared say a word.

Mrs. Black's plastic seat cushion sighed as she lowered herself back onto it. Zoom. Another car passed. Again the bus shook. She ground the transmission into first gear. Normally, that would have brought on a chorus of "Grind me up a pound" and "If you can't find it, grind it," but now no one even breathed. Mrs. Black revved the engine, eased the bus into gear, and we pulled silently back onto the main road. In a low whisper from the back of the bus, I heard Sue say, "She's gonna have to buy me a new radio." She was immediately shushed by the formerly loud Rhonda. It was the first time I had ever seen any of these girls look scared.

When we arrived at school, Mrs. Black opened the door and we all filed silently off the bus. When Sue started through the door, Mrs. Black said in a frighteningly sweet tone, "Have a good first day of school."

When the bus came back at the end of the day to take us home, Mrs. Black was not behind the wheel.

And we didn't see her again until the first day of school, one year later.

While Mrs. Black was our most famous victim, she was not the most intriguing. In junior high there was one driver with whom I had real interaction. More than that, I was partly responsible for her demise.

Her name was Sally. Sally was strange to us because she wasn't an old lady. She was fairly young, probably in her late twenties. Back then it was always hard to tell how old an adult was simply because everyone was older than we were, and, for us, people tended to fall into two categories—kids and adults. Sally was an adult, but she wasn't a member of the beehive-hairdo set. Sally looked more like a young Billie Jean King, and I have to admit that, for a few moments when I first met her, I had a bit of a crush on her. The crush, however, proved to be very short-lived.

Sally was a strange person. None of us could figure her out. I think the first day we had Sally, the burnout girls thought they were going to like her because she was young and had a former-freak-girl quality about her, which I'm sure scared them. A cool bus driver who understood them meant no bus driver to torment on the way to school. And that scared *me*. Because if those girls couldn't torment the bus driver, they'd torment other riders they didn't like. And for some reason, they didn't like me. I don't know *why* they didn't like me, but they didn't. I think it was because they *could* pick on me, since I was harmless both in looks and in nature. And pick on me they did. I could never wear a knit cap to school because they'd always steal it. I'd be sitting in my seat in the morning and one of them would always pull my hat off my head as she passed by. This would make my thin hair stick straight up, because the combination of cold weather, knit caps, and getting-your-hat-pulled-off-your-head friction always turned my hair into an electromagnetic nightmare. Then, playing keep-away, they'd throw my hat all over the bus, and it'd usually end up flying out the window where it would spend the rest of its life being run over by cars and frozen into the slushy road, waiting to be found months later, black and crusty, in the spring thaw. So, for the sake of my hats and my sanity, I really hoped some tension would build between the girls and Sally.

My prayers were answered. A couple of days into Sally's tour of duty, she yelled at the girls in the back of the bus to "put out those stinkin' cigarettes." Someone threw a snowball that had been smuggled onto the bus and it smacked Sally in the back of the head and the feud was on.

I never could figure Sally out. One day, she'd give you the biggest, friendliest smile as you got on the bus because she knew that you weren't one of the troublemakers. Then the very next day she'd stare at you with death in her eyes as if you were one of her worst enemies. You never knew day to day how you were going to be greeted, and it became very unsettling to me. On the days Sally decided she liked me, she'd tell me to sit in the front row so that we could talk. Our conversations usually ended after she'd ask me, "What kind of crap do they make you guys study these days, anyway?" and I'd launch into a description of my classes that lost her interest in about five seconds. She'd always respond with a distant "huh" and that would be that. But at least she was on my side.

That is, until one day, when Sally smashed my lunch.

I was sitting in the front row of the bus, right behind the door. Between the front seat and the steps that led off the bus, there was a three-foot-high metal partition that I always assumed was there to stop you from tripping kids who were getting on and off the bus. Also, the doors folded up and swung into the partition whenever they were opened, so I guess it was supposed to protect any front-row riders from getting their knees and feet whacked at each bus stop.

Well, that morning, the girls were giving Sally a pretty hard time. She had to pull the bus over twice and scream at the top of her lungs, and this was making her grow quite agitated. She started complaining to me.

"What the hell, you know? I mean, what the *hell?*" she kept saying over and over.

Always willing to lend a sympathetic ear, I sat forward and leaned on the partition to listen to her. Chin on my arms, I hung my lunch sack over the little metal wall.

"My dad would have kicked my ass if I had acted like that," she said, shaking her head. "He kicked my ass for a lot of things that weren't half that bad."

Sally's words soon turned into mumbling. I tried to understand what she was saying but couldn't really hear her, between the noise of the bus engine and the yelling of the girls in the back. I kept nodding, however, worried that if I didn't seem like I was listening, she might go off the deep end. Well, as soon as we pulled into the school parking lot, Sally glanced at me as I was leaning forward, then quickly reached over, grabbed the lever that opened the door and angrily yanked the doors open before the bus had even stopped. Before I could react, the doors flew toward me and smashed my lunch flat between them and the partition. I pulled my face back just in time to avoid getting my nose broken. I looked over at her and she was staring straight out the front windshield, tapping the wheel with the smallest hint of a smile on her face and acting like she had no idea she had both destroyed the lunch that my mom had packed for me and almost altered my face. Too stunned to say anything to her, I extracted my pancake-thin lunch and got off the bus. That day in the cafeteria, I sadly ate my flattened ham sandwich and exploded Twinkie and tried to figure out why Sally had chosen me to be her scapegoat that morning.

However, I soon found out that my new role as her whipping boy, upon whom she could alleviate all the frustrations of her job, was officially my new full-time career. During the next week, she'd knock her elbow into the back of my head while returning from a cigarette-gathering mission in the back of the bus, make me miss the bus several times by pulling away when I was about ten feet from the door, and on numerous occasions lurch the bus forward when I was walking down the aisle looking for a seat, making me fall flat on my face. I had become Sally's punching bag and had no idea what I had done to deserve it. And I had no idea what to do.

It all came to a head one day as we drove home from school. The bus was unusually calm. That day in the general assembly, they showed us a VD film and I think we were all deeply disturbed by it. The pictures of large open sores and lesions had stunned even the freak girls, who could occasionally be heard muttering, "God, that was so *gross*." And the result of all this was that no one was hassling Sally. And I don't think she knew what to make of it. She seemed really nervous, as if she thought we might be formulating a plan to pounce on her or for some time bomb we planted under her seat to go off. I guess, like a professional soldier, she had just gotten so used to fighting with us that her mind didn't know what to think in times of tranquillity. I watched as Sally became a twitching, fidgeting mess. Her eyes kept darting up to the mirror to look at us, then her head would snap around, as if she thought she was going to catch us doing something below the mirror's view. But there was no such intrigue afoot. Visions of giant syphilitic sores were still too fresh in our minds for any of us to do anything more than think about what a life of celibacy would be like.

As we started arriving at the bus stops, Sally seemed to grow more and more impatient for everyone to get off. She started telling departing students to "hurry up" as they headed down the aisle for the exit. She'd pull up to a bus stop, slam on the brakes, and say "c'mon, c'mon" as people got off. This made the girls in the back start to wake up.

"God, have a cow, why don't you?!"

"What the hell's the matter with you?"

Sally started to look more panicky. God only knew what kind of scenario she was unraveling in her head. Next stop. Screech! "C'mon, c'mon, hurry up!" She was making all of us nervous wrecks. I couldn't wait to get off that bus but was now filled with a feeling of dread that I, Sally's scapegoat, was not going to get off unscathed.

Finally, we arrived at my stop. Everyone from my street got up and filed out. As my friend George, who was walking in front of me, stepped onto the doorway steps, he dropped his notebook. Papers fell all over the street. He stepped off the bus and bent down in front of the door to pick everything up, blocking my exit.

Well, that was apparently more than Sally could take because all of a sudden, I felt her hand grab my back and push me hard. I flew over the top of George and landed headfirst on the pavement. I saw a flash of white, then a few seconds of black, as if I'd just received an uppercut from the world heavyweight champion. As my eyes came back into focus, I saw the last kid jump off the bus as Sally yelled "Jesus Christ, get OUT!" The bus screeched away from the corner as we stared after it, some of George's notebook papers getting sucked into the air by the bus's sudden departure. As the papers fluttered to the street, I touched my forehead and felt a small rock that had embedded itself into my skin.

When I got home, I told my mom what had happened and she proceeded to call the school and report Sally. The next day, Sally was gone. We found out a week later that Sally had been stoned the entire last week she was driving our bus and had lost her driver's license because of it. That was a major notch for the freak girls. Because not only had they gotten rid of another bus driver, they had completely wrecked her life, too.

And then, finally, there was Steve. Steve was a hippie. I always imagined that when he went in for the job interview, he told the bus company, "Hey, man, being that I'm a young guy and into rock and roll and have long hair and stuff, the kids'll really be able to relate to me." After hearing the stories about our dreaded bus, he probably figured that he would be the guy who was going to perform a miracle and crack the unruly crowd on the Wendell route and possibly have a TV movie made about the experience.

One afternoon, after the freak girls had gotten rid of Mrs. Black for yet another year, Steve climbed onto the bus. He was wearing dirty elephant-bell jeans with big flowery patches on the knees, a peace sign T-shirt, sandals, and love beads. His hair was down past his shoulders and he wore a headband. Everyone fell silent when he stood up in front of us and gave us a big smile.

"Hi, everyone. Peace. My name is Steve and I'm your new bus driver. I know you guys have had trouble before with bus drivers and I can relate to that. I have a hard time with the Establishment, too. Adults can be a real drag." He laughed. "I just want you to know that since we're all almost the same age, I'm here to help you guys. If you ever have any problems with anything—school, your parents, your boyfriend or girlfriend—just come on up front here and when I'm done driving you home safely, we'll rap and see if we can't straighten your head out. Okay? That sound groovy?"

He gave us a sincere smile.

We stared at him in silence. Then . . .

"TAKE A BATH, YOU FUCKIN' HIPPIE FAGGOT!" screamed Sue Clark. Then all the freak girls burst into gales of derisive laughter.

Steve's face went blank, then he looked like he was going to cry. He slid silently behind the seat, started the bus, and drove us home. And for the next few weeks, Steve descended into Hippie Hell. The freak girls systematically destroyed everything Steve stood for, shouting insults ranging from "You were probably too much of a pussy to go to war" to "Get a haircut, you homo." After two weeks, Steve was gone. To this day, I still feel depressed when I think about what happened to Steve. Looking back, he was probably the best bus driver we could have had. He probably could have even been our friend.

But I guess people don't really know a savior when they see one.

But then again, saviors shouldn't be driving school buses.

AND NOW A WORD FROM THE BOOTH . . .

One day, when I was in the eleventh grade, I found out the football team was looking for a new announcer. And I was very excited.

Ever since I was little, I'd always fancied that I had a great announcer's voice. When I was seven, my dad gave me an old reel-to-reel tape recorder that quickly became my favorite possession. I'd spend afternoons talking into the mike, making up compelling in-the-field news dramas full of excitement and a testing of the human spirit.

"This is Paul Feig out in the battlefield where things look relatively calm after a . . . wait. What's that?"

Like all seven-year-old boys, I was very good at making the sound of (a) a bomb whistling down out of the sky, (b) that bomb exploding, (c) machine-gun fire, (d) single-shot handgun fire, (e) the rumbling of a squadron of airplanes coming into range, (f) those same airplanes dive-bombing, and (g) any other mechanical sounds that involved war, death, and destruction. At this moment that I was recording my out in the battlefield drama, I was performing a combination of sounds (a) and (e).

"Oh, my God. It's a bomb. Run for your—" Sound (b).

"Oh, my God, they hit the tank! We've gotta get outta here!" Sounds (f), (a), and (c).

"We're trapped! Quick. We've gotta get to that foxhole." Sounds (b) and (c), with a few (d)'s thrown in for added mayhem.

"Argh, they got Charlie! My leg! They got my leg!" Riff on (g).

End ominously by simply turning off the tape, simulating the destruction of the tape recorder. Let your audience ruminate on the horrors of war.

Repeat. Endlessly.

My dad's old reel-to-reel eventually led to my teenage purchase of a high-end cassette recorder and microphone, upon which I would perform my scripted radio shows in the sad privacy of my Steve Martin poster–covered bedroom. By this time, as I was making my way through the wilds of high school, I had left the art of war to the professionals and was dabbling in two areas of sound pastiche—the detective show and Ed Sullivan impersonations. Granted, Ed Sullivan had been off the air for many years by the time I started imitating him, but since I'd heard John Byner do a funny impression of Ed on the local Canadian TV station we received in Detroit, I was convinced that I could do it, too. What I planned on doing with it was a mystery, but at that time, I somehow assumed the media were clamoring for a sixteen-year-old doing imitations of a guy my peers had no memory of.

"Right here on our show, how about a big hand for President Jimmy Carter!" I'd yell enthusiastically into the microphone, as I hunched my shoulders up in a Sullivan-esque fashion. I would then continue talking like Ed Sullivan as I moved the mike away from my mouth, saying things like "All right, Mr. Carter, right this way," creating the impression that Ed was walking away. When the mike was as far as possible from my mouth, I would go into my half-baked Jimmy Carter impression, which was simply a low-grade imitation of Dan Aykroyd's impersonation from *Saturday Night Live*. I'd talk in a Jimmy Carter–like manner, thanking Ed Sullivan as I moved the mike slowly back to my mouth, simulating the approach of our thirty-ninth president. "Well, thank you very much, Mr. Sullivan. My fellow Americans, today I'd like to talk to you about . . . peanuts." Neither my impressions nor my material were very good but my mike technique was outstanding. And so was my growing resolve that I belonged on the radio.

So, in my junior year, when the opportunity to be the announcer for the football team arose, I jumped at it with a gusto unseen in our school regarding anything except trying to get out the front door after the last-period bell. I marched down to the office of our vice principal, Mr. Randell, to offer up my services. Mr. Randell was a nice guy who'd received a very bad rap at our school. Not only did he have the misfortune to be our vice principal, a thankless job that invites all the abuse that students are too afraid to aim at the actual principal, but he was also cursed with the misfortune of looking vaguely froglike. In retrospect, he really didn't look like anything other than an overweight guy with small features, a large fleshy face, and an underbite. But in the hands of our perennially cruel student body, whose main goal was striking out at any and all authority figures, Mr. Randell's features all added up to the poor guy being assigned the nickname "Toad."

I sat down in Mr. Randell's office and informed him of the great fortune that was about to befall both him and the football team.

"Mr. Randell, I want to be the football announcer."

"Oh, really? Excellent. I've always thought you had a good voice, ever since I saw you perform 'The Parrot Sketch' at assembly last year. I'm quite a Monty Python fan, too, you know." No, I didn't know, but I have to say that the Monty Python comedy troupe's cool quotient took a near-fatal hit with that revelation.

"Oh, really?" I said, not wanting to let any negative energy get in the way of my being offered the announcing job. "They're the greatest."

"They certainly are," he said, chuckling to himself, his mind taking a brief trip through their repertoire. Had he been my age, I could have easily launched us into a one-hour marathon of recit-

ing sketches word for word but, since befriending the vice principal would only result in even more torment from my peers, I
simply chuckled, too, and stuck to the matter at hand.

"So . . . is anybody else up for the job?" I asked.

"No, surprisingly. I thought we'd have a few more students interested in it," he said, a hint of sadness in his voice. "Do you
know a lot about football?"

Without missing a beat, I looked him in the eye and said,
"Yes."

I knew nothing about football. I mean, I knew that announcers always said stuff like "he's at the twenty, he's at the ten, he's at
the five, TOUCHDOWN!" I could do that quite well, having
loudly practiced it over and over the previous evening in my room
until my father came in to tell me that he and my mother couldn't
hear the television. To me, being able to describe what I was seeing on the field would be a nonstop performance of making jokes,
doing funny voices, and keeping the audience rapt as I called out
the action of an extra-point kick. "There's the snap. The kicker
runs up and . . . OOOOHHH! IT'S GOOOOOOOOOOD!"
What more did you need to know about football than that? Nothing. At least not in my book.

"Have you ever been an announcer at a football game before?"
Mr. Randell asked.

"Whenever my father and I watch football, I do the play-by-
play commentary along with the TV." It was scaring me how effortlessly the lies were coming out of my mouth. My father and I
never watched football together, and on the few occasions that I
would turn on a game, my "announcing" the play-by-play consisted of my simply repeating any of the announcer's phrases that
seemed fun to say. Phrases like "Ooo, that's *gotta* hurt" and "Oh,
brother, can you believe *that?*" were the extent to which I had
ever announced a football game. But in my head, at this moment,
that qualified me for a great career in the announcer's booth.

This was not a new way of thinking for me. Unfortunately.

See, ever since I was a kid, I was always convinced that if the pressure was really on, I could do anything. I always imagined a scenario in which I was being held captive by some enemy soldiers who'd have a gun at my head. One of them would say, "If you can play Mozart on this piano, right now, we won't kill you. If you can't, you're dead." And then, because it was a life-or-death situation, even though I had no idea how to play the piano, somehow I'd magically be able to play Mozart. I don't know why I thought this. Probably because there had been a lot of stories on *That's Incredible!* lately about mothers who, when their children were pinned under cars, suddenly developed superhuman strength and were able to lift the autos with one hand. So, I guess I figured that if a housewife can lift a car, I could play a sonata. And at the very least, I had to be able to announce a stupid football game.

Mr. Randell gave me the job and told me my first gig was that Friday night. I left his office very excited. I foresaw great things in my future. From the Chippewa Valley Big Reds football games, it would be a straight shot to taking over for George Kell and announcing the Detroit Tigers baseball games. From there, it was a quick stroll to *Wide World of Sports,* where I would be standing in the field with Jim McKay, announcing downhill skiing as I wore my supercool yellow announcer's sportcoat with the regal WWOS patch on the breast pocket. I knew I could say "and the agony of defeat" as well as anyone else out there. Big things were on the horizon and I owed it all to a guy named Toad.

I spent the next few days practicing in my room and in my car. I didn't bother to read any books about football because I had convinced myself that I'd have a sidekick who would take care of all the details of the game. Every sportscaster has a color commentator, and I knew they weren't just going to stick me in the booth alone. Even Mr. Randell had said there'd be people up there to help me. So what was the point of trying to fill my head with a bunch of mundane rules? Leave that stuff to the support team, I thought. I was there to entertain and enthrall.

My father was quite surprised when I told him about my new job.

"*You're* going to be a football announcer?" he asked in the same supportive tone he'd used the time I told him I wanted to ask my school's head cheerleader to the prom.

"Yeah, they gave me the job."

"But you don't know anything about football."

"Sure, I do," I said, indignant.

"Well, you sure as hell didn't learn it from me. I can't stand the game."

It was true. My whole family had a strange aversion to sports. Except for my grandmother, who was fanatical about the Tigers. She always referred to them as "my Tigers" and would sooner give up her Social Security checks than miss watching a game on TV. According to her, she was always "suffering" along with her Tigers whenever they had a bad season. I've always wondered if it was my grandmother who made professional sports so unattractive to the rest of us. It's like being around alcoholics. The more they get into the booze, the less cool booze seems. Being around sports enthusiasts makes me want to push an amendment through Congress banning all professional sports from our culture. The sight of people either celebrating a victory of their local sports team or getting really upset because their team didn't win has always depressed the hell out of me. I don't begrudge anybody for getting excited about the fortunes of the team they've decided to follow. It's just when it really seems to affect their happiness and satisfaction with their lives that it makes me nervous. I've become enthused over certain play-off series and championships whenever my old Detroit teams were involved, but it was because I no longer lived in Detroit and was homesick for the Midwest. By living in Los Angeles and still rooting for Detroit, I was somehow reconnecting with my past, cheering not for the men on my team but for the place in which I grew up. And if my home team lost, especially to a Los Angeles team, it was as if my place of birth had failed, thus causing me to be a dud, a second-rate citizen put in his place by the bigger, hipper town in which he was now living. In these moments, sports were simply a conduit through which my self-worth passed. And so, for displaced people in this country, I can understand the allure of following your favorite sports team.

But if you're living in the town that your team's in and you're going nuts all the time, then something's gotta be missing from your life.

The night of the football game arrived. I got in my car and nervously headed over to the football field. I had spent the week imagining what my debut was going to be like. I had never been to one of my school's football games, except in my sophomore year when I spent the homecoming game standing by the fence pining over Tina Jenkins, a pretty cheerleader whom I was planning to ask to the homecoming dance on the very day *of* the homecoming dance. And on that day, the announcer's booth had been a faraway and mystical place to me, a small wooden house up at the top of the bleachers. I tried to remember what the announcer for the team had sounded like but couldn't recall ever hearing one. I remember hearing the occasional announcement of a player's name and the score, but beyond that my memory had failed me. I kept telling myself that, despite what the past announcers had done with their jobs, I was going to bring a whole new level of entertainment to the proceedings. I envisioned the people in the stands laughing uproariously at my humorous side comments. I couldn't really think of what any of these humorous side comments might be, but I was sure that in the heat of the moment, I'd be playing that crowd the same way I'd be bashing out Bach's *Goldberg Variations* if a gun were pointed at my head.

I pulled into the school parking lot, which was crowded with cars and families heading over to the field. Seeing them, I started to get a little nervous, but quickly made myself feel better with the realization that these people were all in for quite a treat. They didn't notice me now, but after the game they'd be mobbing me, shaking my hand and saying "Funny, funny stuff" and "I never enjoyed football until tonight. Thank you." The night air was cold and I hadn't worn a warm enough jacket. However, I knew that once I got up into that booth, everything would be great. I had seen the inside of an announcer's booth on an episode of *The Odd Couple,* when Oscar was doing play-by-play with Howard Cosell. The clean white room with the bank of recording and sound equipment against the back wall. The microphones mounted on stands, sitting in front of you on a white counter. The window that revealed your sound engineer, to whom you would confidently nod as you were coming to the end of a commentary so that he could deftly hit the music button just as your story reached its crescendo. I couldn't wait for the game to start and my career to be launched.

I got to the bleachers and looked up at the announcer's booth. I wasn't quite sure how to get up there. I scanned around and saw that there was a rickety wooden staircase leading up to it behind the bleachers. I took a look back at the crowds who were heading to their seats. Moms and dads and little brothers and grandfathers were all decked out in red and white with the politically incorrect logo of our school's screaming Big Red Indian emblazoned on their sweatshirts and jackets. These were the football regulars, people who came out every weekend night to watch their sons and neighbors clash on the gridiron. The world of high school sports and its supporters was as foreign to me as the backstage politics of the drama club was to these people who were now packing into the stands. Would they accept me and my new take on their world? Or would my vocal antics prove too revolutionary for them? Did they want their football straight up and sober, or had they been longing for an unorthodox messiah who would challenge the very way they enjoyed their sport? Unsure, I turned and headed up the stairs to the announcer's booth, the butterflies in my stomach doubling with each creaky wooden step I trod. Whether they were ready or not, this crowd was just minutes away from the new world order, and I was going to be standing at the helm.

I got to the top and opened the door. I was immediately shocked. The booth was nothing like the one in *The Odd Couple*. It was nothing like where the announcers sat during *Monday Night Football*. It wasn't even as nice as the shed in our backyard. It was basically a big wooden box that looked like it had been assembled by the Little Rascals. There were no lights in it, it was made entirely out of plywood and particleboard, and it had no glass windows. The counter where the mike stood was basically a couple of two-by-fours that had been nailed together and then hastily pounded into the wall. A bunch of men in their late forties and early fifties were standing around, wrapped in heavy coats and wearing aviator glasses. They all seemed to have mustaches. When they saw me, they gave me a look.

"Where the hell have you been? You're the announcer, right?" said the biggest mustache man. These guys all looked like the deer hunters who always came into my dad's store to buy bright orange clothes that were supposed to prevent them from drunkenly shooting each other out in the forest.

"Uh, yeah, Mr. Randell told me to get here at seven. I thought I was early."

"No, kid, the game *starts* at seven. Christ, I thought one of us was gonna have to announce it." He shook his head as if my misinterpretation of the time had reaffirmed everything he's ever believed about how the new generation was going to drag the country into anarchy through its stupidity and laziness. "Well, get over here so we can tell you what you've gotta do."

The guy motioned for me to sit on a metal folding chair behind the microphone. The "window" in front of the mike was simply a large, long rectangle that had been cut out of the front of the booth. The wind was blowing in and it was freezing. I realized that my lack of a warm jacket was now going to result in a very uncomfortable evening. I sat down on the ancient metal folding chair and felt a shock of cold penetrate the back of my jeans and immediately freeze my ass. The mustache guys all surrounded me, leaning in over my shoulders and exhaling clouds of breath that bore the distinct scent of Dewar's and Old Milwaukee.

"Okay, here's the team's roster. Jake will be calling out the numbers of the players who make the plays. When he does, you look on the sheet, find the names if you don't know them already, and then make the announcement. You announce the tackler first and then you announce whoever assisted in the tackle. Got it?"

My head was immediately swimming. The tone of voice the guy was using was not the reassuring voice of my mother or my teachers or anyone who was planning on patiently guiding me through an unfamiliar experience. These were a bunch of older guys the likes of which I had seen on construction sites and in VFW halls, the types of guys who I imagined had beaten up hippies in the sixties, guys who supported the Vietnam War and thought the only reason we lost it was because we didn't drop the bomb on the VC. In short, the kind of guys who would have no patience for a teenage male who didn't know anything about the sport of football. I felt a hot flash of impending failure shoot up the back of my neck.

"Do you *got* it?" he repeated impatiently. I could feel him trying to prevent himself from calling me "you little sissy boy."

Completely intimidated, I nodded yes, not having a clue how anybody could ever figure out who tackled who, let alone be able to decipher information as obtuse as who "assisted" in the tackle. But I tried to keep a positive attitude.

"And then I do all the play-by-play, too, right?" I asked.

They looked at me as if I had just announced I wanted to blow them all.

"Play-by-play? Who do you think you are? Howard goddamn Cosell?" This, of course, got a big laugh out of them all, and I immediately had the feeling these guys were quite capable of reenacting Ned Beatty's "squeal like a pig" scene from *Deliverance*.

"You don't do play-by-play over the loudspeaker at a game. Jesus Christ, you'd drive everybody crazy."

The evening was getting worse by the second. I had been in the booth for less than two minutes and already I knew that I never wanted to do this again. The unpleasant, oppressive sound of the marching band drifted up through the open window in front of me, carried along on an icy wind that made my chest tense up. I felt the beginnings of uncontrollable shivering starting to take root in my torso, and I knew that speaking was going to become harder and harder.

"Man, I should've brought my coat. It's cold in here," I said, somehow hoping my discomfort would be a legitimate cause for dismissal.

"Christ Almighty, you didn't bring a *coat*?" said the main mustache guy. "Where the hell did you think you were gonna be? In some goddamn hotel suite?"

Sort of, I thought. I definitely didn't envision that I'd be in a killin' shack that some sadist had dropped on top of the bleachers.

The guys all exchanged incredulous looks, and it was quite clear that we were not going to be best friends by the end of the evening. And because of that, I didn't expect the magnanimous gesture that happened next.

"Pete, give the kid your coat."

As cold as I was, the one thing I knew, with all certainty, was that I didn't want Pete's coat. I didn't want to place anything on my body that belonged to any of these guys, let alone something they were wearing at that very moment. I felt panic rise up in me. It was the same feeling I'd had the time I went camping with a friend's family and forgot my toothbrush and his mother said, "Well, why don't you just use Dave's toothbrush? He doesn't have any germs." I was able to beg my way out of having to use Dave's toothbrush by producing a pack of Dentine chewing gum. However, tonight, Pete's coat was unfortunately inescapable.

"Oh, no, that's okay. I'm not that cold," I said, trying to sound suddenly warm.

"Oh, fer Christ sake, put it on. If you start shivering, you're no good to anyone up here."

And with that, Pete, the biggest guy who had the dirtiest hair and the greasiest pants I'd seen this side of a pit-crew member at a stock-car race, peeled off his plaid hunting jacket and handed it to me. There's a smell you encounter on the occasions when you get into a chain smoker's car on a rainy, humid day and see that his dog, who has just spent the last couple of hours running through a stagnant swamp, is in the backseat. Well, that was the smell I *wish* I was partaking in when Pete's coat came near my nose. In order to have a stinkier coat, Pete would had to have died and been buried in it. I felt faint but knew I didn't really have a leg to stand on when it came to convincing these guys I was just joking about being cold. And so, like a man being handed the gun after the fifth click in a game of Russian roulette, I resignedly took Pete's jacket and put it on.

Before I could fully immerse myself in the wave of nausea that was beginning to overtake me, I saw the cheerleaders head out onto the field with an eight-foot-wide hoop that had been covered with paper. On the paper was painted "Go Big Reds" in big, poorly spaced letters. As the cheerleaders brought the hoop out, the crowd started to cheer. Two of the cheerleaders took the hoop into my school's end zone and held it up parallel to the goalpost. The other cheerleaders ran out around the hoop and started doing their uncontrollable kick-and-leap-into-the-air moves that cheerleaders seemed to do incessantly. The main mustache guy poked me in the shoulder blade and pointed to the list of players.

"All right, it's time to introduce the team. Once the band does its fanfare, you welcome everyone to the game and then introduce the players. As you say each name, they'll run out and break through the hoop. Keep the pace up or it'll take too long."

More prophetic words were never spoken.

I looked down at the list of players' names.

It's here that I need to give you a small factoid about the metro Detroit area. Detroit has one of the largest Polish communities in the country. And a lot of Polish Americans went to my school. And the minute I looked at that list, I realized that every Polish kid in our school was on the football team. Sitting on the counter before me was an endless list of names, none of which were less than ten letters long and all with a definite shortage of vowels. These were names that looked more like "words" a toddler with a bucket of plastic consonants would construct than the proud family monikers of onetime immigrants who fought and struggled to come to our country. Names like Krymnikowski and Pfekotovsky stared out at me like a street map of Warsaw. Before I could even consult with my mustachioed cohorts, the band hit its warbly fanfare and three guys kicked my chair.

"You're on!"

I nervously clicked on the mike and said, "Ladies and gentlemen, welcome to tonight's football game." Even though I was talking into a microphone, I couldn't for the life of me hear myself over the loudspeaker. I heard the crowd cheer. I could only deduce that either they could hear me or a car had just been raffled off. "Is this on?" I asked the guys. Before I could look back at them, I heard someone in the stands yell "Yes," followed by much derisive laughter. It was then that I realized I didn't even know the name of the other team. I guess part of me had assumed that someone would have written up this kind of copy for me so that all I'd have to do was read it out loud and be amusing. I put my hand over the mike and turned to the guys. "What's the name of the other team?"

The men rolled their eyes like teenage girls, making open-mouthed faces that said in an unheard Valley Girl voice, "Oh my God, I can't believe you don't know that." The main guy recovered quickly and yelled at me, "The Cougars! The goddamn Warren High Cougars!"

I moved my hand and said into the mike, "Tonight's game is between the Warren High School Cougars and the Chippewa Valley Big Reds!" The crowd cheered again, and it was at that moment that I realized how easy it was to get a rise out of a football crowd. Momentarily energized, I continued. "And now, let's meet the players!"

The band hit another fanfare and then the snare player did a drumroll. It was all very exciting except for the fact that I now knew I had to take on that list of names. The cheerleaders tensed their grip on the hoop. I could see the players standing in the back of the end zone, lined up, waiting to hear their names, the first player setting himself to sprint forward and burst through the large paper ring. I looked back at my support team.

"Just read the list. Read it in order," the main guy said to me, with a don't-screw-this-up look on his face.

I looked at the first name on the list and dove in. "Mike Krack . . . eye . . . now . . . ski." And indeed, Mike Krackinowski ran up and burst through the hoop as the crowd cheered.

All except for one angry voice from the stands.

"It's Krack-*in*-owski!"

I looked out the window. Sitting two rows from the booth was a very angry mother with a large beehive hairdo wearing a Valvoline windbreaker. She was glaring at me. Her look was so intense that I was momentarily stunned. I felt a finger poke me in the ribs.

"Go on! Keep reading!"

I looked back down at the list. "Bob Stan . . . zow . . . line . . . insky." And out ran Bob.

"It's Stanzo-lin-*nine*-sky!" Another angry parent, this time right under the booth's window, was glaring at me. I felt another prickly wave of panic run up the back of my neck. It was the panic of being trapped, of no escape, of knowing that there was nowhere to go but down. These two names had taken me about twenty seconds to get out and the pace of the players running out of the hoop was not at all what the inventors of the Hoop Introduction Industry had in mind when they first came up with it. Just go back to the list, I told myself. Go back to the list.

"Steven Lip . . . ow . . . . rank . . . in . . . . flaanski." Another player ran through the hoop. Another angry parent yelled at me. Another wave of prickly panic shot up the back of my neck.

It took me five minutes to get through the first half of the list. The crowd became a mixture of angry parents who felt I was destroying the dignity of both their football-playing sons and their families' heritages and students who found the whole spectacle funnier by the second. The football team was staring up at the announcer's booth, the coaches were staring up at the announcer's booth, and the cheerleaders were staring up at the announcer's booth. Each name I was able to mangle brought a less enthusiastic player through the hoop. Through my mispronunciations, I was single-handedly defeating our football team more effectively than any rival school ever could. The fact that their team's announcer didn't really know who any of them were seemed to put the whole idea of their participation in organized sports on trial. Maybe they weren't as good as they thought they were. Maybe football wasn't the be-all and end-all of their lives. Whatever they were thinking, they knew that there was at least one guy in the school who couldn't care less that they could throw or catch a football, that they could run fast and dodge their way through other guys and knock their fellow players down. And that guy was now in charge of the school's sound system.

Finally, the main mustache guy said, "Oh, for fuck's sake," and grabbed the microphone. He snatched the list of names from me and started reading them off quickly. The crowd cheered at my dismissal and the football team ran en masse through the hoop and onto the field. The opposing team ran out and the referees blew their whistles. The mustache guy slammed the list down in front of me, clicked off the mike and said, "Jesus Christ, where the hell did you learn to read, anyway?"

"Uh . . . " I said, quite sure it wasn't the answer he wanted to hear, "at this school."

The rest of the evening was a blur. They spoon-fed me the names of the tacklers and the assistants, and I said them and froze my ass off and never got used to the horrible smell of Pete's jacket. When the game was over, no bonding had occurred between me and the Green Berets up in the booth. They gave me a look that said "don't come back" when the game was finally over, and I hastily made my way down the rickety stairs and sprinted to the safety of my car before the crowds could see me.

That Monday, I was so humiliated that I avoided Mr. Randell at every turn, sure that he had heard about my disastrous job behind the mike. And when the next Friday rolled around, I very happily stayed far away from the football field, sure that restraining orders had been issued to keep me away from the announcer's booth. I never felt more relieved in my life to not be somewhere than I did that Friday night and enjoyed an evening of *SCTV* watching and junk food eating with my next-door neighbor Craig.

The following Monday, Mr. Randell called me into his office.

"So," he said with a very disappointed look on his face, "where were you Friday night? You missed the game."

I was shocked. I couldn't even conceive of anyone's expecting that I would have returned to the scene of my failure. And now, completely embarrassed, I just couldn't bring myself to admit to him that I assumed I had been fired.

"Uh . . . I thought it was gonna rain Friday night and that they were gonna call the game off, so I didn't go."

I sat there for a fifteen-minute lecture on responsibility and what it means for a man to keep his word, basically the same one my dad had given me during Little League. I nodded and looked remorseful the entire time, taking solace in the knowledge that if this was the hair shirt I would have to put on in order to never have to attend another football game again, it was well worth it. And it was still more pleasurable to wear than Pete's coat.

At the end of his tirade, he gave me a very fatherly look and shocked me by saying, "So, I can count on you to show up and announce the game again this Friday?"

I looked at the man and realized that drastic measures had to be taken to escape this Sartre-like situation that the job of being our school's football announcer had turned out to be.

"Mr. Randell," I said apologetically, "I'm afraid I can't announce the football games anymore. Friday nights I have to go shopping with my mom."

THE LAST AND ONLY PROM

Since I was seven, I had a huge crush on the girl who lived next door to me.

Mary was the middle daughter in a family of eight kids and was the same age as me. She, myself, and her younger sister Stephanie comprised what became officially known as the Garage Club. We used to spend every summer in my family's garage putting on plays and haunted houses, as well as the one time we opened a dance studio by making up a few simple steps to the Bo Donaldson and the Heywoods classic "Billy, Don't Be a Hero." We then passed it off as "the latest dance craze" sweeping some other city far from our own, thus ensuring that no one would figure out we had simply invented it in two minutes and then demand their twenty-five-cent tuition back. Once, the Garage Club even raided the garbage Dumpster behind my father's army-surplus store and turned a load of discarded packing materials into a potpourri of sellable items. Cardboard dividers whose purpose in the world of shipping was to keep cowboy hats from crushing each other became actual hats in our garage boutique. It's amazing how the word *Hat* written in Magic Marker on a cardboard divider can actually convince a four-year-old to fork over fifty cents and march off into the street wearing a glorified piece of garbage on his head. Cardboard boxes that once contained musty old canvas tarps miraculously became portable forts, available to any kid in our neighborhood with one dollar of allowance money and the will to cart the thing off on his or her bike. Unfortunately, when I made treasure maps that led the buyer through the most treacherous parts of our neighborhood only to discover that the "X" that marked "the spot" merely marked the spot where I hadn't actually put anything, the plan backfired. Several angry older brothers descended on our garage with their crying siblings, demanding their money back and threatening to close us down if we ever tried to peddle our shoddy wares within the neighborhood again. But the one thing that kept me going, even through these retail hardships, was the fact that I was working side by side with my beloved Mary.

The irony is that I had already married her sister Sharon. It was a simple ceremony, me in my Sunday school suit and Sharon in her confirmation dress, wearing a simple veil made out of a disgustingly dirty piece of drop cloth from my dad's paint bin. Sharon was an older woman, it was true. But we had decided that our love could overcome the one-year age difference between us and make our bond all the stronger. We were married on the back stoop of my house, with my mother performing the ceremony by uttering a quick and nervous, "Even though this isn't real in the eyes of God, I now pronounce you pretend husband and wife," and then handing us a pitcher of Kool-Aid so that we could start our honeymoon on the swing set fully amped-up on sugar. But even during my wedding ceremony, with Mary standing next to Sharon, acting as her bridesmaid, and the three-year-old ring bearer Stephanie wistfully picking her nose at Mary's side, I knew that my marriage to Sharon was merely a sham, a small dalliance on the road to true marital bliss with my future wife, Mary.

Over the years, Mary and I were inseparable. We did everything together, which usually involved some form of torturing her little sister Stephanie. We bonded through cruelty, as many children do, finding our friendship growing each time we invented a new and increasingly insulting nickname for Stephanie. "Zit" seemed to stick the longest and was only improved upon by upgrades in pronunciation. Zit became Zut became Zoot became the performance-dependent *Zooooot* became years of eventual therapy for poor Stephanie. Not that *I* was spared, by any means. Mary called me Fig Newton constantly, and while it never felt like a romantic pet name, at least it showed the world that we were more than just casual friends.

Once, when we were thirteen years old and saw the movie *Aloha, Bobby and Rose,* Mary and my ex-wife Sharon were traumatized and inconsolable at the death-by-cop demise of Bobby at the film's end. Having hated the overwrought teen drama, I found the whole thing rather amusing as we walked home, since the two girls seemed incapable of stopping their crying jags. My inflammatory comment "I don't know, I think Bobby had it coming" was met by Mary's searing glare and a very angry "Shut up, *Pig* Newton!" That one *did* hurt, not so much because I had been called a pig, since I was extremely skinny and not at all piglike, but because she looked so hatefully at me in that one moment. And so I vowed never to upset her again.

My love for Mary seemed to grow exponentially once we hit our teens. Mary was blossoming into full womanhood and I was blossoming into full awkward gangliness. Her breasts and hair grew; my ears, nose, arms, and feet grew, unfortunately in complete disproportion to the rest of my body. I found myself secretly staring moonily at Mary's face as we would play board games like Battleship and Kerplunk and the nerve-jangling Operation. The ease and grace of her hands as she deftly removed a Wrenched Ankle or an Adam's Apple was something to behold. Little did she know that as she was removing a Broken Heart, she was in full possession of mine.

Once, in junior high, my older cousin Leslie taught me how to say "I love you" in French. And so, on Mary's birthday, I bought her an innocuous card and on the inside flap, in what I considered to be unreadable microprint, I wrote the words *"Je t'aime."* Then, to draw attention away from it, I wrote in the place where you're supposed to sign a card a very innocent "Happy Birthday, Your friend, Paul." I gave her the card as we headed home from school that day and told her to open it when she got to her house. My thought process was simple. Mary would see the secretive French "I love you" and process it subconsciously. Then, overcome with years of unrequited love for me, she would rush to my door, throw her arms around me, and profess her undying affection. And so, heart pounding, I sat at home that afternoon, waiting for her to arrive. As the hours passed and our front door was silent, I realized something had gone wrong with the plan. I headed over, wondering if my microprinting was indeed *too* micro, causing my French declaration of love to go unseen. I knocked on her door and was immediately met by Sharon, who looked at me through the screen door with a face that said "I know something that you don't want me to know."

"Hey, Sharon," I said cautiously, knowing something was up.

"Hey, Fig Newton . . ." Long torturous pause. "Geeee tay-meeee!"

Having said this, she burst into laughter, which was followed by the sound of distant laughter inside the house from her older sister Becky and their mother. Sharon fell away from the door, hysterical. Then Mary appeared, with a look that was a mixture of uncertainty, amusement, and disbelief. She cracked the screen door open and looked at me.

"Fig Newton . . . do you *love* me?" It wasn't a tender, rhetorical question but one of true confusion.

"What? No. What are you talking about?" I said, covering way too hard, completely transparent.

"Didn't you write that thing in my card? That French thing?"

"What? Oh, *that?* No, I was practicing writing out some French stuff and my pen got stuck and I used that card to try and make the pen start writing again and I guess I wrote that on there to make sure that the pen was working. Oh, man, I can't believe I wrote that on your card. Ha ha."

She had a look on her face that said she wasn't buying a word of this, and I made a hasty retreat back to my house before she could say anything else. The sound of her sisters and mother laughing escorted me back to my front door. I stayed in my room the rest of the day playing "I Honestly Love You" over and over on my stereo and wondering why I had fallen apart so completely in what could have been a turning point in my life.

As time passed and we went on to high school, both Mary and I got busy with our own groups of friends and our own after-school activities. I became best friends with her older brother Craig, who was four years my senior. And because of this, I was over at her house as much as ever. Craig and I spent most of our time talking about *Star Wars* and making super-8 Claymation films and reading *Starlog* magazine. But being in her house, close to her but not as accessible as before, just made my love for her grow deeper and more profound. In some weird way, she was my ace in the hole. With all the fleeting crushes I had on girls throughout my high school career, having a girl I had grown up with living next door felt like a resource I could eventually call upon once I felt I was ready for a truly long-term and mature, albeit safe, relationship. It was as if she had been promised to me in my youth and we were simply waiting for the right moment in our lives to commence with our deep and predestined romance.

As the end of my senior year approached, it was becoming clear to me that this moment had better come quickly. Simply put, time was running out. In addition to our ill-fated date to my junior high dance, I had already screwed up a year earlier when I invited Mary to attend a Yes concert with me at Olympia Stadium in downtown Detroit. Instead of being honest about my romantic intentions, I presented the evening as more of a "hey, let's go as friends to this concert" event. I guess that in my heart I was assuming that an evening of sitting next to each other, serenaded by the keyboard virtuosity of Rick Wakeman, would cause romance to blossom between us. Of course, this turned out to not be the case, since we ended up being driven to the concert by her older brother John and his friend Tony, two stoners who effectively romance-proofed the whole event by cranking their car stereo louder than a Ted Nugent concert, smoking joints as they drove excessively fast, and keeping me in constant paranoia that we would be pulled over by the police. I imagined my picture splashed all over the front page of the *Macomb Daily* under the headline "Local Business Owner's Son Dies in Drug-Related Car Wreck, Shames Family." But even though the date was a failure in the love department, I could see from the moments in between fearing for our lives and being deafened by Yes's ponderous concert promoting possibly their worst album ever, *Tormato,* that Mary and I were indeed the perfect couple just waiting to happen.

All I needed was the right situation.

And so, one day in May, I decided to ask her to an event that could not be interpreted as anything other than an evening of romance and pronouncements of lifelong devotion . . .

The senior prom.

I did it at the end of her driveway. I hadn't talked to her in a few weeks and when I went over to her house to ask her to be my date, it was with a resolve that had come from years of preparation in front of my bedroom mirror. I knocked on her door and she appeared at the screen.

"Hey, Fig Newton, what's up?" she said the same way she'd said it a million times before.

"Um . . . can you come outside? I need to talk to you."

I don't know if it was something in the tone of my voice or because I had turned my nervousness into an expression of steely calm, but she seemed to sense that I was going to ask her something that was outside the normal bounds of our friendship. We walked away from her house toward the road, chatting a bit about school, as the gravel from her driveway crunched beneath our feet. I had heard that driveway gravel crunch my entire life. It made me think of the years she and I had spent growing up together. My driveway was cement, and so I was always enamored with the way my tennis shoes sounded on her gravel whenever I walked up and down her driveway. It always made me feel as if I were a supercool cowboy, grinding up the rocks beneath my feet as I strode bravely toward my showdown with a bad guy. But on this spring day, a day I had waited years for, the crunching sound was quieter, as if the gravel were trying to help me out by not adding any additional distractions to my heartfelt task.

We stopped at the end of the driveway and faced each other. I stared at her for a few seconds, unable to speak.

"What's up?" she asked in a friendly tone.

When you're a little kid, there comes a moment when you're standing on the edge of a diving board for the first time, staring down at the water, unsure if you'll ever have the nerve to jump into the deep end. Then suddenly something in you just says, Ah, screw it, jump in already. And so I stepped off the diving board and plunged feet-first into the water.

"Mary," I said, "do you want to go to the prom with me?"

She stared at me for a second, then smiled, a smile I had never seen her give me before, and said very sweetly, "Sure, Fig New—" She stopped herself, then . . .

"I mean . . . Paul."

Oh my God, I thought. She actually said yes. The moment I'd waited for my entire life had just happened. *And* she called me by my real name. I'd waited since I was five for her to stop calling me "Fig Newton" and call me Paul again. And now all my dreams had come true in the time it took me to ask her to a school-sponsored dance. I couldn't believe it. I was so happy.

So why did I feel so weird?

Mary smiled at me again. I smiled back and wondered if I was supposed to kiss her. It seemed like the kind of moment in which you were supposed to kiss somebody, but I didn't know if she'd let me and I didn't know if I wanted to. I'd never kissed her before, and it didn't seem right to do it for the first time standing in the same front yard in which we used to play hide-and-seek. And so I simply nodded and said, as romantically as possible, "Okay, great. We'll have a great time."

I walked her back to her door, but instead of walking the way we normally walked, like two people who've known each other all their lives trying to get from one location to another, we were now walking in an "aw, shucks," *Our Town,* shy-young-couple-in-love sort of way: the guy with his hands in his pockets, looking down as he walks slowly and ponderously, and the girl with her arms crossed in front of her as her feet lightly kick at the dirt with each step she takes. It no longer felt as if we were Paul and Mary, the kids who started the Garage Club and took great pleasure in squirting baby lotion down Zit's throat as she lay napping with her mouth open. We now felt more like *Paul and Mary,* the teenagers whom people might now say were "perfect for each other," who were "such a cute couple," and who had "finally gotten together." We got to her door, said good-bye to each other, and then she went inside, but only after looking back at me and giving me another warm smile. As the door shut behind her, I turned and headed home, feeling happy and relieved and excited.

And really, really weird.

At school the next day, my friend Tom was talking about the prom. He had just asked a girl to go with him and was telling me everything he felt I needed to know, especially since I had been bragging that I, too, would be squiring a young lady this year.

"Everybody gets laid on prom night, you know that, right?" he said.

No, I didn't know that. In fact, it had truly been the last thing on my mind. "*Everybody* does?" I asked, thinking that maybe he was joking.

"Sure," said Tom, as if I were crazy. "Why else do you think people go to the prom? To *dance?*"

My head immediately started to swim. For all the times I had imagined Mary and me being in love, for some reason sex had never entered the equation. Whether it was because I had known her since we were babies or because I had seen her cut her foot open once on a piece of glass on her lawn or because she had spent so much time referring to me as a chewy-chewy-rich-and-gooey fruit cookie, the thought of true intimacy with her was an idea that was almost foreign to me. Sure, there was the time last year when her brother John had built a wooden fort in their backyard that quickly became the neighborhood freaks' make-out palace. I had heard that Mary had gone in there with John's friend Al, who was *three* years older than her, and that they had actually made out. But that story had only swelled a Holden Caulfield–esque anger in me, indignation that my sweet and innocent Mary had been forced into a compromising situation with an older man. Truly that couldn't be who she really was. Surely she didn't actually have sexual urges. Or did she? My brain tried to sort things out. Maybe Mary *was* sexually active, I thought. And maybe when I'd asked her to the prom, she'd said yes, knowing that indeed "*everybody* gets laid on prom night."

Over the next few days, as I went about the ritual of renting a tux—making sure that I got a tuxedo shirt with a wing-tip collar so I could look like Robert Redford at the end of *The Sting*—my mind started to fill more and more with panic.

I'm going to have to have sex with Mary after the prom, I thought. After all, it's what *everybody* does. They don't just go to *dance.*

Visions of a ubiquitous pamphlet that had been front and center on the literature table in my Sunday school kept flashing in my brain. In big letters on the front of the pamphlet were the words *Chastity: The Pre-Marital Standard.* Not only was this prom date going to be potentially traumatic, my teenage brain kept thinking over and over, it was also going to get me in huge trouble with God. The more I thought about it, the more I knew first and foremost that I didn't want to get laid on prom night with my next-door neighbor, and the reasons kept coming at me hot and heavy. First of all, where were we going to do this sex thing, anyway? In the car? If so, what about the fact that we'll be dressed in gowns and tuxedos? It had taken me a good ten minutes to get the tux on in the mall fitting room, struggling with the fake tie that hooked in the back and the cumbersome cummerbund, not to mention the tight-fitting pants and oddly shaped shiny shoes that could only be squeezed into with a shoe horn. An attempt at getting undressed in the backseat of a car could quickly turn into the stateroom scene from the Marx Brothers' *A Night at the Opera,* and I knew that if I did indeed have to lose my virginity that night, I didn't want it to be funny. And could I even get naked in front of another person? I'd barely been able to shower in gym class in front of other guys. How was I now going to let someone of the opposite sex see me naked? And what if we got caught, like teenagers always seemed to do in the movies? Would we be in the throes of lovemaking, only to have a flashlight beam shine in our faces, whereupon we'd be forced to scramble about the car in a humiliating, bare-assed panic trying to retrieve our clothes while banjo music played on the sound track and a potbellied sheriff said things like "Well, well, Earl, looks like we got us a regular Romeo here" and "All right, Casanova, what say you and me take a little trip downtown so you can explain all this to the judge?"

And most important, did I really want to have sex with Mary?

In case it's not completely obvious by now, I was a very immature kid, even as a high school senior. Especially when it came to sex. True, I had been indulging in "the rope feeling" for years before my classmates were, but comparing masturbation to sex is like comparing skill at video golf to being a pro on the PGA Tour. Sexually, my mind had never advanced from that wedding on the back stoop of our house when I was five. To me, making out with a girl was about as much of love and romance as I could get my head around, and even that was an overwhelming prospect, the pinnacle of what my backward brain could handle. I mean, I hadn't even figured out how to French-kiss a girl yet. How could I have sex with her? I knew that other kids my age, as well as some much younger than me, were having sex throughout the country, especially in the permissive late 1970s. But no one in my group of friends ever seemed to be preoccupied with "going all the way." Sure, we had our crushes and would stare at the girls with the overdeveloped breasts and feel stirrings within ourselves, but no one I knew was actually getting *laid*. We had all been too busy for four years just trying not to get beaten up and to get decent grades and to get through the days with our dignity intact. Sex was something we knew was in our future, and we were all just fine with it staying there for the time being.

Or maybe it *was* just me.

Maybe all my friends, maybe *everyone* I knew was asking girls out on dates every weekend, getting undressed in front of them, and having sex. After all, we *were* seniors. The government said we were old enough to drive and soon we would be old enough to be drafted and to vote. We were certainly *old* enough to have sex. If we were living a few hundred years ago, most of us would have a wife and kids already, which means we would have had a lot of sex by now. The reality of it all was staggering. Maybe all this time, while I'd been sitting at home with my dad on Friday nights watching *Benny Hill* reruns or hanging out with my friend Craig reciting lines from Monty Python movies for the umpteenth time, everyone around me was engaged in the mature, physical act of love.

I tried to force myself not to think about it. But think about it I did. Constantly.

By the time the prom rolled around, I was a mess. I'd been having fever dreams all week, torturous visions of myself being forced to dance naked through the prom's rented catering hall or marrying a pregnant Mary at gunpoint as my parents wept and God damned me to a life of eternal toil for going against *His* will. I put

on my tuxedo that evening like a man preparing to go before a firing squad with a dress code. I tried to force myself to feel happy,
to look forward to what my mother kept telling me was going to
be "one of the happiest nights of my life." Sure, it was easy for *her*
to say. She didn't know the "everybody gets laid on prom night"
rule. She grew up in an era when most people actually *did* wait
until they got married before they had sex. They had all lived their
lives according to *Chastity: The Pre-Marital Standard.* But not me.
Not for long. No, I was living in a new world, a world of discos
and silk shirts and cocaine and high divorce rates and one night
stands and cheesy guys wearing Angel's Flight pants and gold
chains who had sex in bathroom stalls with women they just met.
Or so I'd seen on *Baretta.* But now I was about to join their ranks.
Because I was about to lose my virginity to one of the founding
members of the Garage Club.

I walked over to Mary's house, stepping through the break in
the bushes that separated our yards. I had jumped through that
spot in the bushes every time I came to visit Mary since we were
kids, sometimes leaping through it wildly, as if I were Superman
breaking through a brick wall. Tonight, however, I did not leap. I
stepped through cautiously, afraid of ripping my tuxedo and afraid
of disturbing whatever was left of my youth that might be cling-
ing to those bushes.

When I went into Mary's house, her parents said hello and we
chatted a bit, but I couldn't concentrate. My ears were ringing. All
I could see were the pictures around the room of Mary when she
was younger. Mary in her Garage Club days. Mary in her Brown-
ies uniform. Mary in her confirmation dress. Mary before she was
old enough to care about sex.

She stepped out of her bedroom wearing a lacy white sleeveless dress. She looked pretty. My stomach tied into yet another
knot.

"Hi, Paul," she said shyly. "You look nice."

I thanked her and told her how pretty she looked, but all I

could think of was how much I wanted her to call me Fig Newton at that moment. She would never want Fig Newton to have
sex with her. Fig Newton wouldn't be expected to know how to
remove a bra or to have a condom in his wallet. Paul, however,
had better be ready to deliver the goods.

That night, as I drove Mary to the prom, I felt like I had a time
bomb in the car instead of a girl. I was having a hard time reading
her. Ever since I had picked her up at her house, she had been acting differently than she ever had before, smiling at me and not
making fun of me. She truly seemed to be in a romantic mood, as
she looked sweetly down at the wrist corsage I had given her and
as she checked her lipstick in the visor mirror. Was this the way
girls acted before they had sex? I wondered. Was this the mating
ritual? Was my grandma's old car going to become our conjugal
cell before the night was through?

And was tonight truly going to be the night our childhood innocence was going to end? Not "French-kissing" end but actually
"everyone gets laid on prom night" end?

We pulled up in front of the VFW hall where the prom was
taking place and saw crowds of my classmates heading inside. I
parked the car in the dirt parking lot. We got out and started
walking. I wasn't sure if I should take her hand or not, and she
didn't appear to know if she should offer it up. And so we walked
next to each other, trying to engage in awkward conversation that
was reminiscent neither of things we would talk about in our pre-
prom date lives nor of subjects full-fledged couples could easily
toss around. Instead, we tried to walk on the conversational razor's
edge, which counted observable things near us as its main topic.
Phrases like "Huh, never been to this catering hall" and "Oh, that's
a pretty dress she has on" and "Careful you don't step on that big
rock" fell pithily from both our mouths as we headed toward the
door. Was this how an evening that ended with backseat sex started,
I wondered? Were guys and girls who would be as intimate as two
people could possibly be in just a few short hours really be point-

ing out other people's outfits to each other and musing over the
location of the prom? I'd always imagined that sex occurred only
after a night of poetry and cocktails, of smoking jackets and dressing gowns, of candle-lit dinners and long stares into each other's
eyes. I didn't see how it could come out of an evening in a rented
VFW hall with each one of us encased in polyester. But maybe I
just wasn't savvy in the ways of the world.

We entered the outer lobby. There was a line of people that
made it impossible to get directly into the dance. I could hear the
strains of The Knack's "My Sharona" echoing around inside the
main VFW hall, a place acoustically ill-equipped for any music
other than the National Anthem. I could see flashing lights and
hear the voices of my fellow students having a good time, clearly
fueled, I assumed, by their excitement about the evening of sex
that awaited them after they left the dance. Some student government kids checked us in as they sat behind a long folding table, the
kind of table that professional wrestlers now throw each other
through in WWF bouts. I looked up ahead to see why we were
standing in line and saw a flash of light. It turned out that before
we could enter the dance, we had to have our prom picture taken.
Judging from the heat I felt coming out of the main hall doorway,
they must have figured that none of us were going to look any
better than we did right then as we entered fresh from our bathroom mirrors and the outside air. Once our blow-dried hair and
made-up faces and synthetic formal wear got into that humidity-
trapping room, we would all emerge looking more like abstract
paintings than people who had spent the better part of the day
getting dressed.

As we got closer, Mary and I watched the other couples pose
for their pictures. Each couple would be placed in a semi-romantic
position by the photographer, who would have them put one arm
around the other's waist, turn toward each other at a forty-five-
degree angle, and hold their free hands tenderly together in front
of them, creating a romantic keepsake of their evening suitable for

framing. Everyone who did it seemed to have been dating for years. They would very confidently hold each other's hands and melt into one another, smiling comfortably for the photographer. Even the fact that the rest of us in line were watching didn't seem to phase them. Clearly everyone in the school was experienced in the world of dating, leaving me with the title of Most Backward Kid at Chippewa Valley High.

When the time came for Mary and me to get our picture taken, I immediately felt the strongest urge not to do it. I didn't feel like I particularly wanted a picture to remember any of this by. And yet to not document it would both insult Mary and possibly turn out to be something I would regret. After all, like it or not, this was my last and only prom. And so Mary and I stepped into the spotlight.

The photographer regaled us with corny photographer jokes, many of which we had already heard him tell every single couple who preceded us. Lines like "Well, well, I knew I'd get to take a picture of Warren Beatty and Farrah Fawcett-Majors one of these days" and "When I tell you, think like a dog and say 'fleas'" were just a few of the "doozies" he served up in a nonstop monologue that we all laughed at even though none of us found him the least bit amusing. The term *captive audience* came to mind, but if this guy wanted to spend his life taking pictures of kids at their proms, then we could at least have the courtesy to laugh at his stupid jokes. He told Mary and me to put our arms around each other and hold hands. We did as he asked. I put my arm stiffly around her waist, as if she were a bag of golf clubs I was trying to keep from falling over. I fumbled to take her hand and ended up intertwining our fingers strangely, making our hands look more arthritic than romantic. The photographer looked at me oddly, giving me a raised-eyebrow that said "What's the matter with you? Don't you know how to hold hands with a girl?" And it was at this moment I realized that I had never actually touched Mary before. I mean, we had played Swinging Statues and touched each other

"It" during tag and probably slapped each other "five" on one occasion or another during our childhood, but we had never made
any prolonged, definite contact. I could tell by the stiffness of her
fingers and by how lightly her arm was around my waist that she
was feeling just as strange about this as I was. And then, when the
photographer came up and shoved us closer together, so that we
were pressed against each other so tightly that we could feel our
hip bones touching and the warmth of our legs connecting through
our clothes, turning our bodies into one unified energy field, I
knew at that moment we were both feeling the exact same thing.

Absolutely nothing.

It was the strangest sensation. I think we both were expecting
to discover something resembling chemistry or a spark of future
passion or even a twinge of connection between us this evening.
But we suddenly both felt like cousins who had been pushed into
a crowded subway car and shoved together by the surrounding
crush. We forced smiles when the photographer uttered the classic "Let's see those pearly whites" and fought not to blink against
the punch of the flash. As soon as he informed us that we were
finished, we quickly moved apart, getting away from the camera
and the eyes of our peers. I immediately shoved my hands in my
pockets and Mary quickly crossed her arms. We gave each other a
supportive smile and headed into the dance.

The evening became one of avoidance. We danced a couple of
fast dances together and then spent a lot of time excusing ourselves to go to the bathroom. But when the song "Please Come to
Boston" by Dave Loggins came on, a song that Mary used to listen to as she beamed at the pictures of Shaun Cassidy she had emblazoned the wall next to her bed with when we were younger, I
knew that I had to ask her to dance. Proms are about slow dances,
no matter what anybody tells you. They're not about sex, they're
not about tuxes and gowns, and they're not about having your
picture taken when you first walk in the door. Proms are for
young adults, former kids who suffered and enjoyed and worked

and goofed off and made their way through the school system since they were five years old just to have one mature moment in a hot VFW hall that would usher them into the next phase of their lives. And because of this, I knew it was my responsibility to Mary as her prom date to escort her through this life ritual. I took a deep breath and went over to her as she stood with her friends.

"Mary," I asked, ". . . you wanna dance?"

"Sure," she said.

We walked out on the floor and positioned ourselves in the midst of our slow-dancing peers. The couples around us were holding each other tight; not a shaft of light or a gust of wind could work its way between their bodies. When Mary and I faced each other, we lightly put our arms around each other and began to sway to the music. However, we left a few inches between us.

As we danced and exchanged a few "fun dance, huh?"'s, we both noticed that all of the couples around us were making out heavily. With mouths open wide enough to administer CPR to each other, they were engaged in the desperate French-kissing reserved only for high school proms and end-of-war celebrations. We both tried to look around for a pair of faces that weren't suctioned together, but there were none to be seen. And so, with nowhere else to look, we looked at each other.

I stared at Mary. There in front of me was the face I had known my entire life. It was the face of my next-door neighbor, my fellow Garage Club member, my longtime playmate, and my best friend. We would not be having sex that night, nor would we ever. That wasn't who we were to each other and we both knew it. I suddenly felt very close to her.

"I'm really glad you came to the prom with me," I said.

"Yeah, I'm glad you took me," she said back.

"Thanks, Mary," I said, giving her a smile.

"You're welcome, Fig Newton," she said, smiling back.

And then we both started to laugh. We laughed not like people who weren't related and not like people who had grown up next door to each other, but like two people who were what we had truly become—brother and sister.

The rest of the evening, she stayed with her friends and I stayed with mine. I was now completely relaxed and was pleased to find that my good friend Dave wasn't getting along with his prom date very well. She had gone off to talk and gossip with her friends and so Dave and I ended up filling our time doing what we had done since we had met in sixth grade—reciting lines from Warner Bros. cartoons and trying to make each other laugh. We regaled each other with Bugs Bunny and Daffy Duck dialogue and seemed to be laughing even harder tonight at things we had already laughed at a million times before.

As the dance neared its end, Mary came over to me and said that she was thinking of heading off with some of her friends. She asked me if I wanted to go with them, strictly because she knew she had to. I didn't want to go with them any more than she wanted me to, and so I said not to worry. I'd tell her mom she was with her girlfriends from school and that everything was fine. We waved good-bye to each other, and then Dave and I decided to head over to the local go-cart track. We stayed there until one-thirty in the morning, driving laps around a dirt track in fast, noisy little cars we could barely fit in, wearing helmets and our rented tuxedos, kicking up clouds of dust and both amazed that we were doing something neither of us had thought could be possible. . . .

We were actually having fun on prom night.

ACKNOWLEDGMENTS

At the movies, only a true geek stays through all the end credits. That is, unless he drank too much pop during the film and has to sprint to the can the minute the words "The End" hit the screen (not that anybody puts the words "The End" at the end of movies anymore—to be honest, I kinda miss them). I've always stayed through the end credits not only because of my geek status, but because I'm always curious to see who helped make the movie I liked (or didn't like). And so, unless you've downed too many bottles of Fanta in your reading chair or there's a weird guy staring at you from the seat opposite you right now, then I ask that you sit through the names of the following people I'd like to thank for helping to make this neurotic little book possible.

First and foremost, I'd like to thank the great Pete Fornatale, my editor, for wanting me to do this book in the first place. I'd also like to extend honorary membership in the Garage Club to Dorianne Steele, Philip Patrick, Annik La Farge and Trisha Howell in thanks for all their help. Lindsay Mergens, Anne Watters, and Jill Flaxman can drink out of my bottle of Squirt any day. And much appreciation to Joni Evans, Andy McNichol, Fred Toczek, Rob Carlson, Gary Loder, and Renee Kurtz for keeping all the bullies from beating me up.

Finally, thanks to Mom for thinking I could do no wrong, to Dad for supportively reminding me that I could, and to Laurie for being more like Mom than Dad.

Oh yeah . . . and to you, for buying this book.

THE END

(See how nice that looks?)